CONQUERING CHAOS

Conquering Chaos

How to lead in a time of extraordinary change

Roy D. Bridges Jr
Tim Kotnour

Heart Ally Books, LLC
Camano Island, Washington

Conquering Chaos: How to Lead in a Time of Extraordinary Change

Editor: Lori Brown
Book and cover design: Artūrs Bremanis

The authors gratefully acknowledge permission to reprint previously published information as Case Study #4, by courtesy of Learning as Leadership.

Published by:
Heart Ally Books, LLC
heartallybooks.com
26910 92nd Ave NW C5-406, Stanwood, WA 98292
Published on Camano Island, WA, USA

ISBNs:
978-1-63107-077-8 (hardback)
978-1-63107-078-5 (paperback)
978-1-63107-079-2 (epub)

Library of Congress Cataloging-in-Publication Data

Names: Bridges, Roy D., 1943- author | Kotnour, Timothy G. (Timothy George) author

Title: Conquering chaos : how to lead in a time of extraordinary change / Roy D. Bridges, Jr., Tim Kotnour.

Description: Camano Island, Washington : Heart Ally Books, LLC, [2025] | Includes bibliographical references and index. | Summary:
"Transformations are hard. Especially when everything around you is on fire. Your organization is in crisis. Pressure from your boss. Rumblings from stakeholders. Demands from stockholders. Disruptions in the marketplace. Deeply frustrated staff and workforce who need to be heard and respected. Who need their dignity. Who need your leadership. Where do you begin? If you're in the middle of a transformation, your days are chaotic. You have one foot in the old business model and the other foot in the new one, trying to incorporate it into the daily work of running your business. It feels like both feet are being held to the fire. Meanwhile, your world is burning. You need a plan and a practical map to lead you through the labyrinth of your transformation's chaos. Conquering Chaos has a proven path that has led organizations out of crisis for years. How? By story. We've shared a detailed look at the inside story of one successful transformation. By experience. We've both faced hard transformations and succeeded. Using the strategic techniques in this book, we've helped organizations not only survive but thrive, in the short term and the long term. By adaptability. We've presented these techniques in a flexible format, so you can customize them to serve the unique needs of your organization's transformation. Five essential views will guide you: Presence. Perspective. Process. People. Dignity. Working through this book, you will learn everything that you need to lead with confidence. Transformations are hard. You got this"-- Provided by publisher.

Identifiers: LCCN 2025048645 (print) | LCCN 2025048646 (ebook) | ISBN 9781631070778 hardcover | ISBN 9781631070785 paperback | ISBN 9781631070792 epub

Subjects: LCSH: Organizational change--Management | Leadership

Classification: LCC HD58.8 .B748 2026 (print) | LCC HD58.8 (ebook) | DDC 658.4/06--dc23/eng/20260211

LC record available at https://lccn.loc.gov/2025048645

LC ebook record available at https://lccn.loc.gov/2025048646

10 9 8 7 6 5 4 3 2 1

To all who strive to make their work and workplace the best they can be for employees and customers, now and far into the future

—Roy

To the NASA leaders and workforce for inspiring us and daring to do the mighty things

—Tim

Table of Contents

Epilogue

For Inquiring Minds...The Details

Illustrations

All of the illustrations in this book were developed in the middle of the KSC transformation in partnership with Roy Bridges, the KSC senior management team, and Tim Kotnour.

The illustrations were developed to build shared understanding in the KSC senior management team. Book designer Artūrs Bremanis refreshed these for consistency of style across the book.

At the end of the day, the secret sauce of success for any organization is taking care of your people.

—Roy Bridges

Leadership is the hardest, least thanked, and loneliest position in an organization. It is also the most important role. You got this.

—Tim Kotnour

The Bottom Line Up Front

You got this

Successful Transformations Are About Dignity

In order to fully understand the message of this book, you must read Chapters 1 and 13. Chapter 1 provides the experience we will learn from. Chapter 13 comes back full circle to show how the fundamental, existential crisis defined in Chapter 1 was resolved. And at the core of the book is this: it's all about dignity.

Dignity

Chapter 1 begins the story with a detailed exploration of the Kennedy Space Center transformation. You must read this first chapter; it is essential to understanding not only the story but the method that arose from the KSC transformation. The book ends in Chapter 13 with a focus on dignity. Roy and his leadership created dignity in

- the workforce;
- the leadership team;
- the internal team supporting the leadership team.

As you read Chapter 1, you will appreciate how the morale of the workforce and leadership teams changed over time. When the transformation started, the morale was low. KSC was told that their historical and fundamental contribution to the space industry was not important. They faced an existential crisis. They were being asked to remove themselves from their calling and were not given a new mission to move to. At the end of the transformation, the morale was high. Significant changes were made. Chapters 2–12 provide a description of the steps to make these changes. Chapter 13 ends the story with the focus on dignity.

You might want to read the book in this order:

- Chapter 1 to understand the transformation;
- Chapter 13 to understand the importance of dignity;
- Chapters 2–12 to understand the steps;
- Chapter 13 to remind yourself about how it all ends.

As you read Chapters 2–12, be thinking about how each of the steps impacts your workforce and leadership teams' morale and sense of dignity.

If you focus on the financial performance alone, you will be missing a key point.

The Overall Model

Our overall premise is that transformations often begin with bad days, but they can become good days if the transformation is worked systematically. Simply, a bad day is a mission failure--a space shuttle crashing, a rocket failing to reach orbit, or a satellite failing to operate. A significant loss in revenue/market share or the failure of a new product or core technology might be your bad day. *But bad days can become good days if the transformation is worked systematically.*

With this book we share our experience as a way to help you conquer your organization's unique chaos. To conquer chaos for your organization is to successfully overcome an existential crisis. Chaos is created by a significant event that makes your current business model irrelevant and unresponsive (e.g., losing a market, primary customers, a primary program, or funding/profit). This chaos shocks your workforce and can lead to feelings of unsurety, disengagement, or a loss of dignity. In this moment, your most pressing leadership challenge is to conquer this chaos: to re-establish your organization's business model and renew—or usher in—your workforce's dignity.

Illustration 0.1 —5 Essential Leadership Tools for Your Transformation

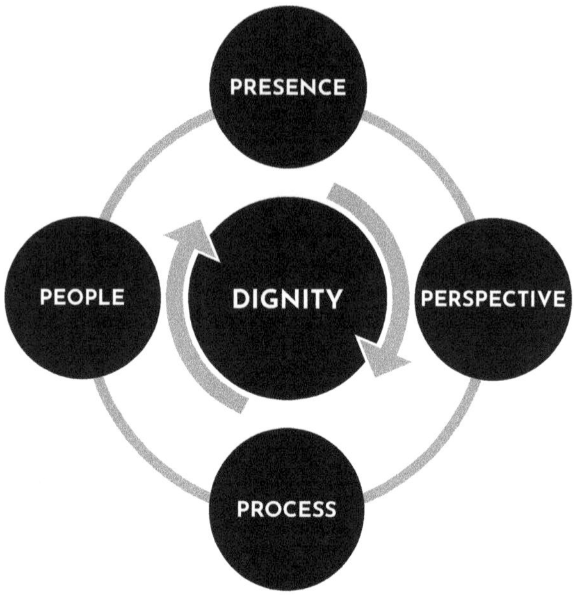

As shown in Illustration 0.1, dignity is created with an authentic leader's presence, perspective, and process, with a focus on the people:

Dignity...Dignity is the heart and soul of your transformation efforts. You need to restore your organization's and your team's sense of dignity.

Presence...Your team and workforce need to feed off your sense of confidence in making the transformation a reality. You must lead by example. You will need to find a balance between sharing a sense of urgency and at the same time giving them a sense of calmness that "we got this."

Perspective...Your perspective (and attitude) toward the transformation will be the driving force. Your leadership team and workforce will be looking to see how you view the transformation. If you are convinced of the need to transform and the initial set of steps, then they will follow you.

Process...Your team will be looking for you to guide them through the change. You need a set of steps to take your team through. Pick the steps that make sense to you and your situation.

People...You know that transformations impact your team and workforce—and transformations are emotional. You will need to understand where your people are coming from. You will need to acknowledge what they are feeling. Your workforce, just like you, will have doubts, will feel unsure. What you communicate to them is indispensable: your job as leader is to ensure they see there is a better tomorrow.

We use KSC's transformation as a way to illustrate these five views.

A transformation is the purposeful, intentional, consistent change of an organization's business model. The essence of this book is that transformations do not happen in a day. A leader or an organization cannot expect to go to one strategic off-site planning session away from the office and make an organizational transformation succeed. Successful transformations and strategy take time—time to think, hold conversations, make decisions, build commitment, take actions, reflect on the results, and adjust the strategy. Furthermore, one set of action items from a strategic off-site is not enough to change the organization's performance.

At the same time, the ideas that emerge from an off-site can be huge. These ideas plant the seed, then get refined and tested over actions and further conversations. As you will learn from KSC's story, some of the conversations held during one strategic off-site led to profound actions over the next several years.

We tell the KSC story to help us and others reflect on the challenges, strategies, methods (processes and tools), and lessons learned in transforming an organization. We use the term "story" to denote the collecting of, organizing, and reflecting on the details and events of KSC's life from 1997 through 2003. When we neared the end of Roy's term as KSC Center Director to discuss this work, he made a very important point: "This story is not about you or me. It is about KSC and NASA. The story is about bringing value to NASA so it can write the next chapter in the NASA book." This story is about a group of people using strategic analysis, thinking, and conversations within the management process to continuously focus on bringing value to NASA and the space industry.

We wrote this book to reflect on our experience. Our intent is not to offer a blueprint or a silver bullet for change. The intent of this reflection is to develop a deeper understanding of the use of strategic management to transform an organization. Our intent is not to develop the single best answer but rather to integrate different models and approaches. The unique advantage we have with this story is that we have a seven-year window to look through that allows us to study the organization and provides in-depth knowledge and experience. It is from this unique perspective that we learn.

Why This Book

We wrote this book to help you lead your organization's transformation.

As you probably already know, whether you are facing one, leading one, or have been through one, transformations are hard. We realize that each organization and each transformation is unique, and we'd like to offer you a framework and a set of lessons learned to help you navigate yours.

The Authors

You are probably asking yourself two important questions:

1. Who are these guys?
2. What qualifies them to help us with our transformation?

Good questions. Here's a quick summary.

Roy D. Bridges, Jr. is a retired Air Force general, former NASA astronaut, and former Center Director of NASA's Kennedy Space Center (KSC). He was at the helm of the Center during the challenging transformation we have used as a window into the workings and possibilities of a real-life transformation. After the KSC transformation, Roy went on to lead three more transformations in different organizations during his remarkable career.

Tim Kotnour, PhD, is now Director of the Engineering Leadership and Innovation Institute of the University of Central Florida. He worked with Roy to navigate the KSC transformation. That experience launched what became and continues to be Tim's own successful career supporting leaders who are navigating their organizations' transformations.

Why Now

This story started when we—Roy as Center Director and Tim as a university-based consultant—worked together on the KSC transformation from 1997–2003. Our shared experience there formed the basis for this book. We both went on separately to new efforts, using the lessons learned and the practices of our experience together. We each continued to learn about transformations, leadership, and strategy with both government and commercial organizations. The KSC case offers a good source of "insider" information that is more easily shared than that of commercial transformations that we each have been involved with.

We are writing and sharing this now to better tell a complete story. Previous works exist that describe the KSC transformation. Those works are more academically focused. They do not include the behind-the-scenes stories that add the emotion—the human factor—to the story. KSC's emotional stories are best told by the person sitting in the leadership role—Roy. Through the benefit of time, we can also see how the transformation impacted KSC then and now, 20 years later. As you will see, this transformation laid the foundation for the future of KSC and the commercial space industry.

After Roy left KSC, I continued to reflect on the transformation process and lessons learned, using the materials we prepared for training sessions to write a more detailed case study in the form of a book (*Transforming Organizations: Strategies and Methods*). You probably have not heard of it. Not many have. It was overly academic and not easily accessible or digestible. But it served its purpose to provide a very detailed documentation of the KSC transformation history. We are building from this previous analysis and reflection.

Years later, I connected with Roy to ask for help by sharing his lessons learned with other leaders. I shared my thanks for his mentorship. I also shared that I wished the original book had been better. The KSC experience could be valuable to others. Roy came to an off-site I was running to share his lessons learned. Listening to Roy again reminded me that we really needed to fix that first, overly academic book.

This book is our "final" attempt to learn and share what we learned from this transformation and the ones that came later. Our hope is that we have presented our lessons learned in a way that you can use today.

How to Read This Book: **What You Need to Know Before Jumping In**

Transformations are hard. We've been there. And we are here to try to make your journey easier. These are some of the ways we're doing that.

The information below is essential to understanding how to get the most out of this book and use it to plan and carry out your transformation. By understanding how the book is organized and using it strategically, you will customize your transformation to suit your unique organization and the people who make it work.

Writing Style

To help you better lead your organization's transformation, we wrote this book to share very personal, firsthand perspectives and lessons learned from the transformation. The story iterates the same ground, but from different perspectives, between Roy, sharing the leader's view of a real-life transformation, and Tim, sharing the processes and tools KSC used and how they can support your organization's real-life transformation. This writing approach enables us to better share the emotions and human impact of the journey while also offering practical advice.

Words

While we try to avoid using jargon, sometimes specific, more technical words are necessary. If we use a specialized term whose meaning isn't immediately clear, we have tried to (1) define it at first mention, and/or (2) add it to our Glossary (p. 301-304) and/or our Abbreviations list. (p. 300)

Formatting

The book is organized so that the important, basic information (like this section) is right up front. At the beginning of each chapter, there is a brief summary of what the chapter covers, followed by deeper details and expanded discussion in the rest of the chapter. There are also occasional sidebars leading you to even more detailed information that you can access at your convenience—now, later, whenever—your choice.

This is the basic structure for each chapter:

- **Your Situation** = Defines the situation you are facing as a leader and "why" the call to action matters
- **Next Steps** = a summary of the very specific steps you can take today
- **Start the Conversation** = a set of questions you can use to engage your leadership team: their answers will begin to form a transformation customized to your organization's unique needs and desires
- **Dig Deeper** = a very detailed description of the "next steps"... these are described from two perspectives:
  - The Leader's Experience...this is where Roy describes "what" he and his team were facing in this transformation and "what" they did
  - The Consultant's Observations...this is where Tim provides a generalized view and description of "how" you can execute the next steps
- **Recommendations** = just what it says
- **Next Steps** = a repeat of the very specific steps you can take today...given what you read you can decide on what you will do next
- **Start the Conversation** = a repeat of the set of questions shared at the start of the chapter. As you work your way through the chapter you may have gained a new perspective on how to answer these questions and what they mean to your organization.

We have used this structure to help make the material directly applicable to what you are facing.

Chapter 1
The Kennedy Space Center Transformation... from a Bad Day to a Good Day for Years to Come

You got this

You are the leader of your organization's transformation. We've been there. A framework can help you think about and guide your leadership actions. In this book, we offer you a framework based on our shared experience with the Kennedy Space Center's (KSC) transformation. By using KSC's story we provide a real-world example of the leadership approaches to address the daily challenges and opportunities you will face along your transformation journey. The KSC example provides situations that you can relate to and learn from.

In this chapter we provide a macro summary of the transformation to provide (1) our credibility and (2) your confidence in what we share in this book. We do not provide all of the details. While you may be a space buff, our intent in this book is to not do a deep dive into the history. In this chapter we focus on the *why KSC needed to change* and the *what they changed* as the context for describing how KSC made these changes. You will need to define your organization's *why* and *what*, and the framework in the remainder of the book can help you develop your *how* to transform.

We use the KSC transformation from 1997 to 2003 as an experience base for learning about transformations and strategy. At times we will share information prior to 1997 to establish the overall context and trends impacting KSC. We use the 1997–2003 timeframe as this represents the time that Roy was the KSC Center Director.

As you read this chapter we want you to be able to see that transformations

1. are hard... and how KSC leadership accepted the challenge
2. start with bad days & end with good days... and how KSC delivered positive results then and now;
3. change the business model... and how KSC was intentional on the new models;
4. face disruptions... and how KSC navigated the disruptions;
5. are a journey... and how KSC systematically went on the journey using strategy;
6. require shared understanding, commitment, and intention... and how KSC made their strategic thinking explicit
7. require making the right changes... and how KSC made the needed targeted changes;
8. require new behaviors... and how KSC leadership drove the culture change;
9. are emotional... and how KSC leadership acknowledged the emotions;
10. require continuous communication... and how KSC leadership consistently shared the story;
11. require leadership... and how KSC leadership was engaged and visible;
12. require transformational leadership...it's all about dignity... and how KSC leadership built the leadership capability.

The essence of the transformation is shown below.

Illustration 1.1—Visual Summary of the KSC Transformation Story

National Environment Driving the Need to Transform

- Lack of national mandate for space
- Push to downsize the government
- Push to reduce government involvement in the space industry

NASA Environment Driving the Need to Transform

- Downsizing shuttle operations
- Shifting ISS philosophy
- Shifting new launch vehicles/ spacecraft efforts
- Shifting space exploration directions
- Focusing NASA on doing research, not operations

KSC's Existential Crisis

- KSC is an operational center, KSC does not do research
- Significant workforce reductions
- Significant reductions in program responsibilities

KSC's Transformation

Delivered the mission while transforming

Made targeted changes
- Transformed processing, launch, and landing operations
  - Transitioned KSC's shuttle operations
  - Established and completed ISS MEIT
  - Consolidated NASA's commercial Launch Services Program at KSC

Enhanced the infrastructure/ spaceport
- Enhanced the office space for KSC Employees
- Established the industrial park outside of KSC Gates
- Established the Cape Canaveral spaceport master plan
- Established the JBOSC with the Air Force

Enhanced technology development focus
- Enhanced spaceport & range techniques
- Participated in shuttle upgrades
- Started to develop a new Checkout and launch control system
- Enhanced KSC's focus on life sciences
- Established ASTWG and ARTWG

Enhanced business operations
- Enhanced KSC's safety focus
- Established the KSC ISO/ business system
- Established and utilized a strategic management process

Ensured the workforce stayed focused on the mission

Enabled Long-Term Success for the Space Industry and NASA

Delivered the mission

Transformed processing, launch, and landing operations
- Continuing to make contributions to the Artemis Program, Launch Services Program, commercial crew, deep space logistics

Enhanced the infrastructure/spaceport
- Preparing the infrastructure for Moon/Mars efforts
- Enabling commercial use of the spaceport

Enhanced technology development focus
- Enhancing and processing systems
- Preparing for the infrastructure on Moon/Mars

Enhanced business operations
- Continuing to evolve operations to the environment

Ensured the workforce stayed focused on the mission
- Maintaining critical skills to enable the mission

Who KSC Is

As shown below, KSC is one of NASA's Centers and facilities. NASA is administered from NASA headquarters, based in Washington, DC. Each of the Centers and facilities has unique capabilities and roles. Since KSC's establishment in March 1962 as NASA's Launch Operations Center, the KSC spaceport has served as the departure gate for most American-manned missions. Some early manned missions launched from Cape Canaveral Air Force Station before KSC was established and while the KSC launch facilities were being constructed. Most unmanned spacecraft were launched from Cape Canaveral Air Force Station, which is adjacent to KSC, since NASA stopped launching them on the space shuttle after the Challenger accident in 1986. The Center was renamed the John F. Kennedy Space Center in late 1963 to honor the president who put America on the path to the moon. A more detailed history of KSC can be found on the Kennedy Space Center website (Kennedy Space Center, n.d.)

Illustration 1.2—NASA's Centers and Facilities

- NASA Headquarters
- Ames Research Center
- Neil A. Armstrong Flight Research Center
- Glenn Research Center
- Goddard Space Flight Center
- Goddard Institute for Space Studies
- Jet Propulsion Laboratory
- Johnson Space Center
- Katherine Johnson IV&V Facility
- Kennedy Space Center
- Langley Research Center
- Marshall Space Flight Center
- Michoud Assembly Facility
- NASA Engineering and Safety Center
- NASA Safety Center
- NASA Shared Services Center
- Neil Armstrong Test Facility
- Stennis Space Center
- Wallops Flight Facility
- White Sands Test Facility

Before we discuss the journey KSC made, we need to understand the "control context" in which KSC existed and how much control KSC had for its destiny as a NASA field Center.

KSC was valued for getting the job done. In response to major program decisions, KSC executed what it was asked to do. As a government entity, it had limited influence on the external environment—its stakeholders and customers—in which it operated. Each level of the hierarchy added a layer of authority that KSC had to respond to:

- The president and Congress set the overall direction for NASA and appropriated resources for it.
- The NASA Administrator and his management team translated the direction into NASA programs. The NASA budget provided a specific amount of money for each program.
- The NASA program managers defined program requirements for the projects that the Centers were to meet and decided how to allocate it to the Centers to support their program operations. Each Center was able to negotiate with NASA HQ for additional funding if needed, but NASA program directors made the final call on what they actually received.

Out of necessity, given this hierarchy, KSC had to be very responsive to NASA and program requests. As he took the job of Center Director, Roy noted this in his remarks in the March 1997 KSC Implementation Plan:

This plan is the initial step in defining KSC's role in current and future NASA endeavors. It will help us lead our Agency responsibilities and see how we fit into enterprise plans. In working the next iteration of this plan, we will develop a clearer focus by prioritizing and concentrating our efforts on critical strategies to assure we achieve our objectives (*Kennedy Space Center Implementation Plan 1997*).

Driven to Change by the Environment (KSC's External Big Why)

To understand and learn from the KSC transformation, it's essential to understand the nature of its external environment, including the political (presidential/congressional) environment, the US space industry, and the NASA environment. These environments defined the challenges and opportunities that KSC faced.

The political environment drivers included:

- ***The lack of focus on space.*** In this time period, there was very little political excitement about space. Involving Russia in the International Space Station was one key political driver. Beginning with 9/11, the focus became homeland security and the war on terrorism. Within the US political scene, the focus was not on space.
- ***The push to downsize the government.*** In the mid-1990s the focus was on reinventing government, budget responsibility, and governmental infighting. With the transition from the Clinton administration to the Bush administration, the focus transitioned to the new president's agenda (e.g., President's Management Agenda). The government was continuing to move to greater competitive sourcing and use of private-sector resources (e.g., FAIR Education Act).

The US space industry drivers included the push to reduce government involvement in the space industry. As the US space industry evolved within the civil/scientific (NASA), military (DOD-related launches), and commercial (communication-type satellites) markets, KSC's opportunities and constraints changed. NASA partnered and interacted with both the military and commercial markets. The overall US leadership in worldwide launches diminished in the early 1990s.

In the early 1990s, the space industry was pushing heavily for the government to play less of a role in the operations of the civil space business. There was a belief that the civil or science space efforts could be a government-supported role, but the government should not play a major role in the "operations" of the civil space business (NASA 1995a). Both NASA and the military began the process of removing themselves from daily space operations. In the military space business, the Air Force was under pressure, like NASA, to remove itself from the space operations business. However, failures and concerns for program terminations led the Air Force to reconsider its approach to the space business (NASA 1999). There was a push to maintain greater engineering discipline and understanding of the space launch business.

Industry's desire helped give rise to the initial push for removing KSC from the daily operations of the shuttle program. Industry believed it could do a better job if the government was not involved. There was a continuous change in the overall philosophy for the government's role in the shuttle program, from government oversight to privatization to commercialization.

Given this external context, NASA faced a challenging environment:

- NASA operated without a strong national mandate, other than partnering with Russia and international partners for political reasons.
- NASA was realigning and downsizing.

As the United States government was pushing to "reinvent" and downsize, the push was happening within NASA as well. With Dan Goldin as the administrator, NASA was making a push to a "Faster, Better, Cheaper" philosophy. NASA met these challenges by continuously shifting its policy/philosophy for (1) the shuttle, (2) ISS, (3) new launch vehicle/spacecraft development, and (4) exploration:

(1) ***Pushing for downsizing KSC's shuttle operations.*** The shuttle philosophy oscillated from government oversight (being in charge of the shuttle program) to government insight (limited to merely monitoring the shuttle program in every aspect except the actual launch, which it would continue to remain in charge of). The philosophy regarding government involvement

in the shuttle program also oscillated across various concepts for privatization and commercialization. KSC was hesitant due to safety concerns for the shuttle process and also the impacts on KSC.

NASA groups were supporting this move out of operations for KSC. A NASA report called for the privatization of shuttle operations and a reduced civil service role in the daily operations of the shuttle processing activities. In February 1995, NASA released the *Report of the Space Shuttle Management Independent Review Team* (NASA 1995a). The intent of the team was "to review the present shuttle operation management and to propose innovative approaches to significantly decrease total operating costs while maintaining systems safety" (NASA 1995a, iii). The team made three conclusions:

- NASA should establish a clear set of program goals, with greater emphasis on cost-efficient operations and user-friendly payload integration, making it possible for shuttle payloads to be more easily processed, tested, and integrated into the shuttle.
- NASA should redefine the management structure, separating development and operations and disengaging NASA from the daily operation of the space shuttle.
- NASA should provide the necessary environment and conditions within the program to pursue these goals (NASA 1995a, vii).

Given this environment, KSC had to re-establish its relevancy to the shuttle program.

(2) ***Exploring different ISS philosophies.*** Various discussions focused on what "ISS complete" meant—what the final configuration of ISS would be in space. The ISS discussion started with the ship-and-shoot philosophy. The ship-and-shoot philosophy was for each ISS component to be made in the factory, shipped to KSC, and then launched without it being evaluated for fit with the other ISS elements. This was another result of NASA's "Faster, Better, Cheaper" motto of the time—just get out of the way and let the contractors do it to save money and time.

Imagine launching a module and it turned out that it didn't fit or functionally work with the other modules already in orbit. NASA needed to hook those modules up on the ground and make sure that everything was working right. The Multiple Element Integrated Testing (MEIT) integrated and tested various elements on the ground before they were launched and assembled in space. Eventually NASA and the program agreed that "ship and shoot" would be an extremely high risk to the long-term success of the ISS.

(3) ***Starting and stopping new launch vehicle/spacecraft development efforts.*** Many efforts started and stopped (e.g., X-vehicles, Next Generation Launch Technologies, Space Launch Initiative, Orbital Space Plane [OSP]). Each one of these efforts focused on developing a new launch vehicle system that would be more efficient, reliable, and safe than the current Shuttle Transportation System.

(4) ***Shifting the space exploration direction.*** In 1997, NASA was highlighting the successes of the Mars Pathfinder and Mars Sojourner rovers. "Mars or Bust" became the mantra. Within a short time, Mars and exploration were de-emphasized.

This unstable environment created an existential relevancy crisis for KSC.

KSC's Existential Relevancy Crisis (KSC's Local Why)

In the mid-1990s KSC had to justify its existence and determine how it fit within a changing NASA—a research-oriented, "Faster, Better, Cheaper" agency. Throughout these years, KSC had to continue to balance safely meeting the operational mission with creating the future—transitioning out of operations and into new roles. This NASA environment in turn created an external environment in which KSC had to justify its operational role and the civil service value in the operations. This direction eventually led to NASA consolidating multiple contracts into a single prime contract for shuttle processing. This privatization push would lead to a push to reduce the number of KSC civil service employees. It also meant KSC would continually face the challenges of inserting its operational knowledge into ever-changing new vehicle development and space exploration efforts.

NASA conducted a zero-based review (ZBR)—a budgeting method in which all expenses, projects, etc. must be evaluated and justified for a new period, starting from zero instead of beginning with the previous budget and making adjustments to it—and dictated a target level of civil service employees at KSC. It was a significant reduction. The intent of the ZBR "propose[d] streamlining functions at the NASA Centers, so each installation becomes a 'Center of Excellence,' concentrating on specific aspects of NASA's mission" (NASA 1995b). In May 1995, NASA released the results of the ZBR. Consistent with the *Report of the Space Shuttle Management Independent Review Team*, the ZBR team recommended adopting operating guidelines. One of them was that "Aerospace operations, including the Space Shuttle, will be performed by NASA contractors."

Prior to Roy becoming the Center Director, there was a senior management meeting in the fourth-floor conference room. The meeting was focused on identifying potential ways in which KSC could contribute to NASA in the future and thus maintain the workforce level. As each idea was shared, the Center Director said no. As this was happening, another senior manager was writing down numbers, then crossing them off. He shared this with someone across the table. I could see the sheet of paper with the decreasing numbers. The number ended up being 400.

After the meeting, I asked another senior manager what the interchange was about. He said it was the projected workforce that would be left at KSC. This was not a specific financial number for the end of the year ... it was more of a strategy discussion. Still, there was clearly a message that KSC's contributions were not valued and the leader didn't want to engage in new roles.

I sat and watched this and was a bit shocked. How could NASA and KSC be devalued? My dad's love of NASA had rubbed off on me and now I was listening to a situation that didn't make sense to me. I wondered how the senior managers at the table felt.

When the numbers were finally official, though not nearly as draconian as that strategic discussion in the fourth-floor conference room, they were overwhelming. They rattled the walls and it became clear that nothing short of a significant transformation of KSC's business model would achieve their goals. The results of this ZBR included these points:

- KSC was appointed the Center of Excellence for space launch.
- The civil service workforce was projected to be reduced by about 1000 employees.
- The contractor workforce was projected to be reduced by about 2000 employees.

Illustration 1.3 highlights the projected shift in civil service workforce at KSC from 1995 to 2003 and the actual numbers from 1993 to 2003. We included the numbers for 1993 to 1996 to share the trends facing KSC.

Illustration 1.3—Projected shift in civil service workforce at KSC from 1995 to 2003

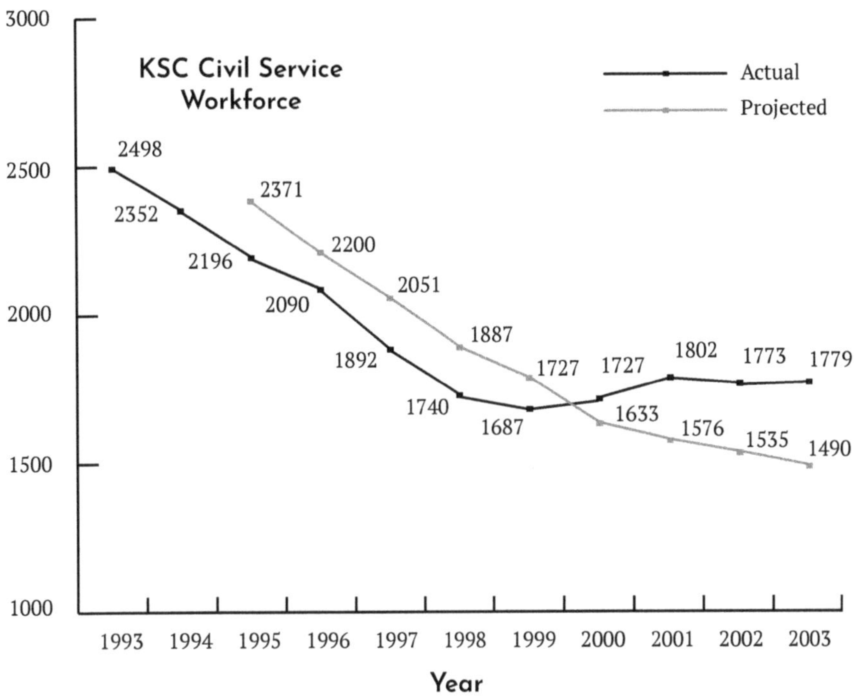

KSC's Response to the Existential Crisis = Transform (KSC's *What Was Changed*)

The KSC transformation is a story of an organization accomplishing many things in a risky environment. The space business is a risky business. As you know, change/transformations are hard. The potential for the loss of life with a shuttle accident raised the stakes for the transformation. The transformation had to ensure current operations were safely executed while KSC was in the process of changing. As shown in Illustration 1.4, KSC transformed from 1997 to 2003.

Illustration 1.4 – Comparison of KSC in 1997 to 2003

Category	KSC in 1997	KSC in 2003
External Environment	Reinvent/downsize government NASA: Goldin, "Faster, Better, Cheaper"; zero-based review (ZBR)	Terrorism and war
KSC's Credibility within NASA	Get the operational job done	Significant number of KSC alumni in leadership positions within NASA Value of operational knowledge is appreciated and sought
KSC Direction	NASA does research, KSC is an operational Center Reduce civil service role in shuttle operations	Space launch operations Center of Excellence Launch Service Program (LSP) lead Spaceport and range technologies designation
KSC Program Affiliation	Shuttle role declining Spacelab role declining	Space shuttle lead for launch and landing operations and insight of contractor for processing International Space Station test and processing lead Lead Center for Launch Services Program (commercial) Biology/Life science payload development and processing Spaceport and range technologies
Spaceport Operations	Shuttle centric	Consolidated contract to provide infrastructure maintenance and support services with Cape Canaveral, which reduced costs with savings available to fund strategic projects State of Florida commits to funding for the business park and a new life sciences laboratory

All of these were accomplished while responding to national political (presidential and congressional) and NASA initiatives, and while downsizing the workforce.

By 2003, KSC's credibility and presence within NASA was significant. KSC "alumni" held high-level management positions within the NASA structure (e.g., Roy Bridges eventually became Center Director at Langley Research Center; Lesa Roe was Deputy Director and then became Center Director at Langley Research Center; Jim Jennings became Deputy Associate Administrator for Institutions and Asset Management within NASA HQ; Dave King became the Center Director at Marshall Space Flight Center). Furthermore, KSC's role of operational knowledge in new vehicle development was supported. Their strategic direction was supported by NASA HQ in principle. Significant program affiliation with roles in shuttle, ISS, and Launch Services Program (LSP) was vibrant. KSC continued to have limited funded roles in the research and development activities.

During this time in a risky business, KSC

- delivered the mission while transforming;
- made targeted changes;
    - transformed processing, launch, and landing operations;
    - enhanced the infrastructure/spaceport;
    - enhanced technology development focus;
    - enhanced business operations;
- ensured the workforce stayed focused on the mission.

These changes enabled long-term success for the space industry and NASA.

Delivered the Mission While Transforming

KSC continued to meet its responsibilities as it transformed. The very nature of a transformation may change the core mission of your organization. Throughout its transformation, KSC focused on meeting its mission. Its core mission didn't change over time, but what the mission was applied to and how the mission was executed did change over time.

KSC executed its long-standing mission of processing the shuttle, ISS, and NASA payloads. Through the strategic management process within NASA and KSC, KSC further expanded its application of its mission to include the Launch Services Program, spaceport and range technology development, and exploration support. Illustration 1.5 (located in *For Inquiring Minds...The Details,* p. 284) summarizes the major efforts KSC implemented to meet the core mission.

Illustration 1.6—Summary of KSC Business Model Changes

Area	Item
Transformed Processing, Launch, and Landing Operations	Transitioned KSC's Shuttle Operations
	Established and Completed the International Space Station Multiple Element Integrated Test
	Consolidated NASA's Commercial Launch Services Program at KSC
Enhanced the Infrastructure/ Spaceport	Enhanced the Office Space for KSC Employees
	Established the Industrial Park Outside of KSC Gates
	Established the Cape Canaveral Spaceport Master Plan
	Established the Joint Base Operations Support Contract with the Air Force
Enhanced the Technology Development Focus	Enhanced Spaceport & Range Technologies
	Participated in Shuttle Upgrades
	Started to Develop a New Checkout & Launch Control System
	Enhanced KSC's Focus on Life Sciences
	Established Advanced Spaceport Technologies & Advanced Range Technologies Working Groups
Enhanced Business Operations	Enhanced KSC's Safety Focus
	Established the KSC ISO/Business System
	Established and Utilized a Strategic Management Process

Made Targeted Changes

In order to align to the new "missions" they were facing, they had to align their products, services, processes, structure, tools, and workforce. They wanted to move to a new business model which balanced processing/launch/landing operations, infrastructure/spaceport, technology development, and business operations (e.g., the back office functions such as human resources, legal, procurement) to support delivering the mission. Illustration 1.6 summarizes KSC's major change in business model elements for these four areas.

Description	Nature of the Change
Create a new method for the government to provide mission assurance	Adapt current model
Conduct a test of the elements on the ground before they are launched and placed in space	Create new products, services, and methods
Consolidate commercial launch services acquisition from across NASA to KSC	Create new products, services, and methods
Provide new, safe facilities for the employees	Create new infrastructure
Enable easier research partnerships with universities	Create new products, services, and methods
Build a long-term perspective to the future needs and path to meet these needs	Create new products, services, and methods
Implement a joint contract across KSC and the AF for providing the base support functions	Create new methods
Provide new technologies to enable safer and more efficient processing	Create new methods
Design and implement upgrades to enhance the shuttle	Create new products, services, and methods
Design and develop a new checkout and launch control system	Create new products, services, and methods
Create a focus on the systems to enable plant growth in space	Create new products, services, and methods
Explore the performance and technology needs to modernize and enhance the operations of spaceports and ranges	Create new products, services, and methods
Increase the daily focus on safely executing work	Create new methods
Provide an infrastructure for systematic business operations and management	Create new methods
Provide a systematic, routine process for defining and executing the KSC strategy	Create new methods

Transformed Processing, Launch, and Landing Operations

Transitioned Shuttle Operations at KSC: The effort was successfully executed. KSC achieved a significant reduction in civil service and contractor workforces, although well short of initial goals. NASA eventually recognized the value of what KSC was contributing across all NASA efforts and suspended the downsizing.

Established and Completed ISS Multi-Element Integration and Test (MEIT): This successfully assured the long-term viability of the ISS, which has been continually supported by crew for over two decades.

Consolidated NASA's Commercial Launch Services at KSC with the Launch Services Program (LSP): The effort was successful and gave KSC a full program that they used to serve all of NASA Centers with excellent launch services. It also paved the way for more private investments in developing new launch vehicles in the long term.

Enhanced the Infrastructure/Spaceport

Enhanced the Office Space for KSC Employees. Early efforts to get rid of trailer parks and boxcars as housing for the workforce offices and labs were successful. With the completion of the multi-story OSBII office building, we reduced substandard housing from over 500,000 ft. square to less than 100,000 ft. square. Instead of boxcars, many small buildings for technical work were constructed in places convenient for the workforce to support processing. Now the workforce is hosted in modern and safe buildings.

Established the Industrial Park Outside the KSC gates. The industrial park has been wildly successful in attracting several large companies to manufacture spacecraft and hardware and hire hundreds of employees into well-paying jobs.

Established the Cape Canaveral Spaceport Master Plan: The plan was developed and was successful. Over time, the spaceport gained significant new customers for the launch and processing facilities and the range. The spaceport became a multiuser facility.

Established the Joint Base Operations and Support Contract (JBOSC) with the Air Force. This was an effort to reduce the number of civil servants managing infrastructure and security contracts at KSC by consolidating everything into one contract and jointly managing it with the Air Force. This ended after 10 years, and the funding that we saved contributed to the success of many of the strategic projects that made KSC what it is today. Also, JBOSC was very significant in giving us a "bank account" to help with the transition. The NASA Administrator, Dan Goldin, did not believe that we would be successful in establishing the JBOSC, but, to encourage us, he said that he would allow us to keep any savings for reinvestment in KSC. That was a huge incentive for our team to achieve the savings. We knew that we would save a lot of money when the JBOSC hired 500 fewer people on day one of the contract to do the same job. In the five years from 1998 through 2003, we saved over $70 million, which we invested in magnet and safety projects.

Enhanced KSC's Technology Development Focus

Enhanced Spaceport and Range Technologies: Created numerous technology development efforts under a new banner for the Center—the Spaceport Technology Center. One example was the Cryogenic Test Bed Facility, which was developed in partnership with the State of Florida. This project was immediately successful in validating the utility of a cryogenic freeze plug technique that allowed crews to change out a shuttle component rather than an expensive, and time-consuming, shuttle rollback from the launch pad. KSC's efforts to create and transfer spaceport and range technologies can be credited in part with the proliferation of spaceports in the US and the transformation of KSC into a multiuser spaceport. While this effort was only partially successful because it began well ahead of its time, many today recognize the value of these technologies in enabling higher launch rates. Today, KSC and Cape Canaveral launch rates keep setting higher records year after year.

Participated in Shuttle Upgrades: KSC made use of its operational knowledge to support shuttle upgrades meant to increase the safety and efficiency of the shuttle. After the Columbia accident, the focus changed to retiring the space shuttle, so only absolutely necessary changes to correct problems in shuttle systems were funded, rather than more extensive upgrades.

Started to Develop a New Checkout and Launch Control System (CLCS): This effort was to create a new checkout and launch control system, for the shuttle. The intent was to increase the safety and efficiency of shuttle processing and launches. As the external environment changed to focus on retiring the space shuttle and developing a new deep space exploration capability for Moon and Mars explorations, the return-on-investment equation changed, and the project was canceled.

Enhanced the Focus on Life Sciences at KSC: In partnership with the state of Florida, KSC enhanced the focus and facilities at KSC for supporting research and technology development of life-support systems in space. This was largely successful, as many experiments have been developed and operated by customers on the ISS over the years.

Established the Advanced Spaceport Technology Working Group (ASTWG)/ Advanced Range Technology Working Group (ARTWG): These working groups established a nation-wide forum to define the needs and requirements for future spaceports and ranges. This failed to achieve full program funding. It was clearly ahead of its time. Looking back at the number of new spaceports and ranges that have been created recently, we can see that these efforts were needed eventually. Today the launch ranges can handle many more launches per year than was possible when this initiative was proposed. Also, there are dozens of new spaceports around the nation and the world.

Enhanced Business Operations

Enhanced Our Focus on Safety. We successfully gained International Standards Organization and the Occupational Safety and Health Administration's *Voluntary Protective Program (VPP)* certification, which helped achieve the best-quality services and products safely. KSC's safety program has resulted in avoiding many mishaps, injuries, and deaths. In terms of mission safety, the establishment of a "world-class" surveillance concept for the Space Shuttle Program allowed us to achieve the desired launch rates and maintain safety with only one shuttle anomaly attributed to KSC processing during the period. The loss of Columbia was well investigated and many improvements were made as a result; however, KSC shuttle processing was not implicated in the cause chain for the mishap. The new Launch Services Program (LSP) for ELVs maintained a near-perfect success record, launching dozens of NASA science missions with a new approach to mission assurance. The MEIT Team did a marvelous job of testing the modules of the International Space Station. Elements built in the United States, Russia, Japan, Canada, and Europe were joined together in space for the first time without major difficulties.

Established the KSC ISO/Business System: This effort focused on documenting and improving the processes at KSC. This was successful. KSC became ISO-certified.

Established and Utilized a Strategic Management Process. The strategic management was used to manage the transformation. This approach also allowed KSC to manage future challenges successfully. For example, they transitioned to a multi-user spaceport supporting many customers. This made previous space shuttle facilities available to support commercial operators. Perhaps most importantly, we trained leaders in strategic management, and they moved to other Centers and NASA headquarters and did incredibly good work.

Ensured the Workforce Stayed Focused on the Mission

Taken together, the trigger events created a context in which the inherent value of the civil service workforce within KSC was questioned. NASA was defined as a research organization, which does not do operations. KSC was defined as an operational Center, which does not do research. KSC faced an identity crisis as well as a funding and workforce challenge. KSC had to address low morale in the workforce (Right Management Associates 1996). The management philosophy at that time focused on doing the assigned job well and being responsive to guidance from NASA headquarters and programs. But KSC needed a vision for the future. KSC focused on making the safe transition to the Space Flight Operations Contract (SFOC) and reducing the workforce. But there was no shared articulation of KSC's contribution in the future. In response to this, a group of employees formed a focus group to help define the problem facing KSC. Illustration 1.7 is the result of this employee group. They pointed to the need for a shared vision.

Illustration 1.7—Employee Concerns

- What is the desired future state/vision for KSC?
- What actions–change approach–will KSC take to go after the future state/vision?
- Employees want leadership action from senior management.
- Employees want to know there is a plan and direction.

Enabled Long-Term Success for the Space Industry and NASA

Transformational leaders know the transformation is about the all-term. The all-term is about today, short-term, and long-term. As the leader, you need to help the organization see how today, short-term, and long-terms are related. Transformations are necessary to meet today's challenges. When done well, they enable amazing tomorrows. See Illustration 1.8 to see how the changes made in the late 1990s and early 2000s are enabling the results KSC is achieving today.

When we were going through the transformation, we were focused on the immediate and short term with an eye on the future (see the strategic thinking principle of managing the all-term discussed in Chapter 7). Some of the changes laid the foundation for the long term. I continued to support KSC and their programs after Roy left. My engagement with them has continued from 1997 and is still going strong as of this writing in 2025. I have the benefit of seeing how the changes impacted the future of the space industry, NASA, and KSC. Some of the highlights include

- The space shuttle returned to flight after correcting issues that caused the loss of Columbia and completed the assembly of the ISS. It did not experience another accident for the rest of its time supporting the ISS with crews and supplies. It was eventually retired to free up resources for new exploration initiatives such as Orion and the Space Launch System. Efforts to provide a United States launch vehicle as a companion to using the Russian Soyuz to rotate crews, provide logistics support, and propulsion to boost the ISS periodically to maintain its altitude resulted in new crew and logistics modules developed by commercial space companies and provided as a service to NASA for a fee.

- The ISS is now in its third decade of continuous human occupation and service without any major problems along the way. This is a testament to the value of the MEIT that KSC ran.
- The Launch Services Program (LSP) has an impeccable record of success in leading NASA's expendable launch vehicle program. The LSP has also led the way to getting more private commercial vehicles engaged in taking NASA payloads to space.
- KSC is highly engaged in assuring that the Orion spacecraft and the Space Launch System rocket will be successful in getting humans back to the moon and beyond.

A recent article, "Once in the doldrums, Florida coast hums with space launches," highlights the long-term impact of KSC on the community:

The [Associated Press] (9/2) reports that Florida's Space Coast has seen a rejuvenation over the past decade, "powered in the past decade by private, commercial companies..." As of last year, "the Kennedy Space Center had more than 12,300 civil servants, private contractors and other employees working at the spaceport, just a few thousand employees short of the 15,000 workers during the heydays of the shuttle program." Along the Space Coast, "new subdivisions have been permitted, new hotels have been built, small manufacturing plants supporting the space industry are under construction in industrial parks and a gleaming outdoor shopping area recently opened in the footprint of the Miracle City Mall. Last year, the Milken Institute ranked the Space Coast metro area as having the second strongest economy in the U.S. using an index based on jobs, wages, and high-tech growth. The ranking for the metro was up 47 spots from three years prior."

(Jackson and Schneider 2022)

Illustration 1.8—Impacts of Earlier Changes on the Long-Term

Focus	Change
Processing, Launch, and Landing Operations	Transitioned KSC's Shuttle Operations
	Established and Completed the International Space Station Multiple Element Integrated Test
	Consolidated NASA's Commercial Launch Services Program at KSC
Infrastructure/ Spaceport	Enhanced the Office Space for KSC Employees
	Established the Industrial Park Outside of KSC Gates
	Established the Cape Canaveral Spaceport Master Plan
	Established the Joint Base Operations Support Contract with the Air Force
Enhanced the Technology Development Focus	Enhanced Spaceport & Range Technologies
	Participated in Shuttle Upgrades
	Started to Develop a New Checkout & Launch Control System
	Enhanced KSC's Focus on Life Sciences
	Established Advanced Spaceport Technologies & Advanced Range Technologies Working Groups
Enhanced Business Operations	Enhanced KSC's Safety Focus
	Established the KSC ISO/Business System
	Established and Utilized a Strategic Management Process

Acronyms for illustration 1.8

CRS: Commercial Resupply Services
CCP: Commercial Crew Program
DSL: Deep Space Logistics
SLS: Space Launch System
VPP: OSHA Voluntary Protection Program
ISO: International Organization for Standardization
EGS: Exploration Ground Systems
NE: Kennedy Engineering Directorate

Long-Term Impacts (2020)
The lessons learned on the approaches for the government to be involved in mission assurance continue to be applied to LSP and the Commercial Crew program
ISS remains in orbit KSC continues to support the ISS utilization by processing cargo
LSP continues to be a vital organization to acquire launch services for NASA LSP lessons learned and people have been transferred to other commercial programs within NASA (e.g., CRS, CCP, DSL)
The enhanced office continues to support the multiple programs being executed at KSC
The office park has become home to new commercial space efforts.
KSC continues to take a long-term perspective to the spaceport After the shuttle, KSC focused on making the spaceport a multi-user spaceport
KSC continued to adjust the base support contract approaches to reduce cost. Using the lessons learned and outcomes, KSC has transformed itself to doing more than government launches; there are significant commercial operations occurring at KSC
The enhanced spaceport is enabling significantly more launches per year.
KSC continues to use its launch vehicle expertise to support the development of the SLS and enhancements to the commercial launch services
As part of the Exploration Ground Systems program (led by KSC), KSC is developing a new launch control and checkout system for SLS
KSC continues to conduct research and technology development on plant systems. These systems are crucial to a sustainable human presence on the Moon and Mars
This expertise is recognized as important to the SLS launch. KSC is assigned the Exploration Ground Systems programs to build the infrastructure for processing and launching the SLS
KSC continues to use the VPP program
KSC continues to use the business and remains ISO certified
Continue to work a strategic management process Transitioned the model to other programs (e.g., LSP, EGS, ISS, NE, DSL)

These current results are not the direct result of the transformation we went through. Our transformation enabled or "built a bridge" to these long-term community impacts by ensuring KSC was still relevant, building the mindset for proactive change, and laying the foundation for the commercial space activities.

In the remainder of this book, we'll explore and understand how KSC made these changes.

KSC's Transformational Approach = Thinking and Acting Strategically (How the KSC Leadership Made the Transformation Happen)

As you can see from the summary of the transformation, KSC made significant changes. These changes were intentionally taken on. Based on what you read, we want you to be able to see that you will need to do the following:

1. Accept that you are here at this moment for a reason
2. Make the first move
3. Fix the current model
4. Respond to unplanned events
5. Create your map to navigate the journey
6. Think strategically
7. Focus your limited resources on the "right" changes
8. Reset your organization's behaviors
9. Gain your workforce's commitment to the transformation
10. Create shared understanding
11. Provide strong leadership presence
12. Ensure your organization knows and believes their actions are making a difference

You must...

Make the choice to transform...it all begins with you and the direction you provide.

Chapter 2
Parachute Into—and Accept—the Transformation

You got this

Your Situation...
Transformations Are Hard

If you are reading this book, you are probably facing a transformational situation. Your senior management team and workforce are looking to see if you are going to recognize and accept the transformation challenge. You may have some doubts...this is good...this means you understand what is at stake. You must *accept* the challenge. Everything you have done to this point will serve you well as you lead your team. Accept that you are here at this time and place for a reason.

You have either been recently hired to lead the transformation or you are the incumbent leader who sees the need to transform the business. Either way, you are sitting in the senior leader's role and may have a sense of

> “*What did I get myself into?*
>
> *How can I make this transformation successful?*”

In this chapter, we share our observations about using the lessons learned from our previous experience to support the KSC transformation. You, too, will use what your previous experience has taught you. We believe you are here at this time and place for a reason. Be confident and make use of the skills and knowledge your previous experiences gave you. Everything you have done up to this point has prepared you for this moment. You got this.

What's Next...
Accept You Are Here at this Moment for a Reason

Standing at the threshold of a transformation can feel overwhelming. But realizing that your knowledge, skills, and past experiences brought you to this time and place can help you accept that you are here at this time for a reason: you are meant to lead this transformation.

Next Steps

To begin your transformation leadership journey:

- Accept that Sometimes We Parachute into the Unknown
- Make Use of Your Previous Experiences
- Be Present and Listen

Start the Conversation

Engage your team in starting the transformation:

What are our past experiences to pull from?

From those experiences, what are we most proud of?

From those experiences, what do we regret the most?

What are the lessons learned?

Moving forward into this new situation, what do we need to start, stop, or continue doing as a leadership team?

Dig Deeper

In this section, we provide the leader's perspective (Roy) and the consultant's perspective (Tim) on the following actions you can take:

- Accept that Sometimes We Parachute into the Unknown
- Make Use of Your Previous Experiences
- Be Present and Listen

Accept That Sometimes We Parachute into the Unknown

The Leader's Experience ... Roy

When things are going well in my organization, I take pleasure in going to work and seeing the workforce at all levels performing well—we are meeting schedules with great quality products and keeping everyone safe. There is plenty of time in the day to do a lot of management by walking around and talking with my people. It is amazing what I learn during those visits—just being present with them, observing and listening—and people seem to enjoy visiting with me.

If I get wind of some problems during these visits, even though the problem hasn't caused a major impact yet, I find it difficult to get people on board to make changes proactively in order to avoid potential impacts. They often don't see the urgency, and they put the needed changes at the bottom of their things to do, therefore putting those changes off. This tendency is normal—and it makes it hard to implement needed changes.

On the other hand, if there is a bad day, it becomes obvious to many that changes are needed, and right now. Mobilizing the workforce to make the changes becomes much easier. Unfortunately, putting off needed changes until an emergency condition occurs can result not only in a problem much more difficult to fix than it would have been to prevent, but also in the current leader being fired and a new leader being selected to lead the change—in a dire or emergency situation.

In my career, I have found myself in the position of that new leader, parachuting into an organization during the worst of times, with expectations from my new boss that I would be able to turn the organization around in record time.

The Consultant's Observations ... Tim

My involvement in the KSC transformation began with a summer research program in 1996, about a year before Roy became the KSC Center Director. The program was the NASA/American Society for Engineering Education Summer Faculty Fellowship Program. Faculty worked at a Center for 10 weeks over the summer. The intent of the program was to help faculty (1) grow their skills and their understanding of the research needs of a NASA Center and (2) deliver research results that the Center needed.

My assignment on this first project was to help the Center understand how to downsize in a "good way." Eventually our focus switched to how to transform—how to downsize the Center in a humane manner and align it to a greater purpose. I didn't have any experience in large-scale transformations or downsizing. I was one year out from finishing my doctorate work at Virginia Tech. I wasn't sure I was ready to do this. So, you may be asking, why did KSC ask me to help them on this effort? I know I was asking myself this question.

Make Use of Your Previous Experiences

The Leader's Experience ... Roy

I attended the US Army Airborne School at Fort Benning, Georgia, for parachute training while I was a cadet at the US Air Force Academy. After much preliminary training, I found myself standing in the door of a large cargo aircraft, watching the ground fly by 1200 feet below. I had developed a fear of falling as a kid while working to harvest and cure tobacco, which involves getting sticks of green tobacco hung up in tobacco barns for curing. These barns are several stories high. My legs were too short to span the poles that we hung the sticks on, so I had to stand on a six-inch-wide board, reach down and take a loaded stick of tobacco, and hand it up to the next level. I saw several people fall out of the barn to the ground below, which caused my visceral fear of falling to develop quickly.

How unlucky for me that I just happened to be sitting in the seat closest to the door on my first jump. I was so tense that when the instructor tapped me on my butt to signal me to jump, I sprang out of the plane like a tightly coiled spring being released. All ended well on that first jump, but I was happy to be going into the Air Force to fly planes instead of being a paratrooper in the Army.

Now, imagine jumping into a combat situation and not knowing exactly what you will find upon landing. That is often what happens to new leaders as they parachute into their new organization after a bad day. Let me give you some examples.

After the Challenger tragedy, my second space shuttle mission was canceled. I had planned to remain as an astronaut to assist NASA in getting the shuttles flying again, but fate intervened. I was ordered to return to the Air Force to command their largest test wing at Edwards Air Force Base, California.

My dream job was to be an astronaut if I could. Now that I was one, I wanted to stay with that. But if I could not continue as an astronaut, I loved testing aircraft and would be happy doing that for the rest of my career.

So I took the position. After I had served in that position for several years, my boss, the two-star general who was the Air Force Flight Test Center Commander, called me to his office one day.

I'd done everything I could do at Edwards. I thought I'd done well enough to get promoted, but I had not been promoted, so I'd kind of given up on that. And when my boss said, "Hey, would you like to have a new command assignment, launching rockets at Cape Canaveral Air Force Station and Patrick Air Force Base, Florida?" all I could think was, “What? Are you kidding me? I would take an assignment launching firecrackers.”

Nobody told me that the organization running the bases, the Eastern Space and Missile Center, was having a bad day. No, I found that out during a visit with my new boss after the change-of-command ceremony. “Roy,” he said, “welcome to your new command. I am excited to have you in charge. I need to give you a few words of caution. The previous commander was fired because he didn’t have enough money in the budget to make it to the end of the fiscal year. He threatened to close the range before the end of the year unless he got a budget plus up. I would advise you to find another approach.”

Oh, my God, I thought. What have I got myself into? It was too late to back out. I was facing a mission impossible. We were already halfway through the year. This was an existential emergency.

Without going into the excruciating detail of what we had to do to make it successfully to the end of the year, we all pulled together as a team, came up with a good plan, and made it work well. Not only did we not have to close the range, but we also developed a plan to recover the items that we had put on the shelf for cost avoidance. At the very end of the year, when some commands turn back money that they can’t spend, we recovered every single item on our list. I also met with the general in charge of the budget for the Air Force Systems Command, our major command, to convince him of how to correct the issue that had led to the budget shortfall. It was based on a misunderstanding. He made sure that this issue would not occur again.

My wife and I threw a “Get Out of Jail” dinner party when the year was over. We wore prison uniforms of black and white stripes and had a dining table centerpiece of bread baked into a ball and chain. What fun.

A few months later, my boss called me again to congratulate me on being on the promotion list to brigadier general.

After several more Air Force assignments, I retired as a major general after 31 years in the service and started looking for a job in the private sector. Imagine my surprise when NASA contacted me and invited me to apply to be the Center Director of the Kennedy Space Center. That was my dream of a great assignment come true—and one that my skills and experience had equipped me for. Yes, I gladly accepted that assignment. Again, I had little idea of the challenges that the organization was facing as I took the helm. I was standing in the door to parachute into the unknown again.

The Consultant's Observations ... Tim

I believe I was asked to support KSC because I made a good impression in the graduate classes I was teaching at the Center. At the time, the University of Central Florida (UCF), where I teach, had a graduate program in Engineering Management that we taught on the Center's property. The previous fall and spring, I had taught two classes for them. I came to understand the KSC situation and KSC people. They got to know me. I think they sensed that I cared, could ask good questions, was a good listener, and could summarize/build a model of what was shared. While I felt unprepared, I was excited to support the KSC team on their journey.

By the way, throughout this first year, I was nervous and kept asking myself *Why am I here? How can I really help them? How can I be most present for them?* I knew I could depend on the people mentoring me (e.g., Jim Jennings, Saul Barton, and senior managers Tip Talone and Shannon Bartell). I was able to make use of my strengths as I developed new skills to help them better. The key was to be authentic and to build trust-based relationships with the management team and supervisors in KSC. I am grateful to KSC for allowing me to go on this journey with them.

Be Present and Listen

The Leader's Experience ... Roy

When parachuting into a new organization, it is often difficult to know who to listen to. My experience with the transformations that I led taught me to listen and learn from everyone. More importantly, the new leader needs to be seen by managers as someone who is open to hearing about everything that is happening from the managers' point of view and who will provide support to correct problems that are preventing the managers from achieving the highest level of performance. The long-term goal is to have everyone working toward common objectives and sharing issues with all on the team. That will take many individual and group conversations to get everyone on the same page.

If a bad day occurs, then the leader must take responsibility and assist the team in finding the best way out of the difficulty. That was crucial in successfully transforming KSC and two other large organizations later in my career. When good days were achieved, I enjoyed spending a significant amount of my workday visiting informally with members of the team and hearing directly from them about current events—again, being present not only physically, but being present in the moment, listening. I had time to do that because they were performing well, and I had plenty of time to listen and help them.

I needed to hear from all levels of the workforce, and not just my senior leadership team. One idea that proved very valuable at KSC was selecting an intern for a short-term assignment working directly with me. The assignments lasted for six months each, and generally the interns moved to higher-level positions when the assignment was over because of their higher visibility to managers across the Centers. The interns helped me to hear what the workforce was feeling about changes that we were making and to take corrective actions if warranted. They also helped me with planning and communicating with the workforce. I had many great interns over the years at KSC.

All these experiences gave me the confidence—and the skills—to take on the next set of experiences and future transformations.

You have a ton of experience to pull from. Be confident in your ability to deliver on this transformation.

The Consultant's Observations ... Tim

For our original project that summer, I worked with Jim Jennings (Director of Human Resources) and Saul Barton (a technical assistant to Jim Jennings). We researched best practices in conducting a transformation by reviewing the literature and speaking with leaders across the KSC community (civil servants and contractors). They pointed to the need for a systematic, strategic approach.

We also conducted employee focus groups. They shared their emotions. At the core they wanted their work at KSC to have a sense of purpose and meaningful contributions. They asked for their "shot at an Apollo"–type moment. From the literature, benchmarking (lessons learned from other transformations) and focus groups, we developed a set of models to help bring clarity to the transformational situation and potential next steps to take.

We shared our results with the Center Director at the time, Jay Honeycutt, and the KSC senior management team. They agreed to begin a strategic planning process. Mr. Honeycutt knew he was leaving the Center soon. He gave us permission to continue the process in preparation for a new Center Director. He believed the current team should have their views thought through before the new Center Director came on.

Shortly after Roy became the Center Director, we (Jim Jennings, Saul Barton, and I) met with him to share what we had learned from internal conversations, internal focus groups, external benchmarking, and review of the research. Roy agreed to our recommendation to take a strategic approach to the transformation. He also shared that he was wondering if KSC had more folks like us who were thinking about how to tackle this transformation. We became part of his team to support the transformation.

This project was truly a "from a small project to a career launch" experience for me. Based on this initial work, I have continuously supported KSC and their programs for the past 25-plus years. I've taken these lessons learned and applied them to NASA HQ, other NASA Centers, and commercial organizations. I've received significant public recognition from this work. One of the big reasons for my promotion to a full professor was the publishing of the original book on the KSC transformation. But it was the transformation itself that added real-world experience to my academic background. It gave me the confidence and credibility to help other organizations. Yes, it does sound like wordplay to say "NASA launched my career," but it is true.

Recommendations

From this chapter we offer a few recommendations on the steps you need to take and questions to engage your team with.

Standing at the threshold of a transformation can feel overwhelming. But realizing that your knowledge, skills, and past experiences brought you to this time and place can help you accept that you are here at this time for a reason: you are meant to lead this transformation.

Next Steps

To begin your transformation leadership journey:

- Accept that Sometimes We Parachute into the Unknown
- Make Use of Your Previous Experiences
- Be Present and Listen

Start the Conversation

Engage your team in starting the transformation:

What are our past experiences to pull from?

From those experiences, what are we most proud of?

From those experiences, what do we regret the most?

What are the lessons learned?

Moving forward into this new situation, what do we need to start, stop, or continue doing as a leadership team?

PERSPECTIVE

You got this

In this section, we explore ways to view your transformation. Your perspective (and attitude) toward the transformation will be the driving force. Your leadership team and workforce will be looking to see how you view the transformation. If you are convinced of the need to transform and the initial set of steps, then they will follow you.

Perspective and presence are closely tied. Your perspective is what your team will see—to the extent that you are present.

Chapter 3
Make the Choice to Move to Good Days

You got this

Your Situation...
Transformations Start with Bad Days and End With Good Days

A bad day can be a mission failure—or an external environmental disruption. Your transformation may be starting with—or will run into—bad days. These bad days will distract your leadership team and workforce. They may feel helpless. Your leadership job is to provide both a sense of urgency to change and hope for the future. You will provide the visible presence that honestly recognizes the realities while confidently sharing the path to the good days in the future. As the wise adage says, "This too shall pass." Yes, these bad days will eventually pass. The encouraging choice in front of you is to have the bad days pass into good days—the good days that you, your team, and your workforce create together.

These are just part of the journey. You will need to recognize and address these bad days systematically:

> "*What is the bad day we are facing?*
>
> *What would a good day look like?*"

In this chapter, we share our observations about the role of the bad days and challenges, and how to use them to move your organization forward.

What's Next...
Make the First Move

Your transformation is probably starting out with a bad day. Your job is to recognize, accept, and understand the bad day and its root causes. This is the start of your transformation journey.

Next Steps

To accept and process the bad day:

- Define the Bad Day...The Case for Change (Triage the Drivers, Trigger Events, and Challenges)
- Retain Your Best and Brightest

Start the Conversation

Engage your team in accepting and processing the transformation by asking them to share their perspectives about:

Why do we need to transform?

What is the bad day we are facing?

What is causing us to have a bad day?

What challenges will we face?

What is going on in our external environment that is driving us to transform?

In the end, what do we hope for in the transformation?

What would a good day look like?

Dig Deeper

In this section, we provide the leader's perspective (Roy) and the consultant's perspective (Tim) on the following actions you can take:

- Define the Bad Day...The Case for Change (Triage the Drivers, Trigger Events, and Challenges)
- Retain Your Best and Brightest.

Define the Bad Day...The Case for Change (Triage the Drivers, Trigger Events, and Challenges)

The Leader's Experience ... Roy

During the period of 1997 to 2003, KSC faced the significant challenge of safely completing its mission while undergoing a major change. This was a daunting endeavor that gripped us every day of the week for the next six years. The difficulty of it has been compared to that of a race car pit crew trying to change the tires on the car while traveling at 200 mph around the track. Clearly, we faced a monumental team challenge.

KSC was being asked to change the way it operated and to reduce its civil service workforce by a drastic 40%—from 2498 employees in Fiscal Year 1993 (FY93—the reduction push began before I became Center Director) to 1490 by FY03 (2003).

For two of those fiscal years (FY94 and FY95), KSC used buyouts—cash incentives to employees nearing retirement age to get them to leave the workforce voluntarily before retirement eligibility. Those were the easy reductions. However, everything else was hard to get. KSC was facing this challenge when I was asked to take the KSC Center Director position.

Before taking the job, I called the head of the shuttle processing organization and asked him if he thought we could successfully make the transition to the new way of conducting shuttle operations. He was convinced that it could be done, but that it would be hard. Others I respected corroborated this assessment.

The real issue was how to give the best of this team hope that there would be exciting work at KSC during their careers. We could not afford to lose our best and brightest young people. It was also clear that reducing the overall workforce at KSC by 40% would require some additional and dramatic changes in the way that we did business.

The Consultant's Observations ... Tim

You need to develop a strategy that aligns your organization's structure, processes, partners, and workforce to your newly defined position. These guidelines will help you define your "right way."

- Your right way includes the processes, structures, and tools by which your work is completed and managed.
- Your right people are defined by your skill needs and the number aligned with your budget.
- Your right time is the proper timing of doing your work to meet near-term work requirements, near-term transition actions to ensure long-term success, and long-term work requirements.

While undergoing a transformation, your organization increases its responsibilities from executing its current business model to creating and operating its future business model while still executing its current business model.

To evolve, your organization must make an investment in the future. The aim of this investment is to either start a new activity or to change the way your business operates. To make this investment, your organization will need to gain new resources—sometimes by moving its existing workforce to a new task and stopping existing work.

This investment will lead your organization to struggle with meeting responsibilities for the current business while trying to invest in new activities for the future. To explain this challenge, we'll use the

"ABC" model developed by Harold Kurstedt (1993). Kurstedt's model says that an organization spends its resources (time, energy, dollars) doing three types of activities:

- Administering the business
- Building the business
- Catering to crises

For an organization undergoing a transformation, the challenge is to find the resources to "build the business"—to invest in its future. These multiple responsibilities can overextend the organization's time, energy, and dollars.

For KSC, this problem was further exasperated because the level of resources—people and dollars—was diminishing. In essence, the "resource pie" was getting smaller while the "work pie" (to invest in the future) needed to remain the same, or even grow. As a result of this transformation effort, KSC personnel had to meet diverse needs.

First, KSC had to continue to meet its mission to ensure the safe, reliable, and cost-effective launching of the space shuttle (*administer the current business*). As this occurred, KSC also had to transition the operational work to a contractor (*build the business*).

Second, KSC had to transform itself into a different KSC (*build the business*). They developed and communicated a strategic direction. KSC defined its future state as focusing on providing its capabilities and expertise anytime, anywhere, to advance space exploration and commerce. KSC's core business was to focus on providing space systems processes, testing and launch techniques, and developing associated technologies. KSC also successfully achieved ISO 9001 quality management standards certification. These efforts consumed resources to lead, manage projects, and complete the work associated with the transformation.

Third, KSC had to deliver on the "new mission" of being a development Center (*administer the new business while building the new business*). KSC was completing new development work. They were using their unique operational knowledge to help space systems developers successfully design and implement new space systems. For example, KSC was playing a major role in developing a new checkout and launch control system for the space shuttle and a new generation of vehicles such as the X-34.

Fourth, KSC had to respond to the normal crises (*cater to crisis*) associated with any organization. For example, an unplanned report or submission to an external agency is a crisis that takes time and resources.

The three areas of *administer the business, build the business*, and *cater to crisis* can drive an organization to overload. Given the declining number of total KSC civil service employees, KSC had to focus these resources in the most effective way.

Retain Your Best and Brightest

The Leader's Experience ... Roy

During this period, the most pressing issue was how to retain our best and brightest and accomplish our mission safely while making this dramatic change. Our desired strategic outcome was to give people hope that there would be exciting work on the other side of this chasm so that our best would decide to stay with us. We needed to create some magnets to attract them to new work.

Ultimately, we were able to reduce our civil service workforce to 1773 (a 29% reduction), over ten fiscal years, from FY93 to FY03. But during that time, what created the greater drama was that the headquarters expected us to reduce the workforce to 1490 by FY03—a 40% reduction—and we knew the Center could not function with such a small staff. However, we were not relieved of this lower target until we had such critical skill shortages that I had to essentially force the headquarters to let me do some hiring for critical skills in FY00 (fiscal year 2000). The increase in workers made FY00 the first time KSC's gains had exceeded losses in seven years—since FY93.

The cultural change challenge can also be seen in the shuttle organization civil service headcount data. We accomplished a 67% reduction in the shuttle organization headcount from FY92 to FY02; the workforce went from 1075 to 354. The contractor organization (USA) was reduced by 10% as well, from 7299 to 6557, over this period. These were the people on the front lines of shuttle processing.

The headquarters also had begun to recognize the value of our workforce at KSC, based on the great work by our team on things such as our new process for testing the new modules for the International Space Station (ISS), the Multi-Element Integrated Test (MEIT), and the early successes after moving the Expendable Launch Vehicle (ELV) program to KSC. These programs were two of the magnets that drew some of our best and brightest because they were challenging and held promise for these skilled and talented people to make major contributions.

The Consultant's Observations ... Tim

KSC had significant expertise in processing the space shuttle and its payloads. This expertise was important to the current operations and could also be important in future space efforts. KSC was under pressure to reduce its workforce in a safe manner. As Roy has shared, this change created a workforce morale challenge. The leadership team was worried about losing the core expertise to deliver the mission now and in the future. The actions described in this book enabled the leadership team to provide the visible actions that the workforce could see the Center as doing. These actions increased the workforce's trust that the leadership was working their future.

Recommendations

From this chapter we offer a few recommendations and questions to engage your team with.

Your transformation is probably starting out with a bad day. Your job is to recognize, accept, and understand the bad day and its root causes. This is the start of your transformation journey.

Next Steps

To accept and process the bad day:

- Define the Bad Day...The Case for Change (Triage the Drivers, Trigger Events, and Challenges)
- Retain Your Best and Brightest

Start the Conversation

Engage your team in accepting and processing the transformation by asking them to share their perspectives about:

Why do we need to transform?

What is the bad day we are facing?

What is causing us to have a bad day?

What challenges will we face?

What is going on in our external environment that is driving us to transform?

In the end, what do we hope for in the transformation?

What would a good day look like?

Chapter 4
Fix What is Broken As a Path to the New

You got this

Your Situation...
Transformations Change the Business Model

In your transformation you will need to change your organization's business model. Yep...saying we need to change the business model is much easier to say than to do. Your current business model has served you well...until the bad days showed up. The change to a new business model is doable if you follow a systematic process.

As you begin the transformation you may be asking:

> "*Why do we need to transform?*
>
> *What parts of the business model do we need to change?*"

In this chapter, we share our observations about how changing the business model is core to your transformation.

To help ensure the successful change to the business model you will need to provide a set of enablers such as

External support	Your customer needs to see the value in the product/service you will be providing in the future
Internal leadership team buy-in	Your internal leadership team needs to support the new business model...they must be willing to make the change
Resources	The financial resources to invest in creating the new model
Internal capability	Your organization must have the capability (e.g., processes, and tools) to deliver the new business model
Human capital	The human capital or workforce to execute the new model
Time	The time to design, pilot, and refine the new model
Stable environment	The external environment needs to be “stable enough” to provide a realistic set of requirements that your new business model needs to meet
Ability to influence the environment	You will need some level of influence on the external environment (customers and stakeholders) to be able to sell your new business to them

What's Next...
Fix the Current Model

Your transformation started with a "bad day." This bad day highlighted the need to change your organization's business model. Changing the business model can be done if you follow a process.

Next Steps

To make changes to your business model:

- Avoid Drastic Measures
- Understand Why You Don't Have Excellence
- Develop a More Relevant and Responsive Business Model Using Your Unique Core Competency
- Provide the Enablers for Successful Implementation

Start the Conversation

Engage your team in exploring new business models by asking them to share their perspectives about:

Where do we start?

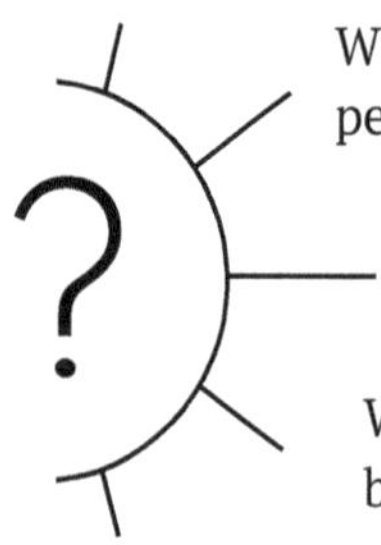

What are the performance gaps?

What is causing these gaps?

What parts of the business model do we need to change?

How can we assure success?

Dig Deeper

In this section, we provide the leader's perspective (Roy) and the consultant's perspective (Tim) on the following actions you can take:

- Avoid Drastic Measures
- Understand Why You Don't Have Excellence
- Develop a More Relevant and Responsive Business Model Using Your Unique Core Competency
- Provide the Enablers for Successful Implementation

Avoid Drastic Measures

The Leader's Experience ... Roy

A "reduction in force" is the most drastic technique for downsizing, as opposed to the use of buyouts or hiring freezes. It means that you are laying off enough employees to meet the target and they will be those employees with the least years of service first. Fortunately, KSC never had to do an involuntary reduction in force. As the push to downsize progressed, I reminded them often that we were encountering critical skill problems that would cause our valuable contributions to suffer and potentially lead to catastrophic incidents. I recommended that they allow for a certain amount of critical-skill hiring—and cease downsizing. The HQ finally realized that they needed a greater number of KSC employees in order to function effectively, and they allowed some critical-skill hiring and stopped the downsizing at a number well above the original target.

During the mid-1990s, the ZBR (zero-based review) pushed for downsizing the KSC civil service workforce to 1490 civil servants. If this extreme reduction had occurred, KSC would not have been able to accomplish its core mission of shuttle, ISS, and LSP, while building the infrastructure for the future and providing operational knowledge to future vehicle development. As a result of KSC's strategic approach and contributions, NASA realized the value of their contributions and ceased the incessant downsizing effort. KSC is now executing the core contribution it defined in the mid-1990s: providing operational knowledge for new designs, current operations, and commercial success.

Looking back at the transformation from the perspective of NASA's Vision for Space Exploration, it's clear that KSC successfully maintained the critical operational knowledge needed for the new effort—the ground-processing of launch vehicles and spacecraft, and developing and operating ground-support equipment and facilities. NASA is now in need of this knowledge, as it helps prepare for the crew exploration vehicle and crew launch vehicle—the next generation of spacecraft and launch vehicles beyond the Shuttle Transportation System—such as the Artemis Program to return astronauts to the moon and eventually put astronauts on Mars.

Finally, the success of KSC can be measured by how well the management team accomplished what it set out to do. As a result of the first series of strategic conversations, the management team defined an overall strategic agenda to transition from its current state. As a result, they retained many of their best and brightest civil servants, who added immense value to KSC and NASA programs.

The Consultant's Observations ... Tim

As shown in the KSC case overview (see chapter 1), KSC made a significant number of changes. **Transformations will fundamentally change your business model.** KSC avoided taking drastic moves by following a set of steps to

- understand why they didn't have excellence;
- develop a more relevant and responsive business model;
- develop and execute a strategy to implement their new business model;
- provide enablers for successful implementation.

You need to transform because something in your current or future environment is making or will make your organization's performance no longer acceptable.

Your organization was running fine, producing the right product or service the right way. Your customer was happy, your internal processes were working well, and your financial performance was going well. Then something changed, or is in the process of changing, in your external environment. A trigger event occurred. A trigger event is the event(s) that fundamentally shifted your relevancy or responsiveness in the industry. Your organization is no longer producing the right product the right way or will no longer be doing so in the future. Before you make a quick change, make sure you are focusing on the right things.

Understand Why You Don't Have Excellence

The Leader's Experience ... Roy

Our "lack of excellence" was driven by external perspectives and decisions. KSC was pushed to develop a new business model to enhance its performance. As the NASA philosophy and programs changed, KSC had to determine the best way to serve. The space Center was being asked to pull out of operations—its primary role. The NASA environment was shifting to be research-focused. KSC needed to evolve, or it would become irrelevant to NASA.

On our journey to attaining the sustained performance excellence needed to support our transformation, the senior management team at KSC followed the path of assessing our business model for position (i.e., relevancy and responsiveness) and alignment. We had the relevant knowledge that NASA needed, but we needed to be more responsive with how/where it was used. Once we clarified their relevancy, we had to assess our responsiveness. As discussed in Chapter 1, we made a series of decisions to enhance our business model based on the gaps we saw in our performance.

The Consultant's Observations ... Tim

As the external environment changes, your organization needs to change its position in that environment. The market may desire a different product or expect your organization to deliver the same product a different way. The inherent challenge is that your organization must continue to adapt. Just because it delivers well today does not mean it will be able to deliver well in the future.

Sustained performance excellence comes from bringing value to your customers. This value comes from externally positioning your organization in the market and aligning its internal workings. Let's take cars, for example. General Motors offers different car models (e.g., Corvette, pickup trucks, SUVs, sedans) for different price points and customers. They target their cars with a certain price point for a specific customer--and that changes over time. Positioning is figuring out what products and prices best fit with each market and customer. It puts your organization in a "good place" for success—today and in the future—as long as you continue to adapt.

Your position is a function of the market, your business model, your customer, and your products and services. Over time, your organization can change its position in the environment by starting new business lines, stopping old ones, or continuing successful ones. Your organization must be able to deliver the right products and services, as defined by the market and customer, and to deliver them the right way. **The fundamental problem your organization experiences during a large-scale transformation is determining what "the right work completed the right way with the right people at the right time" means for your organization to bring value to your customers.**

Develop a More Relevant and Responsive Business Model Using Your Unique Core Competency

The Leader's Experience ... Roy

KSC's senior management team believed our core operational knowledge (see Illustration 7.3—KSC Civil Servant Contribution, in Chapter 7) provided the relevant knowledge to NASA. We also believed we needed to be more responsive in where and how we applied this core knowledge. We believed we could help designers of new launch vehicles and operators of current launch vehicles be successful. We chose to position ourself in emerging roles for developing new systems for ground processing of the shuttle and ISS, supporting NASA mission success using commercial Expendable Launch Vehicles (ELVs), supporting development teams of new vehicles, and developing new spaceport and range technologies.

For KSC, addressing the problem of the right work was a process of flowing requirements down from the mission and vision set forth by NASA and senior management of KSC. The requirements were based on KSC's current, transitional, and future states. The right work included items such as missions, NASA requirements, meaningful work, and products and services the customer desired.

In order to align to the new "missions" we were facing, we had to align our products, services, processes, structure, tools, and workforce. KSC's ever-changing external environment created the need to transform. As discussed in Chapter 1, we had to change the existing business model from being shuttle operations–centric. We wanted to move to a new business model which balanced operations, research, and enabling functions (e.g., the back-office functions such as human resources, legal, procurement), so we

- focused on balancing the business model by providing additional operational knowledge to ISS, LSP, and new vehicle development;
- decided to grow a business line for developing new spaceport and range technologies;

- changed our business model for managing the institutional "base operations."

Once we identified these business model changes (customized to the needs of our unique organization), we needed to develop a strategy to implement the change—and execute it.

The Consultant's Observations ... Tim

Exploring your organization's business model will help you define what the new right work/right way is for your organization. It will help you develop a new business model that will position and align your organization. The works of both Gary Hamel (2002) and Alexander Osterwalder and Yves Pigneur (2010) offer ways to define a business model.

To position your organization to ensure relevancy, your transformation team can assess the external performance of your business model by asking these questions:

1. How well does the market value our organization's products and services?
2. How well are we helping our customers be successful?

Answering these two questions will allow you to understand the external drivers that tell you where your organization needs to change.

Your new business model must position your organization's role (e.g., mission) and contributions (e.g., products and services) in the external environment and industry. Given that you have defined your organization's "right work," you can then explore the "right way to deliver" that work.

To ensure you are responsive to your customer's needs, your new business model must also align your organization's internal elements (e.g., people, processes, tools, and culture) to deliver the needed products and services in a manner your customer desires (e.g., cost, quality, delivery speed). To align your organization, you can assess the internal performance of your business model by asking these questions:

1. How well are the products and services delivered within the customer's expectations regarding cost, quality, and timeliness?
2. How well are we fostering and building meaningful relationships with our key stakeholders for the right products and services?
3. How consistently are we delivering quality or performance?
4. How strongly do our customers trust our organization?
5. How solid is our capability to consistently deliver the new products and services our customers expect from us?
6. How well do we respond to challenges and return to excellence?
7. How consistent and harmonious are our mission, culture, processes, structure, partners, and workforce?

Answering these seven questions will allow you to understand the internal drivers that tell you where your organization needs to change.

Provide the Enablers for Successful Implementation

The Leader's Experience ... Roy

As shared in Chapter 1, we focused our major transformation efforts within four groups:

- the efforts to transform and enhance KSC's operational focus
- the efforts to transform and enhance KSC's infrastructure/spaceport operations
- the efforts to transform and enhance KSC's technology development focus
- the efforts to transform and enhance KSC's business operations focus

For each of these areas, we worked each of the enablers a bit differently, and with varying degrees of success. Each of the moves required different enablers for success.

KSC's transformation efforts had varying levels of success, and these results coincided with how well each effort was supported by the enablers. Illustrations 4.1–4.4 offer detailed information about how the relative presence or absence of enablers affected the short- and long-term outcomes in each of the four efforts above.

1. Illustration 4.1 summarizes how the quality of enabler support affected the successful implementation and outcomes of KSC's efforts to change the operation's business model. For the most part, the operational strategies were successful, aligning with the generally positive presence and support of the enablers.
2. Illustration 4.2 shows that, for the most part, the infrastructure/spaceport strategies were successful—and the support of enablers they had corresponded with the requirements for successful implementation.
3. As shown in Illustration 4.3, for the most part, the development strategies were not fully successful. In reviewing these instances, we can see that they lacked the necessary enablers needed for successful implementation.
4. Illustration 4.4 shows that, for the most part, the business operation strategies were successful—and the support of enablers they had corresponded with the requirements for successful implementation.

Illustrations

You can find the complete four illustrations detailing information about these major transformation efforts in Illustrations 4.1–4.4 in "For Inquiring Minds . . . The Details." on pages 286-292.

As can be seen in the four tables, when the enablers are present (good external support, good internal support, and the right capabilities) the results are good. If you want to increase your chance of success, then ensure the enablers are present or take actions to make them present.

The Consultant's Observations ... Tim

In order to make your new business model a reality, you need to ensure the model fits with

1. the external environment's desires,
2. your organization's desires,
3. your organization's capability to operate the new business model.

Your business model implementation strategy must address any gaps in these three elements.

1. Your implementation strategy needs to account for the external environment's desire, or the lack of it, for the proposed new business model—to consider its "soundness." For example, if the external environment doesn't yet desire the new business model, your organization must validate the need with your customer...they may not see it yet. Through marketing or advocacy building, you need to help them see the need and the value it will bring them. After all, who knew we "needed" a mobile device with a camera, apps, etc.? Marketing and advocacy can help make your customers the biggest cheerleaders for where your organization is headed.

2. Your implementation strategy must also address how much your senior management team or organization wants the new business model. This is important because lack of organizational desire will doom the new business model to failure. If your management team does not want it, they will not support it.

   Hopefully, at this point, your senior management team will see the urgent need to change. They now need to buy in to the specific change. You can evaluate your senior managers' level of support for the change on a continuum, from "totally disagree with" to "indifferent" to "totally agree with the change." As you know, senior managers (and all humans) can be really good at slow-rolling changes they don't want to make. Some senior managers will openly push back and challenge the new model. Some will publicly give their nod of support, but then in their daily actions they (1) ignore the idea, (2) slow-roll it, or (3) even sabotage the change. On the positive side, the senior management team can also be superfans for the change.

As you think about your new business model, be thinking about where your senior managers may fall on their level of support. Based on this, define a strategy to best engage them in exploring the new model. Involve the management team in the process to define a new business model to help gain their support.

At some point, if your management team doesn't support the new direction, then you have a few options:

1. Continue to understand their concerns.
2. Refine the new business model.
3. Change the management team.

3. Finally, your implementation strategy must also account for your organization's capabilities (e.g., processes, tools, and workforce) to deliver the new business model. **If your organization does not have the capability, it must create the capability. Otherwise, it will not be able to deliver.** Your transformation team needs to create the strategy to develop your new business model.

Based on this evaluation, you can define your implementation strategy.

Illustration 4.5 summarizes the different cases that can emerge from the varying levels of external acceptance, internal acceptance, and internal capability. For each case, specific strategies need to be taken based on the decision your management team makes about what the new business needs to be. The decision will have an impact on your organization's performance.

Each of KSC's business model changes required varying levels of change. Each also had varying levels of external support, internal support, and internal capabilities. To make these changes, KSC designed and implemented strategies. In addition to these strategies, KSC had to ensure the success of the business model changes. We'll explore these different business model changes more next when we discuss the need to create the conditions for successful implementation.

You need to provide the enablers—the things that help make it possible for you to achieve your goal—for successfully implementing your business model. This challenge focuses on making sure your strategy can succeed. Your organization needs to provide enablers such as external advocacy and resources.

External advocacy is the external support of your organization's transformation. This support comes from important entities such as the board of directors, major customers, government stakeholders. For example, KSC needed to gain external advocacy from NASA HQ, NASA program managers, other NASA Centers, and the State of Florida. This external advocacy would help create the sense of urgency to provide the resources necessary to drive the transformation.

Resources (time, people, dollars) are the next enablers for successfully implementing your new business model. These resources are needed to invest in aligning the external desire, internal desire, and internal capabilities.

Illustration 4.5—Business Model Fit Evaluation: Situation, Decision, and Potential Impacts

The Situation				
Case	External Need	Internal Want	Internal Capability	Description
I	Yes	Yes	Yes	Ideal
II	Yes	Yes	No	Capability cap
III	Yes	No	Yes	Lack of interest or strategic intent to pursue the business
IV	Yes	No	No	Customer need being unmet by organization
V	No	Yes	Yes	No market
VI	No	Yes	No	Delusional
VII	No	No	Yes	Unneeded capability
VIII	No	No	No	Potential for disruption

Potential Decisions	Potential Impacts from the Decision
Execute and sustain capability	Sustained performance
Build capability	Keep market
Move on	Lose market
Move on	Lost opportunity
Make intent	New market
Ignore	Lost opportunity
Build intent and capability	Seize the market
Make intent	New market
Move on	Resources available for other efforts
Create the market	Potential for new market Potential for wasted investment
Change intent	Focus management's energy and resource on another business
Invest in the market	Potential for new market Potential for wasted investment
Change intent and market need	Potential for new disruptive market creation Potential for wasted resources
Abandon capability	Potential to miss an opportunity
Focus on today's business	Performance in the short run Potential for missing a market
Explore for possibilities	Potential for new market Potential for wasted investment

Recommendations

From this chapter we offer a few recommendations and questions to engage your team with.

Your transformation started with a "bad day." This bad day highlighted the need to change your organization's business model. Changing the business model can be done if you follow a process.

Next Steps

To make changes to your business model:

- Avoid Drastic Measures
- Understand Why You Don't Have Excellence
- Develop a More Relevant and Responsive Business Model Using Your Unique Core Competency
- Provide the Enablers for Successful Implementation

Start the Conversation

Engage your team in exploring new business models by asking them to share their perspectives about:

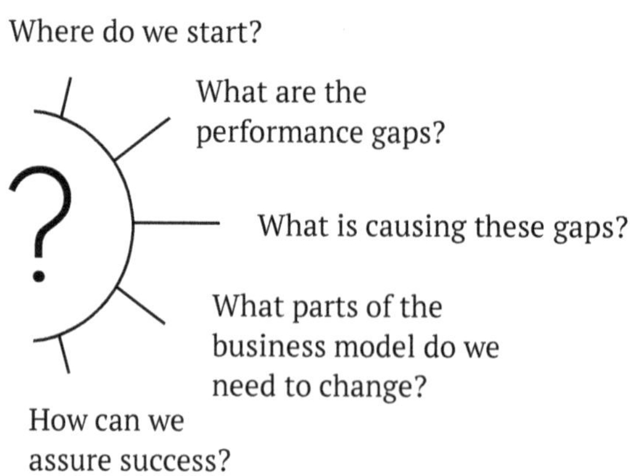

Chapter 5
Lead Through the Unplanned

You got this

Your Situation...
Transformations Face Disruptions

As you lead your organization through the transformation, you will face disruptors. You have a choice on how you respond to these challenges. Your workforce will be watching how you respond. You can calmly respond and make use of these disruptors to move your organization to the future.

You obviously don't have a choice on what disruptors show up at your door. You do have a choice on how you respond.

Make the choice to respond strategically.

You will need to be thinking about

> "*What disruptions/risks can impact our transformation?*
>
> *How can we proactively plan for the disruptors and the frustrations that come with the disruptions?*"

In this chapter we share the significant issues that arose for KSC's transformation and how they responded—and how to prepare for the disruptions in yours.

What's Next...
Respond to Unplanned Events

You will run into unforeseen disruptors. As you know, life can throw us curveballs at times. Transformations are just like life...you will get curveballs or disruptors thrown at you and your team. Your team will be looking to see how you respond to these disruptors. You can provide stability and calmness with your response.

Next Steps

To manage these disruptors, you can:

- Remain Flexible and Adaptable
- Plan with Scenarios
- Focus on the Controllable
- Provide a Response to the Disruption
- Establish and Use an Escalation Philosophy

Start the Conversation

Engage your team in preparing for and responding to disruptors by asking them to share their views about:

What disruptions/risks can impact our transformation?

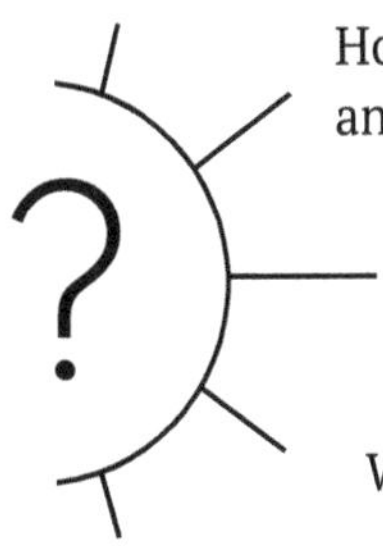

How can we proactively plan for the disruptors and frustrations that come with the disruptions?

What are the potential futures we may see?

What are the best, worst, and most likely cases?

How can we ensure we stay flexible to the changes in the external environment?

Dig Deeper

In this section, we provide the leader's perspective (Roy) and the consultant's perspective (Tim) on the following actions you can take:

- Remain Flexible and Adaptable
- Plan with Scenarios
- Focus on the Controllable
- Provide a Response to the Disruption
- Establish and Use an Escalation Philosophy

Transformations do not always go smoothly. There are often unexpected disruptions.

Remain Flexible and Adaptable

The Leader's Experience ... Roy

KSC's success can also be measured by its agility or ability to stay aware of and continuously understand the ever-changing external environment. KSC had to be flexible and adaptable to the changes in direction both NASA and KSC experienced. As shown in Illustration 5.1, KSC's direction changed over time.

The Consultant's Observations ... Tim

The KSC Senior Management Team proactively worked the disruptors and frustrations. They held regular conversations throughout the transformation (off-sites and internal strategic meetings), worked scenarios (projections of what could happen and what they should do if it did), and created opportunities for the team and workforce to reflect upon and refine the KSC transformation strategy.

Illustration 5.1—Various Directions Provided to KSC

Item	Various Directions Provided to KSC
Civil Service Workforce	• Downsizing by reducing presence of civil service employees in shuttle processing, leading to an initial reduction in force • No reduction in force • Hiring more civil service employees
Shuttle Processing Model	• Government control with assistance by support contractor and contract control by KSC • Commercializing shuttle processing (with transition to SFOC, contract control by JSC, and surveillance by KSC); full KSC government control is only for launch and landing operations)
ISS Model	• Ship-n-shoot (where very limited testing is performed at KSC) • Multiple element integrated testing (MEIT, where various elements are tested at KSC in an integrated fashion) • Various definitions of what "station complete" meant—what the final configuration of ISS would be in space

Plan with Scenarios

The Leader's Experience … Roy

In leading KSC through the transformation, I used scenario planning to help the team envision the potential future for KSC. The team was pretty set in their ways. NASA was flying shuttles for some time and this brought stability to the team. We were not facing a period of instability and uncertainty. Scenarios helped us think about plans for uncertain futures.

In my first off-site with the KSC senior management team I started the team with a strategic scenario question: What is the future scenario you want for KSC? On the one extreme, we could be a museum for space. (This scenario was not a very compelling future). On the other extreme we could be a national asset that continues to make a difference for NASA. This was the more compelling scenario. In between these two extremes were many options. I posed this question to the team to start them thinking about what type of future we wanted to create. These scenarios, while simple, painted the picture perfectly: if we didn't transform we would become a museum. None of us wanted that. These scenarios helped create the case for proactively defining and pursuing the scenario we wanted.

We again used scenario planning a few years later, in 2000. We had been working the transformation for a few years. Our team started to have doubts on the moves and investments we were making. They weren't sure that all of the moves were necessary. We couldn't see how the moves were important to ensure our contributions no matter what external scenario emerged.

We explored four different scenarios. For each scenario we understood the drivers and (1) the steps we need to take to create or avoid the scenario and (2) the actions we would take if the scenario emerged. When we looked at these actions across the four scenarios, we developed a "transformation philosophy." This was general guidance on what we needed to do to ensure our success, no matter what external scenario emerged. As a team, we needed to believe that we had control of our future. Realizing there were many potential futures that we could influence was huge in helping the team to continue the hard transformation work.

The Consultant's Observations ... Tim

To proactively identify potential disruptors, one technique they used was the scenario-planning process (Schwartz 1991). This scenario-planning process helped the team explore the potential futures in NASA and KSC. They explored four scenarios and identified a common set of actions to increase the probability that they were prepared for the future and decrease the probability that they were not prepared for the future. These scenarios provided the macro set of disruptors and risks KSC faced overall.

A scenario captures the potential futures your organization may face. These potential future scenarios can be used to better understand what will favor or act against your organization's transformation. From this understanding, you can focus on specific strategies and actions to help create the future you desire. Our scenario-planning approach was to

- forecast the most likely future scenarios that could affect or were within the scope of the KSC's desired outcomes;
- analyze the outcomes against the future scenarios;
- assess the scenarios as to whether they supported or inhibited our outcomes (good, bad, neutral);
- decide what we wanted to do about the scenario: do nothing, influence the environment, prepare for the environment, or a combination.

For KSC, the list of scenarios became very long. There needed to be a way of assessing the scenarios against each other and ending up with a list of scenarios in which we wanted to invest an effort. Illustration 5.2 provides a summary flow of the scenario thought process. From these scenarios, we identified implications and challenges. The implications and challenges identified the strategic items the management team needed to address.

Illustration 5.2—Scenario Thought Process

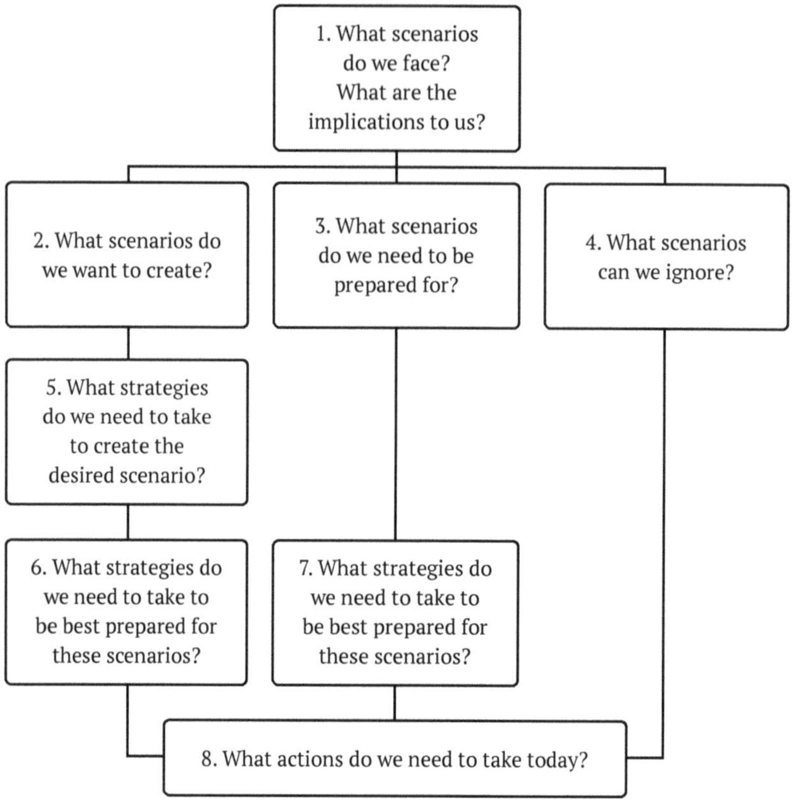

Focus on the Controllable: 9/11 Observations

The Leader's Experience ... Roy

There can be tragedy as well. On the morning of September 11, 2001, my senior staff and I arrived at Dodgertown by bus for a several-day off-site to review progress and make mid-course corrections to our strategic road map. As I was hanging my clothes in my hotel room, I noticed that the TV news was showing a smoking skyscraper in New York City. Then a second one was hit.

I was stunned and grieved about the loss of innocent lives in New York as well as at the Pentagon and the airplane crash in Pennsylvania. Clearly, we had to change our plans. Instead of a multi-day off-site at Dodgertown, we elected to get back to KSC where we needed to address the risk of more attacks in addition to continuing our strategic discussions. After meeting at lunch to review the situation, we abandoned our off-site location and headed back to KSC to prepare for the aftermath of this attack on the nation.

In the days after the attack, details about the hijackers started to become available. They had trained to fly. We didn't know if there were more lurking in the shadows and planning attacks on other national icons such as the space shuttle. A shuttle on the pad was vulnerable to attack from either the air or from the sea, and it wouldn't take a large airliner to cause a disaster. A light airplane flown by a single suicide pilot would get the job done. We had a lot of workers at the pad as we prepared the shuttle for launch. I worried about how to protect them so that they could focus on the critical work they were doing.

I worked with the Air Force, our security contractor, and the state to strengthen our defensive posture. We eventually had armed helicopters and flights of Air Force fighters to protect the shuttle during critical portions of the countdown and launch, as well as a much more intense security screening posture always, and a more structured launch-viewing procedure rather than just letting hundreds of cars enter the Center and park on the causeway. Fortunately, although the Air Force did have to force down several intruding aircraft as a precaution, these all proved to be non-terrorist intrusions, and there were no casualties as a result.

I had guns installed on our helicopters and trained the crews. After the shuttle rolled out, they flew the helicopter out to the launch pad, landed in an open area near the shuttle, and stayed on alert. The idea was that they would act like a hockey goalie and position themselves between an incoming aircraft and the pad. Shots would be fired only if the plane continued to fly directly toward the shuttle.

The NASA Administrator was furious when he learned about my armed helicopters. He called me at home one evening. He yelled at me so loudly that my wife could hear him from the other room. He was worried that we would shoot down some innocent person. When I finally could get a word in edgewise, I said, "Dan, we had to do something to protect our workers at the pad. I didn't ask your permission because I wanted you to have plausible deniability." He let me continue with our protective measure.

The Consultant's Observations ... Tim

As Roy shared, the events of 9/11 had a significant impact on KSC as it did with everyone. The KSC senior management team was just starting their off-site when the news of 9/11 broke. The leadership team had a choice about how to respond to the events. They chose to focus on what they could control. We did continue the off-site; we just changed locations.

In hindsight, this was a brilliant move by Roy. We didn't get stuck in things that were out of our control. We focused on what we were expected to do—our job. I think this also gave a sense of calmness to the team. Your calming presence during these disruptors will provide confidence in your team that they can handle this.

Provide a Response to the Disruption: Columbia Observations

The Leader's Experience ... Roy

There was a professional tragedy, too. On February 1, 2003, as I was escorting the NASA Administrator and other visitors at the Shuttle Landing Facility to witness the landing of STS-107, which was the 113th flight of the Space Transportation System program, we heard the Mission Control Center calling Columbia several times to establish radio contact. At the time for Columbia to arrive over the field and announce her arrival with the signature double sonic booms, there was only silence. I knew immediately that Columbia was lost, as the shuttle is never late to arrive unless the worst imaginable accident has occurred. I knew in my heart that seven people had just died.

I told the NASA Administrator that we had had a bad day and needed to adjourn quickly to a secure facility to investigate the situation and take appropriate actions. He agreed.

Back in the Launch Control Facility, we saw that reporters on TV were showing strange sightings of flaming debris raining down over east Texas. Clearly, this was the worst imaginable accident that I had feared.

After assuring that the crew families were secure and briefed on the accident, we began what would be a multi-month effort to recover Columbia and her crew and return them to KSC. Teams were dispatched to Texas and Louisiana to organize this mammoth undertaking, supported by teams from many other federal and state government agencies.

We also supported the Accident Investigation Board, looking into the cause of the accident and corrective actions that we would need to take before flying again. There were funerals and memorial services to plan and attend.

The details of bringing Columbia home are well presented in the book *Bringing Columbia Home* by Shuttle Launch Director Michael D. Leinbach and Jonathan H. Ward. The team was exceptional. Despite the hardships of the job, they persisted, day after day. Walking through the briars of East Texas, finding all these little pieces of the shuttle—it was traumatic, to say the least. They were sleeping in tents, in stables that were used for rodeos. The Forest Service moved in a lot of their infrastructure: tractor trailers—one would have showers in it, and another one would have food service—and things like that to serve these people, month on month on month.

Michael Leinbach was one of the key leaders of this team, and they stayed the course. They wouldn't let anything get in their way. They kept plowing through until we'd recovered all the essential pieces—all the crew stuff, which we put into a special area because that's all sensitive. They recovered the bodies of the crew. They also found the pieces of the shuttle that helped us confirm exactly what had happened.

We were able to lay out the remains of Columbia in a hangar at the Shuttle Landing Facility. The recovery of those remains was critical to confirming that a piece of foam from the shuttle's external tank had fallen off the tank and hit a critical area in the leading edge of the wing. The resulting hole allowed superheated plasma to enter the wing during shuttle reentry and caused structural failure.

We planned the memorial service for Columbia and her crew to take place on the runway at KSC, where she was supposed to land. I was involved in a critical decision on the morning of the event. We wanted to position the audience in the open on the runway to let them get the full effect of the ceremony, but bad weather threatened. It was cloudy, and rain was possible. After consulting with my weather officer, John Madura, the world's best weather forecaster, I elected to position the guests on the runway, out in the open.

As the ceremony started, I found myself sitting opposite the Florida governor, Jeb Bush. He was on the stage, and I was in the front row of the audience. I was startled by a large raindrop hitting me on my head as the ceremony started. I saw that the governor had noticed my flinch, and I just raised my hands palms up in resignation. It would be what it would be. We were committed. He smiled.

The ceremony continued without any serious rain interference. At the conclusion and at the exact time of day that Columbia should have landed, a low-level flight of four T-38 jets appeared out of the fog, heading down the runway. As they passed, they executed the missing man formation. One of the jets pulled up into the sky and disappeared into the clouds.

It was a dramatic conclusion. I had trouble keeping my composure.

There were many people grieving at the organizations supporting NASA and the Space Shuttle Program. I toured the shops at KSC, like the shop that sewed heat-resistant quilts for the shuttle. Everyone at that shop and many others worried that something that they may have done had caused the mishap.

We kept up a lot of communications during this time to reassure people that we would get to the bottom of this tragedy and explain the causes to them. These communications and the publication of the accident report eventually helped them to realize that, while we all shared in our collective failure to keep Columbia and her crew safe, none of the actions by members of the KSC workforce were implicated in the cause of this accident.

At the end of the investigation, for the entire workforce of KSC, we organized a tour of the hangar where Columbia's remains were laid out on the floor. We took them out on buses and allowed them to walk the floor to see the results.

We obtained permission to organize and properly store the remains in the Vehicle Assembly Building so that we could support research efforts to improve our spacecraft of the future.

The Consultant's Observations. ... Tim

After the accident the Center's senior management team had to focus on bringing stability to KSC and also work the root causes of the accident. The senior management team continued to deliver the mission and also work the transformation in light of the accident.

Establish an Escalation Philosophy

The Leader's Experience ... Roy

In my military and astronaut experience I learned the importance of having open communication channels to share concerns. On my shuttle flight (STS-51F, Spacelab 2) the importance of communicating emerging challenges crisply got reinforced for me.

As we left the launch tower, we were moving more than 100 miles per hour as our tail cleared the launch tower. We completed the roll maneuver so that we were upside down and then completed the throttle down and throttle up to clear the max dynamic pressure region. At approximately two minutes into the ascent, the solids burned out and made a "whoosh" sound as they separated from the shuttle to parachute back into the ocean, where they would be retrieved by special retrieval ships and returned so that they could be reused. You might say, okay, something could happen to us, for sure. But I wasn't thinking about that. I felt sure we would make it into space. This was the fulfillment of my lifelong dream. I was on top of the world.

The ride during the first two minutes was somewhat rough, with considerable vibration. Imagine a cat trying to hang on to a window glass. That's kind of how it felt. We were getting jostled around. It wasn't uncomfortable, but I'd never felt anything like it. None of the simulators did that, of course. So this was an unusual feeling that I had never experienced before. You were just hanging: you had a tiger by the tail, and you were just trying to hang on. But once the solids separated, everything smoothed out, and the only noticeable feeling was the steady increase in g-forces through the chest as we accelerated.

As we approached 2g's, I explored the overhead panel. I wanted to see if I could reach the overhead switches easily under g-loads, as this condition could not be simulated on the ground—simulators can't simulate 2g's or 3g's, like we were going to experience. So I was trying—could I reach that switch if I had to get to it?—and as I reached over my head for the last row of overhead switches, I felt the g-load suddenly decrease, accompanied by warning lights and sounds. When this happened, Gordo didn't have time to look at my hands. I knew he'd seen me do something, so if he'd had time, he probably would have looked over at me with a look that said, *What did you do?*

Then we got the call from Mission Control. "Challenger, Houston. Abort to Orbit." (ATO) We started an emergency procedure to respond to the loss of one of our three engines. Gordo turned the abort switch to ATO and pushed the button to activate our guidance system for ATO. We started a fuel dump of our orbital maneuvering system fuel to reduce our weight and give us a better chance of making it into orbit. Now we had to hope that we would achieve sufficient velocity before running out of fuel to be able to stay in orbit. If not, we would have to Abort Once Around and land at Edwards AFB without achieving orbit. Since we were the first (and ultimately the only) shuttle to lose an engine going to orbit, we were now into the unknown. Would the fuel line low-level sensors work as designed, as we would surely deplete all of our liquid propellants? If not, the turbo pumps would cavitate, overspeed, and likely destructively fail. So we were all busy — and we were all mortally worried.

After getting the necessary actions underway after we began the ATO, Story and I simultaneously said, "This is starting to feel just like another sim. They're not supposed to be doing this stuff to us." We had lost the engine approximately thirty seconds after passing the last chance to land at the Transoceanic Abort Landing site (TAL) in Spain. Had it happened thirty seconds sooner, we would have set a transatlantic speed record of thirty-seven minutes from Florida to Spain. Thankfully, we left that record for someone else to set.

"Challenger, Houston"...Then we got another troubling call from Mission Control. "Challenger, Houston. Limits to inhibit." This was a terrifying radio call. It was definite, clear, crisp. "Limits to inhibit" was a switch on the center console that would inactivate our engine safety shutdown software. We had never used that switch in our many simulator sessions. Gordo threw the switch. Now we were unprotected from overtemperature and other serious conditions in the remaining two engines.

After the flight we learned that our Booster Officer in Mission Control, Jenny Howard, saw a troubling signature in one of our remaining two engines that matched the signature of the failed engine. She told the Flight Director and CAPCOM to go Limits to Inhibit to avoid another engine failure. The failure was in an over-temperature sensor that failed hot, sending a signal to the computer that the engine had reached the temperature that is too high for safety, causing the engine protection software to shut down the engine. When two of three sensors voted hot, the shutdown was activated. One more failing and we would have another engine down.

Fortunately for us, Jenny Howard saved us from a bad day, as we had not yet reached a velocity where we could get to orbit on one engine. That caused other concerns for me. Before the flight, I had approached our lead flight director on behalf of the crew to request permission to schedule a simulator session to validate a downrange abort-landing site. He asked why. I said, "It would be needed in the event of a two-engine failure before we reach a velocity where we can get to orbit on one engine. All previous missions launched into a 28.5-degree inclination orbit. We are the first to use a 49.5-degree inclination orbit. The previously validated downrange abort site will not work for our inclination."

He said, "That's an unrealistic failure scenario. Get out of my office and quit wasting my time."

But my granddaddy and an alligator had taught me to always have a backup plan. I scheduled the simulator session anyway. I validated the computer code to enter in the event of this failure: we would have guidance to land at Souda Bay Naval Air Station on the Greek island of Crete. I had the hexadecimal code written on my kneepad. Now I might actually have to use it.

As we neared orbital velocity, the shuttle throttle automatically moved from full thrust to a value that would sustain a maximum of 3g's. We all nervously watched the velocity indicator, as the value at Main Engine Cutoff (MECO) would determine our fate—enough to stay in orbit or an Abort Once Around. "MECO." Then the shuttle main tank separated, and bam! bam! bam! the attitude-control jets in the nose and tail fired to separate us from the tank.

I carried this experience with me as I led KSC. As part of our emphasis on our culture and specifically safety culture, we established "safety walkdowns." I asked our team to routinely conduct a safety walkdown by visiting their people and facilities to see if there were any major safety concerns. I did the same myself. This provided an opportunity for our employees to have a channel to escalate any concerns they had. When we found and fixed a safety concern, we rewarded the individual escalating the concern with a "Gold Dollar Award." This was a coin that provided a simple but meaningful reward and recognition for their willingness to share concerns. Sharing concerns is vital to a transformation.

The Consultant's Observations ... Tim

The disruptors can come from any direction and any level. Not all disruptors will show up at your door: some will show up to your individual leaders. You and your team will need to have a set of guidelines for how to handle these disruptors. An escalation philosophy—a plan describing why, when, and how to bring awareness of a disruptor to the attention of the leader and team—can provide these guidelines. In working with KSC during this transformation, we didn't make this explicit. Much later on, while I was working with a program manager, the importance of an explicit escalation philosophy became apparent. We are offering this as a lesson learned. An example escalation philosophy is given below.

Illustration 5.3—Escalation

You need to escalate because...

- No one likes surprises
- It is your responsibility to escalate problems to enable the leader to make timely decisions and allocate resources to the most important places
- You are all counting on each other
- You can't assume everyone knows what you know

Escalate the problem to your manager if...

- if the next management level heard it, they would be surprised negatively
- if the outcome will go external (e.g., beyond the program to HQ)
- if it affects more than your unit
- if it significantly impacts the cost, schedule, or risk above your level/sphere of control/authority
- if it requires significant resource changes that you cannot authorize
- if it is a roadblock that will keep the organization from being able to move forward

Communicate the Problem & Solution in Steps...

- At the moment you know about the disruptor...share the problem for awareness
- Within 24 hours...share the background and potential resolutions being worked
- Within a week...share the final resolution plan with impacts and next steps

When You Need Help, Be Definitive

- Be clear
- Explicitly state when you need help and the help needed

The intent of this escalation philosophy is to help your team solve the problems that emerge.

Recommendations

From this chapter we offer a few recommendations and questions to engage your team with.

You will run into unforeseen disruptors. As you know, life can throw us curveballs at times. Transformations are just like life...you will get curveballs or disruptors thrown at you and your team. Your team will be looking to see how you respond to these disruptors. You can provide stability and calmness with your response.

Next Steps

To manage these disruptors, you can:

- Remain Flexible and Adaptable
- Plan with Scenarios
- Focus on the Controllable
- Provide a Response to the Disruption
- Establish and Use an Escalation Philosophy

Start the Conversation

Engage your team in preparing for and responding to disruptors by asking them to share their views about:

What disruptions/risks can impact our transformation?

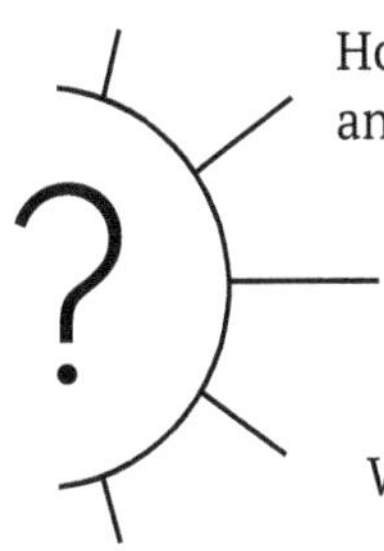

How can we proactively plan for the disruptors and frustrations that come with the disruptions?

What are the potential futures we may see?

What are the best, worst, and most likely cases?

How can we ensure we stay flexible to the changes in the external environment?

PROCESS

You got this

In this section, we share a set of frameworks and actions for you to lead your organization through their transformation. Think about this section as a road map to your transformation journey. We provide a set of steps you can use to guide your team. Pick the steps that make sense to you and your situation.

Your team will be looking for you to guide them through the change.

Chapter 6
Navigate the Journey Strategically

You got this

Your Situation...
Transformations Are a Journey

You are charged with leading your organization through its transformation. When we go on a journey, we use a road map to help us navigate from where we are to where we want to be. To get there, you can follow a systematic process or transformation road map to arrive at your final—and better--destination.

You may be thinking:

> *Where do I start?*
>
> *What are the stages or phases to the transformation?*

In this chapter, we reflect on the phases and swim lanes—the major buckets of items to deliver on to navigate your transformation.

What's Next...
Create Your Map to Navigate the Journey

Transformations are complex and can be hard to execute. You have a choice on how you respond. The best response to a transformation is a strategic response.

Next Steps

To respond strategically you can:

- Get Everyone on Board the Transformation Journey
- Assign a Process Guide to Help the Team Stay Focused
- Focus on Four Transformation Swim Lanes as You Navigate Four Phases
    - Swim Lane 1: Execute Today's Mission
    - Swim Lane 2: Continuously Set Strategy
    - Swim Lane 3: Make the Strategy Real
    - Swim Lane 4: Enable the Transformation
    - Navigate Four Phases

Start the Conversation

Engage your team in developing a strategic response by asking them to share their perspectives about:

Where do we start?

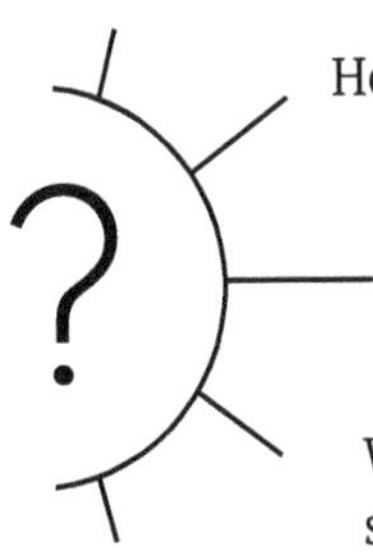

How ready are we for this transformation?

How willing are we to go on this transformation journey?

What process will we use to guide our leadership actions?

What milestones do we need to accomplish?

Dig Deeper

In this section, we provide the leader's perspective (Roy) and the consultant's perspective (Tim) on the following actions you can take:

- Get Everyone on Board the Transformation Journey
- Assign a Process Guide to Help the Team Stay Focused
- Focus on Four Transformation Swim Lanes as You Navigate Four Phases
    - Swim Lane 1: Execute Today's Mission
    - Swim Lane 2: Continuously Set Strategy
    - Swim Lane 3: Make the Strategy Real
    - Swim Lane 4: Enable the Transformation
    - Navigate Four Phases

Get Everyone on Board the Transformation Journey

The Leader's Experience ... Roy

We needed everyone in the top leadership team and at all levels of management engaged to work such an intimidating challenge. Even if I could come up with some magic potion, I would need everyone to get on board to create a KSC that we would all want to migrate toward. While an off-site would help us get started, we would need to meet often and be open to getting everyone engaged and sharing their perspectives.

And we had to find time to do this without harm to the day job: space is hard. We needed everyone to focus to avoid some catastrophe that would further complicate our situation and perhaps cause stakeholders to try to derail our strategic plan.

We've detailed a lot of the elements of our strategic plan and road map in earlier chapters. Each element of our plan required immense effort, without any guarantee of success. Keeping up the effort required us to encourage each other as we made progress. We also needed to spend a fair amount of time measuring progress with good metrics to keep our eyes on the ball and correct for any issues that would inevitably crop up along the way.

I am proud to say that we were successful. Some of the things that we did made sure that KSC is still relevant today and is playing a major role in NASA and the nation's space program.

The senior leaders also had to commit to engage consistently in discussions, both during off-sites and in follow-up meetings; to review progress; and to deal with inevitable obstacles and disruptions that cropped up along the way. Most of them had a full plate of work already, so it was tempting for some to try to avoid being drawn into these crucial conversations.

Solutions to the disheartening issue that NASA heaped on us were not immediately obvious, and time was of the essence: buyouts and hiring freezes were already causing many in the workforce to leave. We desperately needed to keep many of our best and brightest for our effort to be successful in the long run.

The Consultant's Observations ... Tim

Roy was intentional in engaging his leadership team in the transformation. He involved the senior management team in

- identifying the issues facing KSC,
- setting agendas for the off-sites,
- bringing products to the off-sites,
- actively participating in the off-sites,
- crafting and sharing messages with the workforce,
- leading initiative teams.

Roy also had the senior management team work together to craft the all-hands messages to be shared with the workforce. The core messages and images shown in Chapter 7 were developed by the senior management teams. The key to success was the entire senior management team working the transformation together.

Assign a Process Guide to Help the Team Stay Focused

The Leader's Experience ... Roy

As KSC's senior leaders and I began meeting at off-sites to address how to construct an exciting future for KSC, the task looked almost impossible. Just getting everyone to engage, given the perceived hopelessness, was daunting.

The team had engaged a strategic planning expert, Tim Kotnour, to teach and mentor the team through the process. But one of the most critical decisions had been made before I arrived. Tim was engaged to help us devise a strategic plan and road map to a future that would appeal to everyone in the workforce so that we could retain the best and brightest of our people. Tim was an expert guide for our team. Also, a mid-level civil servant, Jenny Lyons, was added to the Center Director's staff to help us keep a focus on the strategy and road map on a day-to-day basis as we moved forward with actions to implement them. Given the press of the day job, it was too easy to be diverted without someone helping us to stay focused. Jenny, Tim, and others acted as our "pit crew" to help us stay focused. We all feared that many of these skilled and knowledgeable employees would leave for greener pastures if we were unsuccessful. This would be destructive and would seal our fate in its current state.

Tim helped us outline what we needed to do. Our vision, strategy, and road map had to be widely perceived as worth doing and doable. It had to restore the sense of purpose, value, and dignity of the KSC workforce. It also had to be acceptable to and supported by the wider community, that is, the chain of command up to NASA headquarters, our sister Centers in NASA, and civic leaders, to include elected officials in local, state, and federal governments.

Tim helped us make sure that whatever we came up with to guide us to a successful future had to be strategic, as opposed to minor, transactional actions. A strategic focus would assure that it was purposeful, intentional, and consistent.

The strategic management approach allowed KSC to manage future challenges successfully. For example, over the next twenty-plus years, they transitioned to a multiuser spaceport supporting many customers. This made proviso space shuttle infrastructure available to support commercial operators. Now, these companies are able to use shuttle infrastructure, lease shuttle launch pads, and build their facilities on KSC property "inside the gates," bringing more jobs to the area and more knowledge and progress to the world.

The Consultant's Observations ... Tim

As Roy shared, he and his team used both internal and external experts to support the journey. I was the lucky one to be part of the journey with them. I think my role was more about

- understanding the team's concerns,
- asking the right questions at the right time,
- developing models to help the team find their own path.

Periodically, Roy would also bring in outside experts to provide a training seminar. These seminars brought new perspectives that helped the team find their path. Under Roy's guidance, the senior management team made use of best practices and perspectives to develop the KSC path forward.

Focus on Four Transformation Swim Lanes as You Navigate Four Phases

The Leader's Experience ... Roy

Transformations are complex. They are even more complex when you are operating in a complex business with human lives at stake. We had to transform while also executing the very important shuttle missions. Space is a hard, risky business. We couldn't take our eye off the shuttle ball. But we also had to move forward systematically.

When I got to KSC, there was a lot of discussion on what needed to be done. Many folks suggested we undertake a reorganization (i.e., change the organizational structure and reporting chains of command). I resisted the reorganization call as the first move. I didn't think we really knew what the core problem and opportunity were. We needed to find and fix the root causes to our current challenges. I also knew that a quick fix or one big move would not create a sustainable positive future for KSC. We were going to face the challenge of delivering a complex, risky business while changing how we did this and creating new lines of business. We were going to be stretched thin. Our leadership challenge was to help our workforce understand and manage these multiple efforts.

I wanted to take a systematic approach to

- **Deliver the mission.** We needed to continue to safely process the shuttle while changing how we did this.
- **Set our strategy.** We first needed to stabilize and triage the current situation. We had to develop a strategy to deal with the current situation we faced. Once this foundation was laid, we were able to think about our longer-term future. We held a series of strategic off-sites and conversations to set our strategy. Our strategy was not set in a single off-site. Each off-site we built from the previous one and took the learnings from our initiatives to explore what was next.
- **Take action to create the future.** We needed to do more than think and talk about our strategy. We needed to take actions

that would create our future. In some cases these changes were to enhance how we processed the shuttle. In other cases we were trying to develop fundamentally new contributions.

- **Enable the transformation.** As you can imagine, the above three swim lanes took a lot of coordination and energy. This was a major change-management effort. We spent time building our capabilities and team to manage these changes.

We intuitively led the KSC workforce in these four swim lanes.

The Consultant's Observations ... Tim

A **strategic response** involves implementing a **strategic transformation path** containing four swim lanes:

- **Execute Today's Mission** focuses on delivering your mission and meeting your customers' requirements. You cannot drop current operations during the transformation. This current business provides your foundation for moving forward.
- **Continuously Set Strategy** focuses on developing and evaluating your organization's overall strategy (e.g., vision, business model, change path to the future). You cannot view setting strategy as a once-a-year activity. This is an ongoing, continual requirement.
- **Make the Strategy Real** focuses on implementing specific efforts to make the strategy a reality. Your current business model and your new business model implementation strategies must be implemented concurrently.
- **Enable the Transformation** focuses on supporting your organization in understanding, accepting, committing to, and executing the transformation. The leader needs to focus on guiding behavior, managing the portfolio of improvement initiatives, learning, and providing a change infrastructure—a team that provides internal consulting to support the senior management in making the transformation happen.

In looking at the KSC transformation, we'll see that KSC implemented a strategic transformation path.

Swim Lane 1: Execute Today's Mission

The first swim lane of the strategic transformation path is to execute your current mission.

Your organization needs to continue to meet its commitments to its customers. The credibility and trust your organization has with its existing customers is the basis for moving forward. If your organization fails to meet its current commitment, there is no basis for new customers to trust your capability. Current customers are the source of the revenue to invest in the future.

KSC continued to meet their responsibilities as it evolved to new roles. "Today's mission" changes over time. The very nature of a transformation may change the core mission of your organization. Throughout its transformation, KSC focused on meeting its mission. Their core mission didn't change over time, but what the mission was applied to and how the mission was executed did change over time.

KSC executed its long-standing mission of processing the shuttle, ISS, and NASA payloads. Through the strategic management process within NASA and KSC, KSC further expanded its application of its mission to include the Launch Services Program, spaceport and range technology development, and exploration support. See Chapter 1 for a recap of how KSC delivered its mission.

Swim Lane 2: Continuously Set Strategy

The second swim lane of the transformation path is to continuously set strategy.

Throughout the transformation, your organization must continue to evaluate the external environment and internal performance in order to set strategy. One of the first steps in achieving successful change and transformation is to create a vision of the future (Kotter 1996; Kanter et al. 1992). The strategy must be adapted over time to reflect changes in the environment. Chapter 8 will provide a more detailed discussion of the strategic planning function.

As we previously stated, KSC chose to take a strategic management approach to the transformation. A key element was the use of a continuous series of strategic conversations (e.g., strategic-planning off-sites). Illustration 6.1 provides a summary of the annual strategic-planning off-sites held by KSC senior management. Each strategic off-site had a major theme.

Illustration 6.1—Summary of KSC Strategic Off-sites

<table>
<tr><th>Strategic off-site</th><th>Strategic off-site Date</th><th>Theme</th><th>Products</th><th>Transformation Phase</th></tr>
<tr><td>1</td><td>Fall 1996</td><td>Understanding strategic context</td><td>Initial need to change and strategic issues for new Center Director</td><td>Understand the need for change</td></tr>
<tr><td>2 & 3</td><td>Spring 1997</td><td>Need for Change & Vision</td><td>Roy's first off-site with this team
Senior management teams established to define the "from-to" view of KSC</td><td>Strategic exploration & visioning</td></tr>
<tr><td>4</td><td>Sept. 1998</td><td>Make it so!</td><td>Spaceport technologies vision</td><td>Strategic exploration & visioning</td></tr>
<tr><td>5</td><td>Sept. 1999</td><td>Teamwork and reorganization</td><td>KSC 2000 reorganization plan</td><td rowspan="4">Strategic implementation & strategic adjustment</td></tr>
<tr><td>6</td><td>Sept. 2000</td><td>Deploying the Vision</td><td>Scenario Planning—Change Path</td></tr>
<tr><td>7</td><td>Sept. 2001</td><td>Planning Our Future</td><td>Strategic resources review
Metrics tied to road map</td></tr>
<tr><td>8</td><td>Sept. 2002</td><td>Focusing Our Path</td><td>Alignment to new NASA direction and administrator</td></tr>
</table>

* *(Note: even though specific dates are listed, significant strategic conversations took place before, after, and in between the off-sites.)*

Swim Lane 3: Make the Strategy Real

The third swim lane of the strategic transformation path is to make the strategy real.

Strategy is more than the physical document or plan. Strategy is made real by the decisions and actions an organization takes to invest time, energy, and resources in moving itself to its vision as defined in its strategic plan. KSC did more than talk about its strategy; they made the strategy real by taking a series of actions to position and align the organization.

One conversation or decision to implement an action led to the next action being taken. The KSC in essence took a series of "stepping stones" to navigate from where it was to where it wanted to be. You can argue the goodness of the actions. But the real point is to highlight the need to have the right strategy and to ensure that the resulting efforts are aligned with the strategy by

- improving the mission;
- improving the organization and transforming the management process;
- partnering.

KSC made the strategy real by improving the execution of the core mission (i.e., provide space systems processes, test and launch techniques, and develop associated technologies). They focused on ensuring they continued to deliver this core operational role in a way that the customer expected. They also were investing to enhance their emerging technology development role.

Swim Lane 4: Enable the Transformation

The fourth swim lane of the transformation path is to enable the transformation.

The leadership team needs to enable the organization to successfully balance executing today's mission, continuously setting strategy, and making the strategy real. These actions are gleaned from understanding best practices in the literature and reflecting on KSC's approaches.

To make the transformation successful, KSC enabled it by:

- guiding behavior,
- managing the portfolio of improvement initiatives,
- learning,
- providing a change infrastructure.

Specifics of these actions to enable the transformation are described in greater detail in Illustration 6.2.

Illustration 6.2—Specific Actions Associated with Enabling the Transformation

Guiding behavior

- Drive accountability: make sure folks do what they are supposed to do. Ensure accountability is met for the initiatives that move the organization forward
    - Gain involvement and commitment
    - Make decisions (raising, framing, and deciding the tough issues)
    - Build a unified team
    - Communicate continuously

Managing the portfolio of improvement initiatives

- Put the big picture together of the why, what, and how of the transformation
- Connect the dots among the different improvement initiatives
- Reinforce the strategic message in all that the organization does

Learning

- Improve understanding about the external environment, organization, and change
- Gain knowledge from self and others
- Listen to an honest broker— a consultant or internal trusted rep who brings data with very little bias for a specific course of action

Providing a change infrastructure

- A team that provides internal consulting to support the senior management in making the transformation happen.

To help us identify the items to focus on to increase our probability of success, we searched for best practices such as these:

- An organizational transformation is redefining an organization's business (e.g., mission and products/services) and the way the business is operated (e.g., processes, technology, people, and culture) (Davidson 1993).
- Your organization needs to overcome the common barriers to change (Grove 1999).

- Other authors have identified critical factors necessary for successful large-scale changes (Appelbaum, Simpson, and Shapiro 1987; Cameron, Freeman, and Mishra 1993; Kanter, Stein, and Jick 1992; Marshall and Yorks 1994; National Academy of Public Administration 1996). Their findings highlight the need for an organization to (1) clearly understand the change's forces or drivers, and (2) design actions that produce positive results and minimize negative ones. Sink and Morris (1995) offered a model of successful change.

We used many different models to help guide our actions.

Navigate Four Phases

Illustration 6.3 is a graphical representation of the strategic response. It illustrates the four phases of the transformation and the four swim lanes and how each of the four swim lanes must be applied in each of the four phases. As your organization goes through the transformation, these swim lanes are the four items your leader and his/her team need to keep their eye on. If your leader reviews their daily calendar, they will be focused on one of these source areas: delivering the mission, setting strategy, making the strategy real, or enabling the transformation. The transformational leader needs to focus on these four areas to ensure the transformation is successful. These are the high-level focal points.

Illustration 6.3—Strategic Response

Transformation Phases

	Swim Lanes	Understand the Need for Change	Strategic Exploration & Visioning
1	Execute Today's Mission	• Current work	• Current work
2	Continuously Set Strategy	• Define scenarios • Assess healthiness	• Set strategic • direction
3	Make the Strategy Real	• Fix the "crisis" elements	• Define initial problems to solve and implement quick wins
4	Enable the Transformation	• Identify staff • Show visibility • Create a model	• Define the decision process • Communicate with stakeholders

We can define a transformation from a life-cycle perspective. This transformation life cycle has phases much like an engineering project. The management implication from the transformation life cycle is that your team must understand which phase they are in and manage the transformation activities accordingly. These phases are as follows (see the four phases at the top row of Illustration 6.3):

Phase 1: Understand the need for change. During this first phase, you need to understand the state of the external environment and where your organization is within that environment. Your management team defines

- the important trends in the environment impacting your organization;

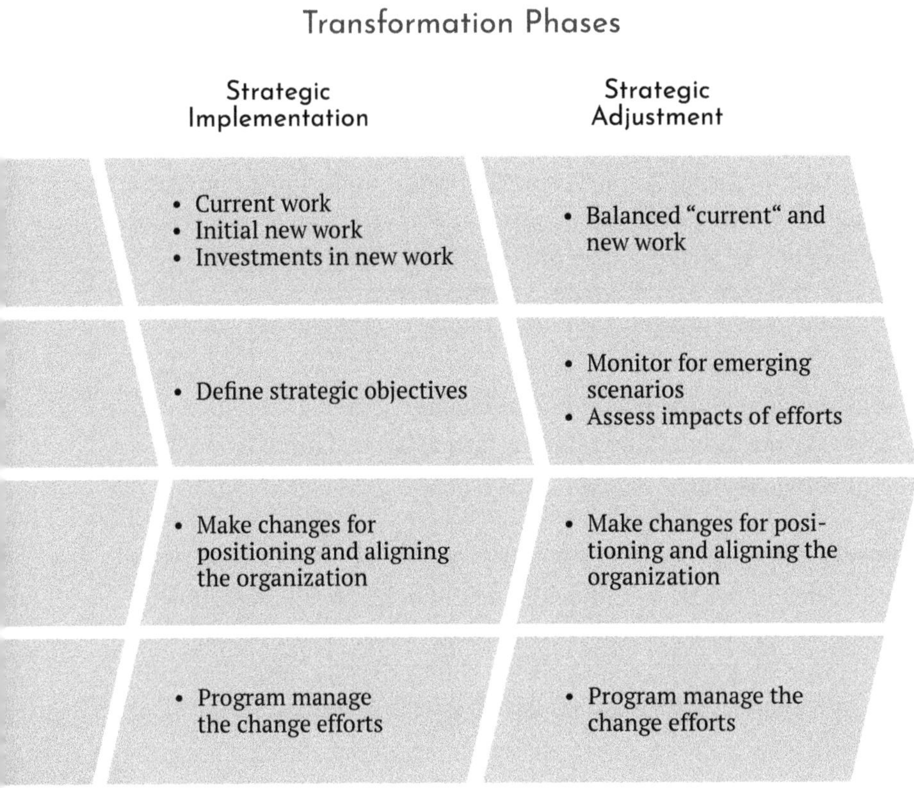

- the significant trigger event that is driving your organization to transform;
- the unacceptable state of your current business model.

In this phase, you make your case for change. During this phase your team needs to make the explicit choice to take a strategic approach and set strategy for the transformation.

Phase 2: Strategic exploration and visioning. During this second phase, your team will go through a series of strategic analyses and conversations to better understand

- where your organization is;
- where your organization wants to be (i.e., vision);

- how to achieve your vision or move from your current state to your desired state of the organization.

This phase is where the initial strategic planning of the transformation takes place. Your management team holds conversations to explore its external and internal environments and business. In this phase, your organization develops and refines new future business models and strategies to move forward. This strategic plan becomes your baseline strategic plan, which is continuously readjusted.
You will also take "triage actions" in this phase:

- to minimize the impact of the current challenges in your organization
- to respond to the initial trigger events
- to lay the foundation for more systematic and fundamental change

Phase 3: Strategic implementation. During this third phase, your team makes its vision a reality. You take actions here to position and align your organization with your strategic plan. To implement your strategic plan, your organization takes on strategic initiatives—the efforts to enhance existing or develop new products, services, or capabilities.

In this phase, your strategy includes the concurrent operation of your current business model and your new business model implementation strategy. **This is the hardest part of the active transformation. You have one foot in the old business model and the other foot in the new one, trying to get it incorporated into the daily work of running the business. Remember that this is going to be tough on everyone, so be prepared. Bring extra patience and compassion.**

Phase 4: Strategic adjustment. During this fourth phase, you continue to implement the new strategy while monitoring the external environment and your internal performance. You will also continue to adjust the strategy as needed.

Within these phases, there are specific actions you will need to take. These actions are unique to each phase and swim lane of the transformation. Throughout these phases, your organization must enable the transformation (i.e., change management is essential throughout each phase) and make strategic decisions. Obviously, there is overlap in the phases.

Recommendations

From this chapter we offer a few recommendations and questions to engage your team with.

Transformations are complex and can be hard to execute. You have a choice on how you respond. The best response to a transformation is a strategic response.

Next Steps

To respond strategically you can:

- Get Everyone on Board the Transformation Journey
- Assign a Process Guide to Help the Team Stay Focused
- Focus on Four Transformation Swim Lanes as You Navigate Four Phases
    - Swim Lane 1: Execute Today's Mission
    - Swim Lane 2: Continuously Set Strategy
    - Swim Lane 3: Make the Strategy Real
    - Swim Lane 4: Enable the Transformation
    - Navigate Four Phases

Start the Conversation

Engage your team in developing a strategic response by asking them to share their perspectives about:

Where do we start?

How ready are we for this transformation?

How willing are we to go on this transformation journey?

What process will we use to guide our leadership actions?

What milestones do we need to accomplish?

Chapter 7
Create a North Star (for Shared Commitment)

You got this

Your Situation...
Transformations Require Shared Understanding, Commitment, and Intention

During your transformation, your senior management team and workforce need to believe in the why, what, and how of the transformation. They need a story that gives them confidence to know where their organization is headed and how to get to a new future. By crafting and sharing a strategy, your workforce will see there is real leadership in their organization.

In the previous chapter we outlined four phases and four swim lanes. One of the swim lanes was to be strategic. You can think strategically about your transformation by answering the following question:

> "*What does 'thinking strategically' mean?*"

In this chapter, we will share what *think strategically* meant to KSC.

What's Next...
Think Strategically

You've made the choice to respond strategically to the transformation need. You and your team need to think strategically.

Next Steps

To think strategically you can:

- Create Safe Spaces for Meaningful Conversations
- Lay in Your Strategic Intent (Vision, Mission, Goals, Guiding Principles)
- Use Six Strategic Thinking Principles to Guide the Conversations
  - Principle 1: Understand Environments
  - Principle 2: Focus on Outcomes
  - Principle 3: Manage the All-Term
  - Principle 4: Balance Responsiveness with Proactivity
  - Principle 5: Synthesize Multiple Viewpoints
  - Principle 6: Align Goals, Objectives, Strategies, and Measures

Start the Conversation

Engage your team in strategic thinking by asking them to share their perspectives about:

What does thinking strategically mean?

How well are we defining our internal and external environments?

How well are we defining our desired outcomes?

How well are we managing our all-term?

How well are we balancing being responsive and proactive?

How well are we integrating multiple viewpoints?

How well are we aligning goals, objectives, and strategies?

How well are we connecting the dots?

Dig Deeper

In this section, we provide the leader's perspective (Roy) and the consultant's perspective (Tim) on the following actions you can take:

- Create Safe Spaces for Meaningful Conversations
- Lay in Your Strategic Intent (Vision, Mission, Goals, Guiding Principles)
- Use Six Strategic Thinking Principles to Guide the Conversations
    - Strategic Thinking Principle 1: Understand Environments
    - Strategic Thinking Principle 2: Focus on Outcomes
    - Strategic Thinking Principle 3: Manage the All-Term
    - Strategic Thinking Principle 4: Balance Responsiveness with Proactivity
    - Strategic Thinking Principle 5: Synthesize Multiple Viewpoints
    - Strategic Thinking Principle 6: Align Goals, Objectives, Strategies, and Measures

Create Safe Spaces for Meaningful Conversations

The Leader's Experience ... Roy

We decided to take on this challenge using a strategic-management approach consisting of many strategic conversations. As I stood before the senior staff at the first strategic retreat, I felt invigorated at having such a talented team to make the transition. They were individually superb. The problem was that each was focused on the day-to-day business of getting the next mission off. I needed to help them visualize the future and understand that we could make the future better if we could see a future that we liked as a team and were willing to work to achieve it.

We did achieve that goal, but many, many conversations were required over the next six years to complete the task. The conversations took many forms, from strategic off-sites with senior staff to town hall meetings with the broader workforce, as well as other techniques that will be discussed in this chapter and later in more detail in Chapters 10 and 12. I participated in several hundred conversations with our workforce and stakeholders each year. These were crucial to setting our plan and goals and then making them happen.

Remember that we did not have a cookbook or recipe to guide us, but we did have talented consultants like Tim Kotnour, who was with us every step of the way, helping us to see the next steps to take.

The Consultant's Observations ... Tim

Having routine strategic conversations is important, but equally important is the need to have these conversations in an environment in which people can talk openly and honestly. The individuals in the conversation must feel that they can share their opinions without fear of repercussions. If people are afraid of the ramifications of sharing their thoughts, they will not create new paradigms or share "unfavorable" assessments of the external environment and the internal workings of the organization. By *unfavorable*, I mean the conversations that go against the perceived thoughts of the leadership or power team. Many "unspoken" conversations will be left hanging.

The needed conversations that get to core issues will be held in the halls and in small groups, not in the larger management team where actions need to be taken. You need open, honest conversations to raise and answer the fundamental issues facing your organization. **Without open, honest conversations, strategy is destined to fail; commitment and involvement in the strategy will decrease.**

At KSC, the group at times struggled to have meaningful conversations in a large group setting. The better open and honest conversations happened in smaller settings and in one-on-one meetings with the KSC Center Director. The Center Director would then share these concerns with the broader team and seek their support for strate-

Illustration 7.1—Example of Weekly Strategic Conversations

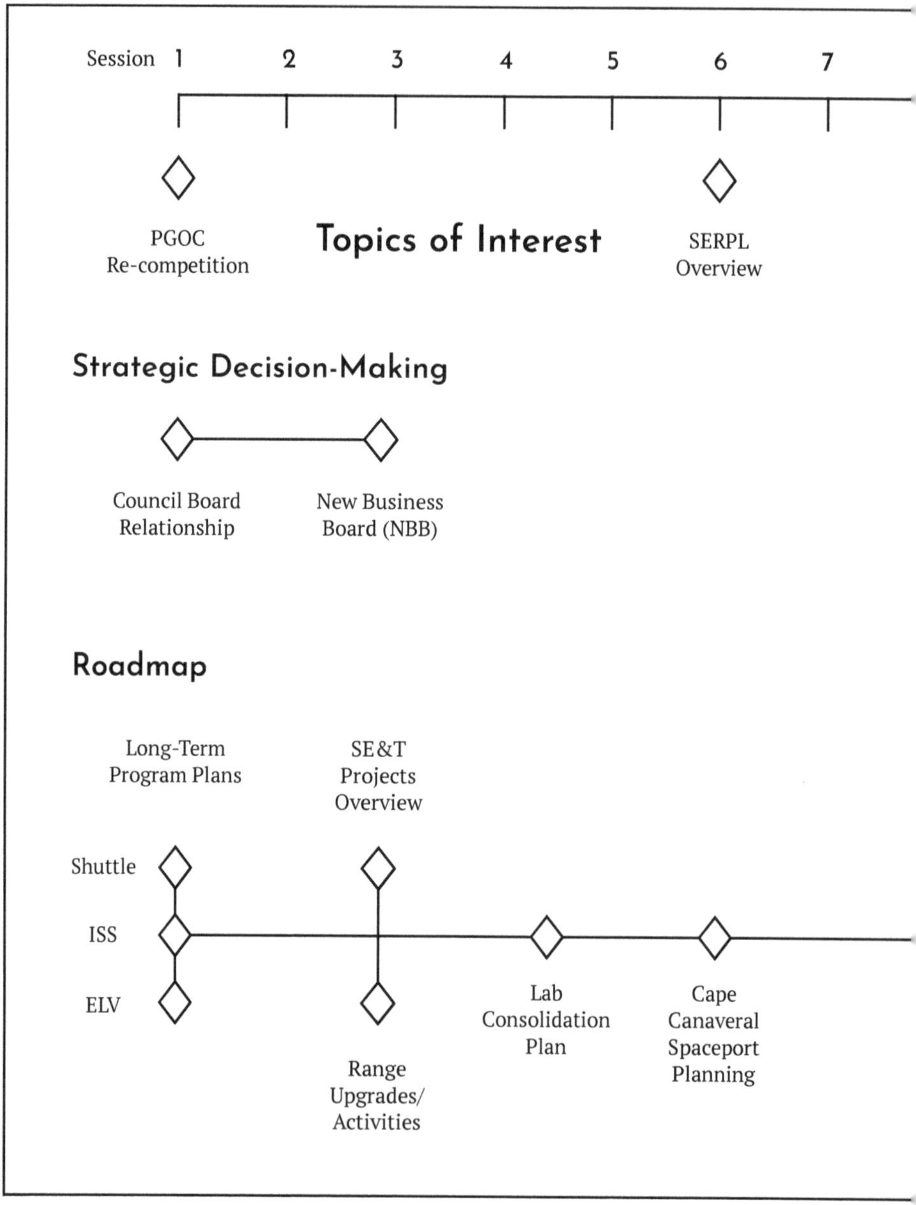

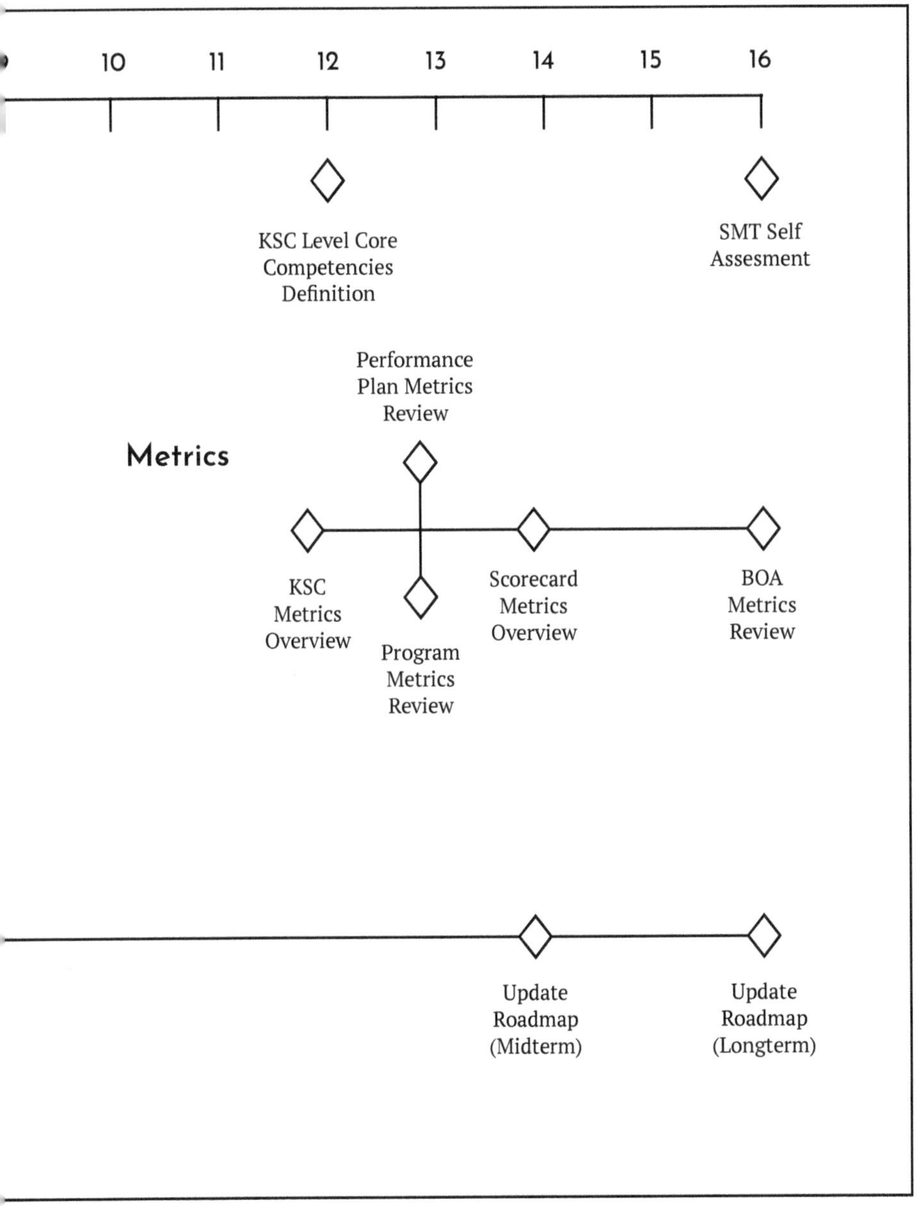

10
11
12
13
14
15
16
KSC Level Core Competencies Definition
SMT Self Assesment
Performance Plan Metrics Review
Metrics
KSC Metrics Overview
Program Metrics Review
Scorecard Metrics Overview
BOA Metrics Review
Update Roadmap (Midterm)
Update Roadmap (Longterm)

gic changes to address them. This contributed to strategic directions that were more fully supported.

One challenge in holding continuous strategic conversations is finding the time to devote to them. Annual management strategic off-sites are one tool to hold these conversations, but the problem with annual strategic off-sites is that they are annual—they happen only once a year. And once the strategic off-site is over, people go back to work on their daily, routine issues.

An organization needs to find a way to hold strategic conversations on a routine basis. To help hold continuous conversations, KSC implemented a "strategic Friday" concept, where the senior management team would routinely meet to discuss strategic issues, not the normal everyday status of operations. Illustration 7.1 provides an example schedule of the strategic items to be discussed during a series of strategic Fridays. This was developed by the KSC strategic planning manager, Jenny Lyons.

Lay In Your Strategic Intent (Vision, Mission, Goals, Guiding Principles)

The Leader's Experience ... Roy

To work within this external environment and associated challenges, KSC responded strategically. The senior management team responded to my strategic questions about how the Center wanted to change. Starting in 1997, the senior management team held a series of strategic conversations, from which the basic philosophy or direction was born. This direction focused on eight key elements:

1. Changing KSC from shuttle-centric to multi-program-centric
2. Recognizing the knowledge contribution of KSC's civil servants
3. Systematically transitioning the workforce from one program to the next
4. Defining KSC's core business
5. Defining KSC's guiding principles (i.e., values)
6. Defining a proactive approach to its destiny
7. Defining KSC's products and services
8. Defining a road map to the future.

Details follow.

First, KSC defined the desire to change from being shuttle-centric. Illustration 7.2 highlights the nature of this change from the Center's past to its future. Following the first off-site with me as the new Center Director, teams of senior managers developed this chart to signify the need to change KSC. Following this first management off-site, four senior management teams defined the past and future states of KSC. The senior management teams integrated their findings into an overall philosophy to be a multi-program-centric Center.

Illustration 7.2—KSC's Future: Capabilities, Expertise, Services

KSC's Future: Capabilities, expertise, services

Past		Future
INFRASTRUCTURE	→	MULTIPROGRAM CAPABILITIES
Apollo/ELV/Shuttle		Multipurpose, Flexible and Responsive
EXPERTISE	→	CUSTOMER-FOCUSED
Operations Focused		Tailored, Cutting Edge Engineering/Business Processes, Tests, and Techniques
SERVICES	→	DEVELOPMENT SERVICES
Launch and Payload Operations		Launch and Payload Processing Techniques and Technologies
AT KSC	→	ANYWHERE, ANYTIME

Second, KSC defined and recognized the knowledge contribution of its civil servants. It focused on "bearing fruit" for NASA now and in the future. KSC understood its roots and heritage. It focused on using its operations knowledge and expertise to continue to support current operations and to enhance the development of future vehicles, payloads, spaceports, and ranges. Illustration 7.3 is the chart senior managers developed to define the value of KSC's operational knowledge. Their vast operational knowledge value, in addition to applying to processing, integrating, testing, and launching the shuttle, could be applied to: (1) helping designers design new launch vehicle and spacecraft systems, and (2) enabling mission and commercial success of operations (e.g., supporting the expendable launch vehicle commercial business with NASA).

Illustration 7.3—KSC Civil Servant Contribution

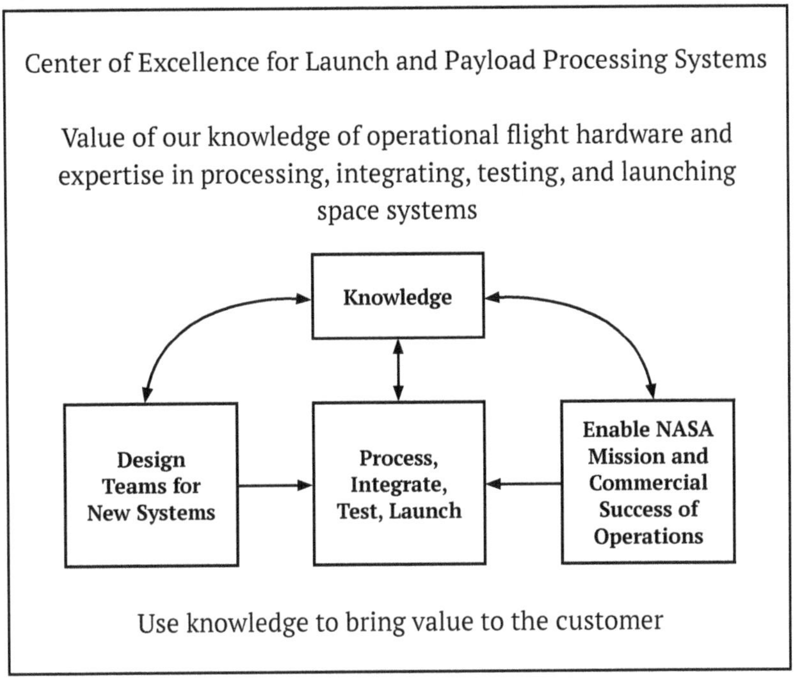

Third, KSC defined an approach for systematically transitioning the workforce from one program to the next. Illustration 7.4 shows the original concept of transitioning and evolving the KSC workforce. In this original concept, KSC would help transition shuttle operations to a new contract management approach and then eventually privatize the shuttle fleet. This was the nature of the conversation in the early and mid-1990s. Consistent with the role of operational knowledge (see Illustration 7.3), the workforce would then use their operational knowledge on other NASA development efforts. They participated in these programs until the programs were canceled. KSC would continue to choose other paths to use their operational knowledge to support NASA.

Illustration 7.4—Yesterday, Today, Tomorrow

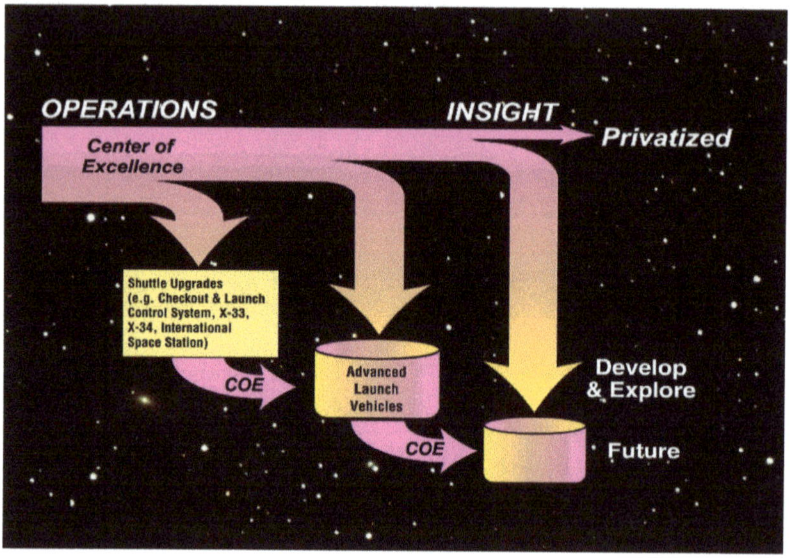

Fourth, KSC defined its core business. This core business statement (see Illustration 7.5) emphasized the operational role of the space Center. The business statement also recognized KSC's history and competence at designing and building the infrastructure needed for the spaceport operations (i.e., processing, integrating, launching, and landing launch vehicles and spacecraft). Again, this core business statement was developed by a team of senior managers during a strategic management off-site. This highlighted the push for KSC to further build its development capability. This new emphasis on the development capability was a key addition to KSC and part of the KSC vision—a vision to move beyond just operations.

Figures 7.2-7.8

Figures 7.2-7.8 were developed by teams of KSC senior managers to signify the need to change KSC.

Illustration 7.5—Core Business

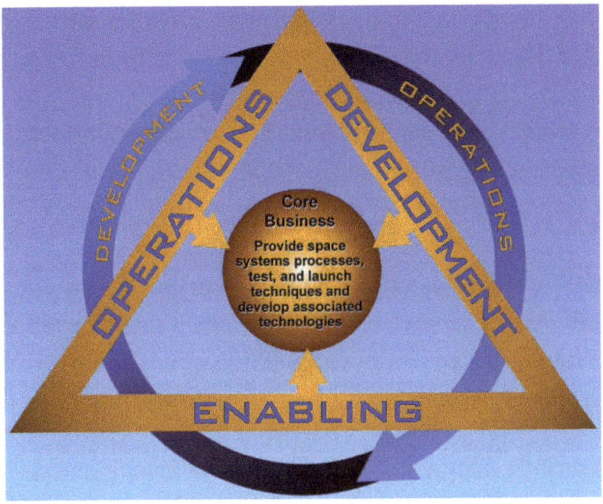

Fifth, KSC defined their guiding principles. These guiding principles are shown in Illustration 7.6. As we'll see later, these guiding principles led to a series of specific actions to reinforce them.

Illustration 7.6—Summary of KSC's Strategic Intent

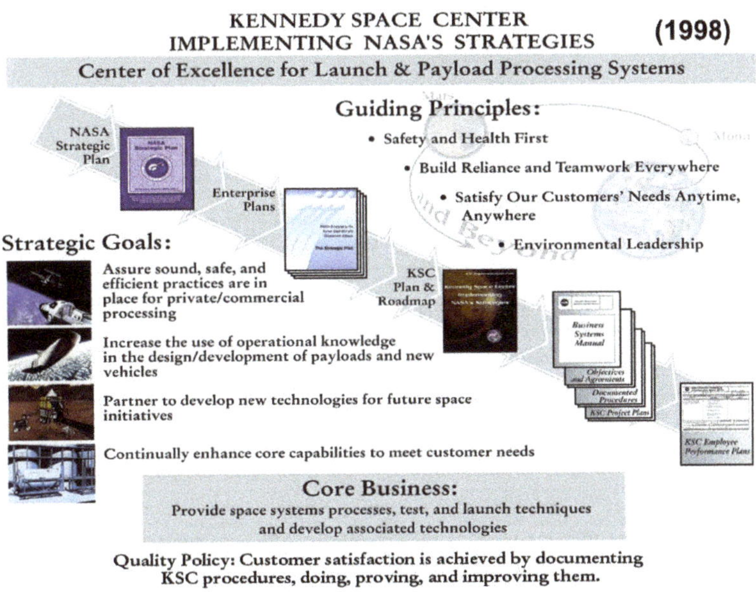

Sixth, KSC defined a proactive approach to its destiny. KSC wanted to be both responsive and proactive in its work with NASA. As a field Center, KSC clearly understood the need to be responsive to NASA's direction. NASA and its program provided to KSC the work to be completed. KSC provided implementation plans on how it would meet programmatic requirements. KSC also wanted to—and did—become more proactive in helping influence NASA's strategic direction.

Seventh, KSC defined its products and services. (See Illustration 7.7.) KSC defined this view to connect the development products with the products and services it delivered to the operational customers—for example, Fluid System Technologies includes things to improve the storage, loading, and unloading propellants of spacecraft. Again, a key part of KSC's vision was to increase KSC's involvement and capability in technology development and science. They wanted to ensure these efforts were aligned to its customers' ground operations, such as testing of spacecraft systems to assure that they are functioning correctly and repairing any malfunctioning system.

Illustration 7.7—KSC External Lines of Business and Product/ Service Lines

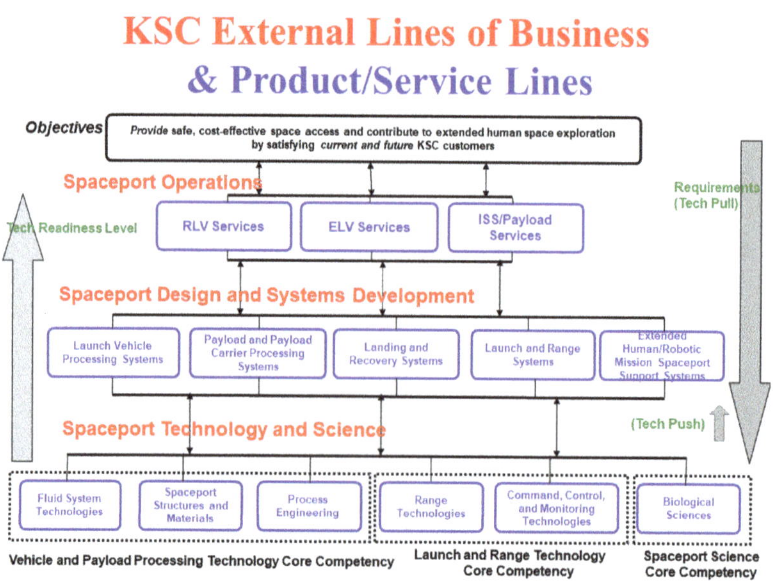

Eighth, KSC defined a road map to the future. As shown in Illustration 7.8, this road map defined the goals, objectives, and key strategies for KSC to accomplish. This road map was a strategic product that defined the specific accomplishments that would have to take place to implement the strategic intent.

Illustration 7.8—KSC Road Map

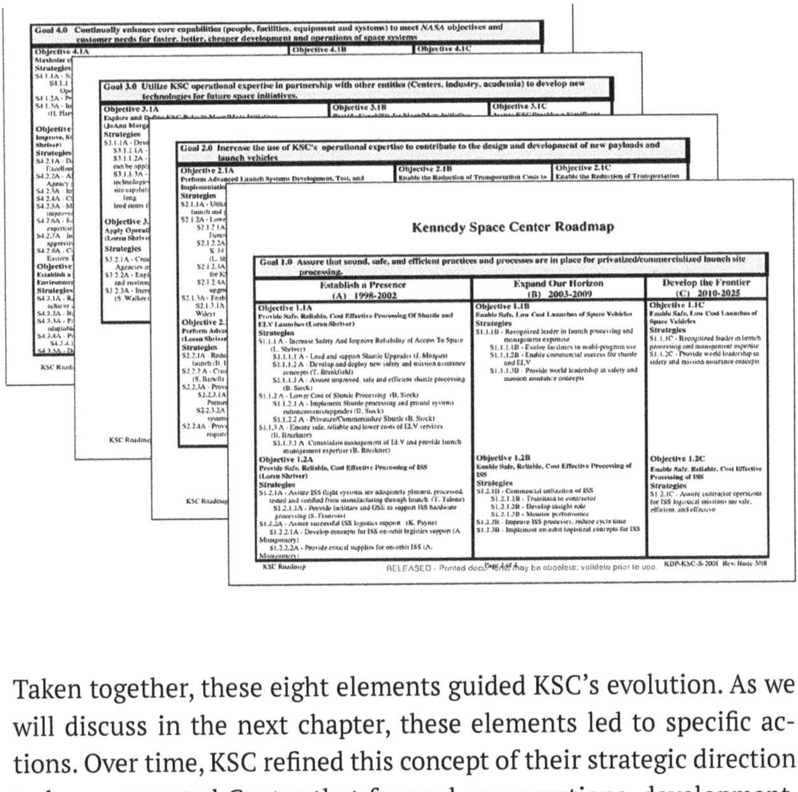

Taken together, these eight elements guided KSC's evolution. As we will discuss in the next chapter, these elements led to specific actions. Over time, KSC refined this concept of their strategic direction to be an accepted Center that focused on operations, development, and enabling functions. The push to increase the development function became a major focus for KSC.

The Consultant's Observations ... Tim

Strategic conversations focus on your organization's ever-changing external environment and how well your strategy is working. The aim is to adjust your strategy to your external business environment. To help your organization determine its future, you can provide a "north star" or overarching context using items such as vision, mission, goals, and guiding principles. Having clarity and commitment to these four elements provides a way for the team to make decisions.

The Vision

To improve life here, to extend life to there, to find life beyond: this was the NASA vision. So that all of NASA would have one shared vision, we made this vision our own and used it to guide us.

The Core Mission

As the Center of Excellence for Launch and Payload Processing Systems, we saw our core business (i.e., mission) to be to provide

- space systems processes,
- test and launch techniques, and
- to develop associated technologies.

The Four Goals

As a team we needed to reach a consensus on the value that we could bring to NASA, now and in the future. After much discussion, we settled on the following four goals:

- Goal 1: Assure sound, safe, and efficient practices are in place for private/commercial processing.
- Goal 2: Increase the use of operational knowledge in the design/development of payloads and new vehicles.
- Goal 3: Partner to develop new technologies for future space initiatives.

- Goal 4: Continually enhance core capabilities to meet customer needs.

The Four Guiding Principles

We also settled on the following four guiding principles:

- safety and health first
- build reliance and teamwork everywhere
- satisfy our customers' needs anytime, anywhere
- environmental leadership (protecting the natural environment and resources)

Use Six Strategic Thinking Principles to Guide the Conversations

The Leader's Experience ... Roy

At an operational Center, it is common to be so focused on getting that day's job done correctly and safely that you have trouble setting aside time to be looking ahead at where you need to be in the future and taking actions to get there. Thinking strategically means asking what we want to accomplish, recognizing what steps need to be followed in order to achieve it, and methodically going about getting those things done rather than doing a few things to solve a problem today and another tomorrow but having no idea of what you should be doing for the future to be successful. Taking the time to think and act strategically is critical to be ready for what the customer will need from KSC in future years.

The Consultant's Observations ... Tim

Six strategic thinking principles can help guide your thinking—as the leader, you must connect the dots. To help manage the transformation challenges, implement the strategic response, and implement the leadership roles, you must think strategically. From the KSC experience we extract and describe six strategic thinking principles:

1. Understand your internal and external environments.
2. Focus on your desired outcomes.
3. Manage your all-term.
4. Balance responsiveness with proactivity.
5. Synthesize multiple viewpoints.
6. Align goals, objectives, strategies, and measures.

As we'll see, KSC implemented these principles in their strategic-planning road map.

The glue that holds these six principles together is the concept of connecting the dots. As a leader, you must understand and communicate the connection of the results of strategic thinking.

Strategic Thinking Principle 1: Understand Environments

The first principle is to understand environments. This principle highlights the need to understand the current and future environments and the implications of these potential environments to your organization (Schwartz 1996).

Many future potential environments exist, some more positive than others, for your organization. Strategic thinking involves defining what the potential future environments are, what they mean for your organization, and what your most desired environment is. To do that, you will create scenarios.

Scenarios are a combination of both projections of what is known and extrapolations beyond what is known. They are a "story" of what the world and/or your organization could be like in the future.

Many methods exist to create a scenario. One method is to identify the best, worst, and most likely cases. Another method is to identify the important variables and explore different combinations of them.

Understanding environments is a process of sorting out what potential scenarios face your organization. Once that is done, your team needs to define the more favorable scenarios, the scenarios you need to be prepared for, and the scenarios you can ignore.

From these imagined scenarios, your team can develop strategies to either create the favorable scenarios or to ensure your organization is ready for an unfavorable scenario. In the end, your organization needs to take action to position and align itself.

In the 1997 KSC strategic management off-site, KSC Director Roy Bridges presented potential scenarios facing KSC. He asked the management team which scenario they wanted to create. They began to explore what their future might be like. They struggled with the thought of becoming a government-owned, contractor-operated Center. They believed they could contribute more to NASA. They began to focus on the environment they wanted to create for themselves. Again, in 2000, KSC used a scenario-planning process to help define and understand the potential scenarios facing NASA and KSC. The management team used these scenarios to better understand their path to the future.

Strategic Thinking Principle 2: Focus on Outcomes

The second principle is to focus on outcomes. This principle highlights the need to define your desired outcomes and align decisions and actions with these outcomes. Desired outcomes are the results your organization needs to achieve from the perspective of its customers, key stakeholders, and employees. Once outcomes are defined, you can implement the remainder of the strategy process. Desired outcomes drive the strategy.

As stated earlier from a transformation perspective, KSC defined its contributions to NASA using its four goals. These outcomes—the achievement of these four goals—led to the KSC road map (see Illustration 7.8), which defined its strategies, tactics, and actions.

Strategic Thinking Principle 3: Manage the All-Term

The third principle is to manage the all-term. This principle highlights the need to understand the relationship among your current, short-term, and long-term states—the "all-term"—of your organization. In order to manage the all-term, your team needs to think, align resources, and take actions to

- meet today's mission,
- transition to the short-term state of your organization,
- transform to the long-term state.

Your organization needs to invest in actions today that will create its future. You may not see the results of the action now, but you will be laying the foundation for the future you desire.

To transform KSC, senior management needed to answer a set of questions. The questions focused on where KSC was, where it wanted to be, and how it could get there. The transformation of an organization involves understanding its current state and defining its ideal future and transition states. The transition state is the time when the organization is balancing its current- and future-state missions and core businesses.

Illustration 7.9 shows the three states of KSC over time. The strategic direction as developed in strategic planning defines the requirements and time frames during which actions are taken to move the organization to the transition and future states. KSC used this model to define their actions to ensure that current, short-term, and long-term needs were met. By defining the long-term state, they could then work backwards to develop the path from the future to today. They also worked from today to the future to make sure the path was doable from where they started.

Illustration 7.9— KSC Was Undergoing an "All-term" Transition

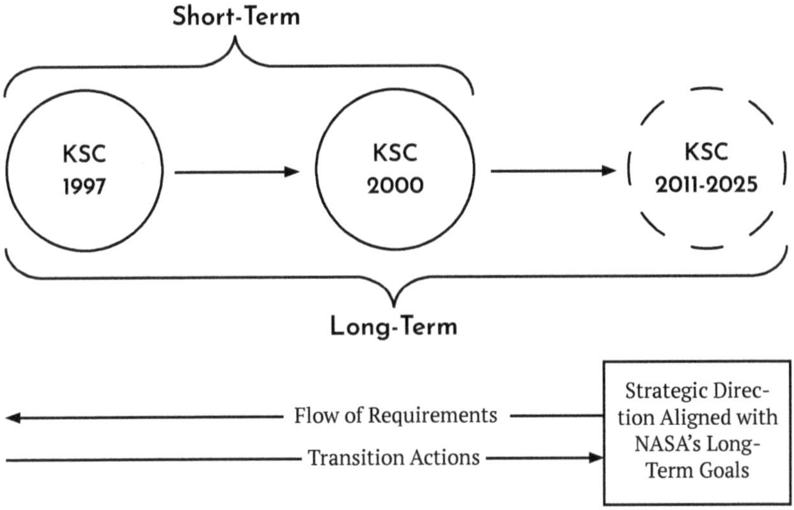

In 1997, KSC was operating in an oversight mode—where the government is in charge of all activities and is supported by the contractor—for the Space Shuttle Program. However, they were being driven by pressure from the NASA Administrator to move to an insight mode—where the contractor is in charge of all day-to-day processing activities. The radical downsizing of the KSC workforce became the predominant pressure to make it happen as soon as possible. This came to be in the short run as the SFOC was implemented, and was sustained until the last shuttle flight landed. Under insight mode, KSC provided quality control technicians to observe critical items and report any issues to KSC management as well as the contractor. The government was only fully in charge for the launch countdown and landing. This remained the method used for the rest of the life of the Space Shuttle Program.

During strategic planning, employee focus groups identified the need to define the state beyond the short-term transition to the SFOC. That is, the employees wanted to know what the long-term state was. The long term was about determining what we wanted to do strategically to bring new programs to KSC to be able to keep some of our best and brightest. That was what the strategic planning was all about. It helped us define a future that would be attractive to the remaining workforce.

Therefore, KSC had to strategically think about and understand

- where KSC was in 1997;
- where it needed to be in 2000;
- where it desired to be in the long term;
- how these three were related;
- what actions were needed to achieve each of the three states.

Again, this strategic-thinking principle was made real in the KSC strategic road map. For each time frame, the objectives and strategies described what needed to be accomplished to create KSC's state in that time frame. (See Illustration 7.8.)

Strategic Thinking Principle 4: Balance Responsiveness with Proactivity

The fourth principle is to balance responsiveness with proactivity. This principle highlights the need to be responsive to meeting your current requirements while at the same time trying to influence the requirement-setting process: trying to get your organization's key stakeholders to make reasonable demands and restrictions that don't contradict each other and/or create impossible situations.

All organizations are part of a larger system. For example, some organizations are divisions or business units in a larger organization, or a field Center of an agency (e.g., KSC of NASA). Being part of that larger system, your organization must be responsive to the direction of the guidance provided by your headquarters. Responsiveness is also important for your organization to meet your customers' needs.

A reactive response focuses on defining how your organization can meet the needs and requirements of your headquarters or your customers. In addition to being reactive, your organization needs to be proactive—anticipating what may be needed in the future. By being proactive, your organization helps your parent organization define its future. Being proactive is defining your future requirements and bringing potential solutions to these requirements.

KSC was extremely responsive. As an operational Center, they had had very few program leadership responsibilities assigned. The program managers defined requirements and KSC defined how they would meet them. KSC was also looking to influence NASA's long-term plans by being proactive with ideas that KSC had about their shared future. They wanted to influence both today's and the future's strategy.

This thinking moved itself into the strategic arena as well. NASA Administrator Dan Goldin asked KSC Director Roy Bridges to develop a strategic plan for KSC. Roy called for KSC to be further responsive and proactive.

Strategic Thinking Principle 5: Synthesize Multiple Viewpoints

The fifth principle is to synthesize multiple viewpoints. This principle highlights the need to integrate many viewpoints and inputs into the strategy-setting process. Many factors will influence the strategy during this process. Each factor needs to be understood and integrated.

KSC developed its goals, objectives, and strategies to ensure that a set of outcomes was achieved. The set included bringing value to NASA and customers, accomplishing the future state and core business, overcoming sacred cows and concerns, and meeting the KSC guiding principles.

NASA goals and objectives were the primary drivers for KSC actions. The sacred cows were the items (internal and external) that prohibited KSC from achieving its future state and from meeting the

NASA goals/objectives. Among the sacred cows that KSC defined to be eliminated were

- organizational self-reliance (each program at KSC relied primarily on their own workforce and contracts—there was little sharing across the organization);
- excessive user/customer documentation (too much paperwork);
- excessive oversight, meetings, and formal reviews (they take too much time away from getting work done);
- red tape (slow response, lack of flexibility);
- risk avoidance (because you don't get to the moon by avoiding risk).

The concerns were items that had to be managed for KSC to move forward. The concerns included

- maintaining skills and expertise;
- being unable to hire new employees;
- retaining good people;
- providing pricing flexibility to customers.

These items were integrated into the KSC road map.

Strategic Thinking Principle 6: Align Goals, Objectives, Strategies, and Measures

The sixth principle is to align goals, objectives, strategies, and measures. This principle highlights the need to "connect the dots" of your strategy to drive the transformation. To help your organization understand and give meaning to actions, you need a clear alignment of your goals-objectives-strategies-measures "dots." Illustration 7.10 shows the flow-down sequence from the mission/vision to the strategies.

As you can see in the previous section (Lay in Your Strategic Intent), the "Our Four Goals" statements point to the enduring contributions KSC wanted to make. By defining these types of enduring goals, the workforce could see what their daily efforts contributed to. The workforce could also see how KSC's contributions to these four goals evolved over time. Specific objectives and strategies were then defined to accomplish these four goals. KSC's strategic road map helped document the alignment of vision, mission, goals, objectives, and strategies. KSC developed a scorecard (i.e., set of measures) to understand how well the goals, objectives, and strategies were being accomplished.

Illustration 7.10—Relationship Among Mission, Vision, Goals, Objectives, Measures, and Strategies

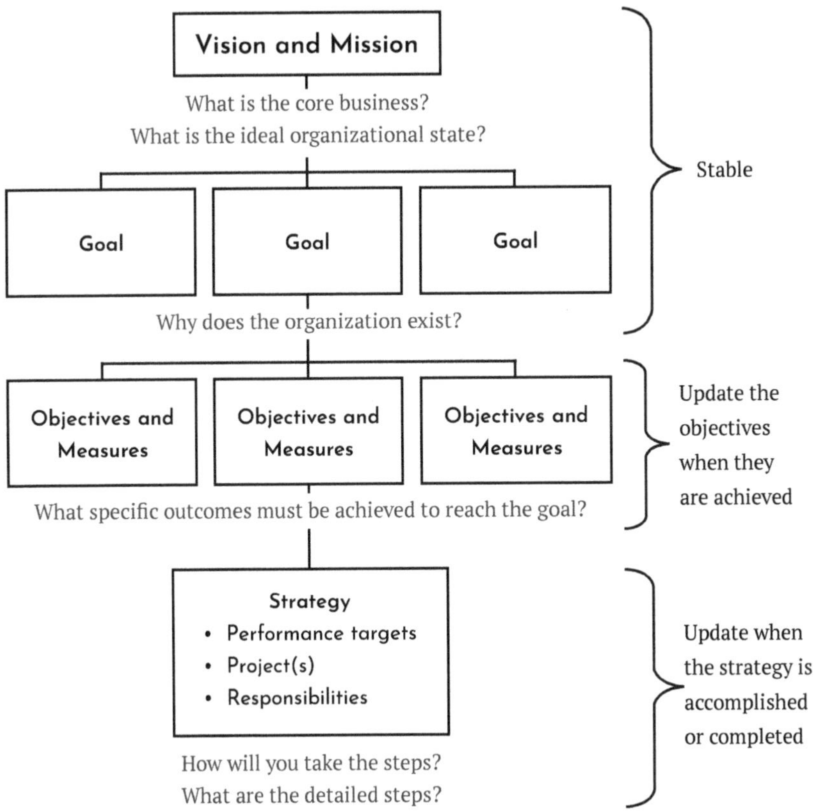

A cautionary note is needed on this principle. Just about every organization I have supported with strategy work has wrestled with these terms. If you ask 10 people for definitions, you will get 20 different answers. We ran into this as well with the KSC team. We established and used a common language set. Illustration 7.11 shows we can define the terms in the set in relation to the transformational situation you are facing.

Illustration 7.11—*Definition of Common Strategy Terms*

Term	Our Definition	Example: Personal Life
Mission	The core business the organization is engaged in. The mission can be defined by describing: • why the organization exists, • what the organization does, • how the organization does the why and what	• To live as a well-rounded and supportive family
Vision	• The desired end state the organization would like to achieve in the future	• A self-sufficient and supportive family that makes a positive difference in the world
Goal	• The major outcomes or value your organization delivers for its stakeholders • Goals tend to be loftier statements that do not change very often	• Live a healthy life for my family and my self
Objective	• A targeted performance level your organization must achieve in a given timeframe • Objectives point to the measurable results to be achieved	• Reduce cardio risk failure • Reduce body weight • Increase muscle mass
Strategy	• The set of efforts to execute to meet the objectives • Strategies could be a process, project, or simple action	• Exercise daily • Eat better
Measure	• The expected tangible result from taking action • Measures provide a way to understand how well the strategies, objectives, and goals are being achieved	• Body weight • Number of days exercising each week • Number of calories consuming each day

Your role is to help the organization see how the mission, vision, goals, objectives, strategies, and measures are aligned.

Recommendations

From this chapter we offer a few recommendations and questions to engage your team with. You've made the choice to respond strategically to the transformation need. You and your team need to think strategically.

Next Steps

To think strategically you can:

- Create Safe Spaces for Meaningful Conversations
- Lay in Your Strategic Intent (Vision, Mission, Goals, Guiding Principles)
- Use Six Strategic Thinking Principles to Guide the Conversations
    - Principle 1: Understand Environments
    - Principle 2: Focus on Outcomes
    - Principle 3: Manage the All-Term
    - Principle 4: Balance Responsiveness with Proactivity
    - Principle 5: Synthesize Multiple Viewpoints
    - Principle 6: Align Goals, Objectives, Strategies, and Measures

Start the Conversation

Engage your team in strategic thinking by asking them to share their perspectives about:

What does thinking strategically mean?

How well are we defining our internal and external environments?

How well are we defining our desired outcomes?

How well are we managing our all-term?

How well are we balancing being responsive and proactive?

How well are we integrating multiple viewpoints?

How well are we aligning goals, objectives, and strategies?

How well are we connecting the dots?

Chapter 8
Drive Accountability for Change

You got this

Your Situation...
Transformations Require Making the Right Changes

In the previous chapter, we shared the idea of *thinking* strategically. But just thinking strategically won't cut it. You need to make the strategic thoughts a reality by taking action. As an old adage says, "Vision without action is daydreaming." You need to translate the thoughts to actions. You can use a strategic management process to *act* strategically in a systematic way.

As you think about your strategic management process, you should think about these questions.

> "*What strategic acts or moves do we need to take?*
>
> *What process can we use to identify and make the strategic acts or moves a reality?*"

In this chapter, we reflect on the strategic management process KSC defined and used.

What's Next...
Focus Your Limited Resources on the Right Changes

Your team has made the choice to think strategically. You need to convert these strategic thoughts to results by taking action. A closed-loop strategic management process (see Illustration 8.2) can help keep your team members accountable for making the changes a reality.

Next Steps

Make Targeted Moves

1. Make Use of Expertise for New Roles
2. Reduce Costs through Partnering
3. Make Investments in Capabilities
4. Reinforce Guiding Principles
5. Continuously Engage with Stakeholders

Use an Eight-step Strategic Management Process to Drive Accountability

1. Set strategic intent
2. Deploy the strategic intent
3. Set strategy
4. Deploy resources
5. Execute the strategy
6. Deploy results
7. Review performance
8. Deploy learnings

Start the Conversation

Engage your team in acting strategically by asking them to share their perspectives about:

What strategic actions or moves do we need to make?

What is our process to set and execute our strategy?

Dig Deeper

In this section, we provide the leader's perspective (Roy) and the consultant's perspective (Tim) on the following actions you can take:

Make Targeted Moves

- Make Use of Expertise for New Roles
- Reduce Costs through Partnering
- Make Investments in Capabilities
- Reinforce Guiding Principles
- Continuously Engage with Stakeholders

Use an Eight-step Strategic Management Process to Drive Accountability

- Set strategic intent
- Deploy the strategic intent
- Set strategy
- Deploy resources
- Execute the strategy
- Deploy results
- Review performance
- Deploy learnings

Make Targeted Moves

The Leader's Experience ... Roy

KSC intentionally took a set of "moves" to act strategically, including

- making use of expertise for new roles,
- reducing costs through partnerships,
- making investments in capabilities,
- reinforcing guiding principles,
- continuously engaging stakeholders.

Make Use of Expertise for New Roles

Spaceport and Range Technologies Example

Creating new roles for our experts and for the Center required thinking out of the box—and into the future. One key initiative was deciding to establish a spaceport and range technologies organization and identify high-priority projects, as KSC needed a role in NASA's research rather than being viewed as an organization doing only operations.

During initial off-site discussions of what to do in this area, we had difficulty convincing ourselves that we could convince headquarters of the importance of doing this. Before reconvening the next day, I went for my three-mile run on the beach and had an amazing revelation. Of course, there would be many spaceports in the future, and the business of putting spacecraft into orbit would evolve from just a government activity to broader commercial businesses. This was just a vision with no concrete proof, so it was still a tough sell. But today there are 13 spaceports in the United States and many more around the world. All need the latest and best technologies for getting their space vehicles prepared and launched safely and efficiently. We identified some key projects and had some sterling successes. NASA HQ amended the Center's mission to recognize its role in developing "spaceport and range technologies." This was only partially successful, as it was well ahead of its time.

Life Science Payloads Processing Facility Example

After visiting the current facility that we leased from Cape Canaveral when I first arrived at KSC, I decided that we needed a new facility to process life sciences payloads for the space shuttle and ISS. The facility was totally inadequate in both size and capability for those types of payloads. Also, I felt that the number of payloads in this area would greatly increase after the ISS reached full operational status over the next few years, after we completed construction.

Given how tight budgets were for the ISS, which was overrunning its initial budget projections, I doubted this idea would be well received at NASA HQ. I decided to take new Florida Governor Bush up on his pledge to be an advocate for space and KSC. First, I had to make this a win-win proposition for the state of Florida, as without it, funding a building for us on KSC had little chance of passing in the legislature. (See results in "Industrial Park Example," page 149.)

MEIT Example

One of the most significant new projects that we worked with the ISS Program Office to develop was called the Multi-Element Integrated Test (MEIT). Initially, the ISS modules from the United States, Japan, and others would come to KSC for launch preparations—but almost no testing—under the "ship-and-shoot" philosophy adopted early in the program. MEIT changed that when we replaced ship-and-shoot with it. MEIT would connect the modules on the ground and make sure that all the interfaces and systems were tested to assure that they would work well when attached on orbit.

We also developed tests for the ammonia thermal control system with fluid installed. This required an extensive modification to the ISS Processing Facility to assure it could be done safely. KSC engineers migrated over from the Space Shuttle Processing organization to design and implement these tests. Simulators had to be designed and built to assure that the Russian elements would work well, with particular attention to docking mechanisms. These tests were spread out over the entire program and involved many modules over the years until the ISS was completed. Many of the complex payload systems were also well tested.

The history of constructing and operating the ISS, now in its third decade of continuous occupation, is that MEIT was a phenomenal success. No critical problems have been encountered during construction and operation. Over the years, many of the systems have been maintained and upgraded successfully on orbit.

Expendable Launch Vehicle Program Example

Another key program was bringing the NASA Expendable Launch Vehicle Programs to KSC. KSC did provide some launch support services for Expendable Launch Vehicles (ELVs), but the Glenn Research Center and the Goddard Space Flight Center managed the programs for NASA-procured vehicles, and the United States Air Force managed programs for several other types of vehicles hauling primarily national security payloads. Selling this idea to NASA headquarters as a key strategy proved difficult but eventually was successful. I convinced NASA HQ that consolidating these programs at KSC would be a win for NASA, customers of these vehicles, and KSC. It would give KSC a large, important program to manage, and we had the expertise to do a good job.

This program attracted several of our brightest engineers and managers. KSC worked with many other Centers that were responsible for building NASA spacecraft to assure that we provided timely and flawless launch services. This certainly increased the awareness of value that KSC added to the overall NASA mission. It has a near-perfect record of launch successes over the years.

Reduce Costs through Partnering

KSC made the strategy real through partnering. The management team realized that KSC could not execute its strategy by itself. There were other techniques that we developed to help with the reductions, especially the financial reductions, that were required. An important one was getting agreement from the Air Force to combine the infrastructure support for both KSC and Cape Canaveral Air Force Station.

JBOSC Example

Creating JBOSC—the Joint Base Operations and Support Contract—was something that I brought to the table. I had run Cape Canaveral while in the Air Force, so I had a good idea of how the infrastructure and security were supported on that side of the river. The initial impetus was to reduce the number of civil servants managing infrastructure and security contracts at KSC by consolidating everything into one contract and jointly managing it with the Air Force. Naturally this idea wasn't initially very popular among the group of KSC employees involved in managing KSC's contractors for these tasks. But as the concept matured, they realized that their expertise would still be needed to manage the contract, but in a new way. I also felt that we could get this job done much more cheaply under JBOSC.

As mentioned earlier, Dan Goldin didn't think that I could be successful with this initiative and gave me his pledge to leave any savings in our Center budget as an inducement. I was thrilled, as that money would allow us to fund many strategic projects that would be critical to our overall success. After getting the Eastern Space and Missile Center Commander on board, I met with officials at the headquarters of both NASA and the Air Force and obtained their support.

Then we formed a joint team to build the Request for Proposal (RFP) and evaluate those that were submitted. We also created the Cape Canaveral Spaceport Management Office to manage the contract and populated it with personnel from both units. We also had a board of directors jointly chaired by the Eastern Space and Missile Center commander and me to review the progress and resolve issues after contract award.

The primary problem that we encountered initially was making sure that organizations were charged correctly for work that was done. This was complicated, as KSC did have some facilities on Cape Canaveral. KSC needed to be charged for support provided to them. Eventually the contractor set up a system that worked well.

We competed the contract. On day one of the new contract, the contractor hired 500 fewer people than we had had in our previous separate contracts. NASA allowed KSC to keep the savings in our budget. This generated over $70 million over the first five years that we could use to invest in other important strategic projects over the first five years of JBOSC, such as our initial spaceport and range technology development projects, a new line of business for KSC. This was a huge win for KSC.

Taking Care of Your People Example

Another fruitful idea was to talk the headquarters into investing in new buildings to replace dilapidated and unsafe trailers and converted boxcars to give our workforce safe and modern workspaces. It also significantly reduced the cost of maintaining the facilities. That was initially deemed to be impossible, but after a close call from a hurricane, NASA and congressional leaders got on board.

Make Investments in Capabilities

Industrial Park Example

Another idea that we pursued successfully was convincing the state of Florida to invest in building a business park at KSC on some old orange tree groves. This land surrounding KSC was part of the wildlife refuge and was supposed to remain undisturbed. I had noticed that some of the area right outside the gates had been cultivated as citrus groves back before the Center was formed. I came up with the idea of an industrial park adjacent to the areas of KSC inside of our security gates. We convinced the wildlife refuge manager to let us use this disturbed land adjacent to the KSC industrial Center.

Access to all this land was by dirt paths used by farmers back in the day. Those would have to be upgraded with a paved road. We modeled a new road that would bypass the secure entry gates, which would be moved inward much closer to the KSC industrial area to allow the new road to pass through the old orange groves. It would connect with both of the main roads to KSC and also create an alternative route to the KSC Visitor Center, which was a much easier access to this popular tourist attraction in the community.

I presented this idea to Governor Bush. He liked it and assigned the lieutenant governor to escort me around the capital and introduce me to influential members of the legislature. I found advocates, and the project took off and was eventually funded. The state built the road through the park as well as a new life sciences facility, the very capable Space Experiment Research and Processing Laboratory (SERPL), in the new industrial park. The state leased SERPL to us for the same price as we were currently paying the Air Force for their dilapidated and inadequate hangar on Cape Canaveral. This $30 million investment set the stage for many benefits over the years for KSC and NASA.

It took years for the industrial park to attract new businesses, but now it is home to several high-technology businesses, which built massive manufacturing facilities and hired hundreds of people into high-technology jobs.

Reinforce Guiding Principles

In addition to these key strategic projects that were in the heart of our strategic plan, we also focused on strong efforts in support of our guiding principles. For example, we began a push to become one of the largest organizations to achieve OSHA's Voluntary Protection Program Star status. We were successful and convinced our large contractors to achieve this status.

We also set up a program to require every supervisor and manager to conduct a safety walk-down of one of his or her workplaces every month. We trained them on how to do these and how to record results. Emphasis was placed on touring the location of any previous safety incident or injury and reviewing corrective actions to prevent future safety problems. We also encouraged them to swap walk-downs with other managers and supervisors to get fresh eyes on the areas and to include junior personnel on these to mentor them on how to make work areas safer.

Another project in line with our guiding principles was to do a better job of reporting our new technology projects. It was amazing to see, but in 2001 KSC was awarded NASA's Commercial Innovation of the Year Award as the number one Center for technology reports. KSC also won the Federal Laboratory Technology Transfer Award for the Southeast Region.

We developed a comprehensive set of metrics to track the status of all our day-to-day operations as well as our strategic projects and reviewed them frequently with the entire leadership team in attendance. We had to restart this effort a few times before we got it right. We eventually settled on a comprehensive set of metrics that not only analyzed the status versus our goals but also tracked any related problems or issues.

Continuously Engage with Stakeholders

Since many transformations start after a bad-day event or series of events, they are not optional, nor are they easy. Despite overwhelming evidence that major changes are needed, many leaders and stakeholders tenaciously hold on to the status quo. Reasons vary but, generally, they like the current position and have some fear of the impact of changes. Plus, many are busy just getting the day job done. Transformations also often result in some type of disruption that must be addressed.

At KSC, the need to refocus on going to an insight mode of dealing with space shuttle operations and giving the contractor more day-to-day authority was used by NASA to cut back on civil servants and save money to spend on research. Creating a new vision and selling it to the workforce and stakeholders was crucial to the success of KSC and NASA, as KSC civil servants were key to making a success of many NASA programs.

Moving talented people out of the shuttle organization to more strategic projects was essential to achieving success. The Center had not been through a reorganization process in decades and clearly was not aligned to take on the new strategic projects such as MEIT for the ISS, starting up the Launch Service Program (LSP) for expendable launch vehicles, and creating a spaceport and range technology development center. We began a major reorganization that was called KSC 2000.

I found out that one of our key stakeholders was very upset about this initiative. I went to the annual Goddard Dinner in our nation's capital and ran into an officer, a friend from my days in the Air Force. He said, "I hear that you are planning on leaving KSC." I was shocked and denied it but needed to get to the bottom of this rumor.

My boss was visiting KSC a few days later, and I brought up the issue to him. He said, "George Abbey is not happy about your reorganization and communicated his criticism to Dan Goldin. Dan has started looking for a replacement for you." I told my boss that I could easily find another job if they wanted me to leave, but I couldn't lead the Center through the major changes required without his and Dan's full support. A few days later he said that Dan wanted to apologize to me and wanted me to stay on as Center Director.

Interestingly, I had briefed George Abbey, JSC Center Director, on my reorganization plans in a one-on-one session in his office, and he didn't react negatively at that time. I later heard that he was concerned that he would be required to reorganize JSC if my efforts succeeded. JSC had not been through a major reorganization in a long time, either. Not long after all of this, George got fired because of the ISS cost overruns, and Dan Goldin took me to breakfast and asked me to become the JSC Center Director. After much thought, I decided that the timing was not auspicious, as Dan would be leaving soon, so I turned down the opportunity.

As you navigate your transformation, keep in mind that stakeholders like George Abbey can get you fired if you fail to get them on board with your strategic plan's initiatives. That can be a difficult process that may require many conversations with them to address any of their concerns. A stakeholder can be either internal or external—anyone who can impact or be impacted by your organization. Some are more important than others.

The KSC reorganization helped us to put our best people displaced from the shuttle operations team into our important new positions that were crucial to our success. The process of selecting new leaders for the new positions gave a lot of our people opportunities for promotion and revitalized them and the Center. **At the end of the day, the secret sauce of success for any organization is taking care of your people**. When people are given priority, training, and opportunities to lead, they will perform amazingly well.

Summary: the Value of Partnering

As shown in Illustration 8.1, KSC partnered with the US Air Force, the Cape Canaveral/KSC spaceport community, the State of Florida, and the education community (e.g., community colleges and universities). These partnerships were driven by the strategy of expanding its mission focus beyond current programs, with the primary focus on operations.

The Air Force partnership resulted in the JBOSC for base operations (National Academy of Public Administration 2002) and the desire to pursue advanced spaceport and range technologies (Office of Science and Technology Policy and National Security Council 2000; NASA and US Air Force 2003; NASA and US Air Force 2004).

The partnership with the space community led to the first joint master plan for Cape Canaveral and Kennedy Space Center.

The partnership with the state and the educational system led to the establishment of tighter ties to researchers and research facilities. This led to the establishment of the Space Experiment Research and Processing Laboratory and Florida Space Research Institute.

Illustration 8.1—Major Partnership Efforts

Air Force

1997		1998-2000	
JBOSC Grand Strategy for Unified Launch Base Support (for government use only pitch) Establish AFSC & NASA Partnership Council to understand infrastructure and common use	July 15, 1997	Cape Canaveral Spaceport Steering Team Mission: to enable unified actions to provide safe, world-class launch processing, payload processing, launch, support services, test operations, and technology development services that meet or exceed customers' expectations	August, 1999
		Joint assessment of the customer satisfaction issues across KSC and CCAFS to understand how KSC/CCAFS would work together to provide better service their customers.	August 5, 1999
		Fifth Annual Florida Space Launch Symposium	November 16 -17, 1999

Spaceport--Comprehensive Master Plan for Cape Canaveral Spaceport

1999-2000		2001-2003	
Master planning I Integrated Product Team formed within NASA	September, 1998	Security issues under review	September, 2001
IPT expanded to include AF, Navy, FSA	November, 1999	Comprehensive Master Plan for Cape Canaveral Spaceport released	2002
Federal Spaceport Master Plan concept agreed to	March, 2000		

State Legislature

1999-2000		2001-2003	
Space Summit at KSC Ideas to pursue: SERPL, CCS One-Stop-Shop, Education Memorandum of Understanding, Comprehensive Master Plan	January, 2000	Florida Space Summit II	July 30, 2001
Established MOU with Spaceport Florida Authority to explore the concept of Space Experiment Research and Processing Laboratory	1999	SERPL groundbreaking	February, 2001
		Funding for SERPL announced	March, 2001

Education

1998-2000	
Florida Space Research Institute (FSRI) established	1999
MOU to establish working relationship with KSC, State of Florida, and FSRI on the Advanced Learning Network Concept	August 3, 2000

The Consultant's Observations ... Tim

You will face the challenge of aligning your strategy + actions + results.

KSC acted strategically by managing the set of improvement initiatives—the program to help solve the transformation problem. These strategic initiatives focus on aligning customers, products/services, processes/tools, structure, and skill mix. Your organization needs to understand existing processes, define requirements for new processes, and evaluate the existing processes against the requirements (Brynjolfsson, Renshaw, and Van Alstyne 1997). Given the different types of change needed (Davidson 1993), your organization must match the improvement initiatives with its need (Gadd and Oakland 1996; Lawler, Mohrman, and Ledford 1998; Sink and Morris 1995). You can use an eight-step strategy process.

Use an Eight-Step Strategic Management Process to Drive Accountability

The Leader's Experience ... Roy

Once we had created our road map as discussed earlier, I thought it was critical to hold ourselves as an organization accountable for achieving each and every element of it. To do that we had to create metrics for every level of the organization, and tie them to each element. Then we had to review them regularly and take corrective action where we were not making sufficient progress. I was surprised that KSC used very few metrics so it was difficult initially to get metrics that actually did hold people accountable. We restarted several times, but we did eventually achieve success. Part of holding people accountable was to tie their performance reviews to their success in helping us make progress. We also came up with a system that did exactly that, the Goal Performance Evaluation System (GPES). When I presented my annual review to my boss, I put together a large three-ring binder full of metrics to every important element and reviewed each one. He not only tolerated the length of the review, but complimented us on how rigorous we were in assuring that we achieved great progress toward our goals.

The Consultant's Observations ... Tim

As defined earlier, a transformation is the purposeful, intentional, consistent change in your organization's business model. To implement a strategic response, your organization can follow a strategic management process. **Strategic management is a continuous process aimed at aligning everyday actions with your organization's long-term direction.**

Using a strategic management process produces positive results (Pekar and Abraham 1995; Taylor 1984; Waalewijn and Segaar 1993; Wilson 1994) including long-term growth, profitability, and a sustained competitive advantage. However, barriers to strategic management exist (Hahn 1991; Sandy 1991; Waalewijn and Segaar 1993; Wilson 1994).

As shown in Illustration 8.2, strategic management is defined to contain eight functions supported by three core elements. This is a closed-loop cycle. Set Strategic Intent provides the start of the closed-loop process. The outputs from one step are the inputs to the next step. This becomes a closed loop when the outputs of Step 8, Deploy Learnings, are used to refine the Strategic Intent in Step 1. Each of the 8 steps are further defined below.

Illustration 8.2—Strategic Management Process

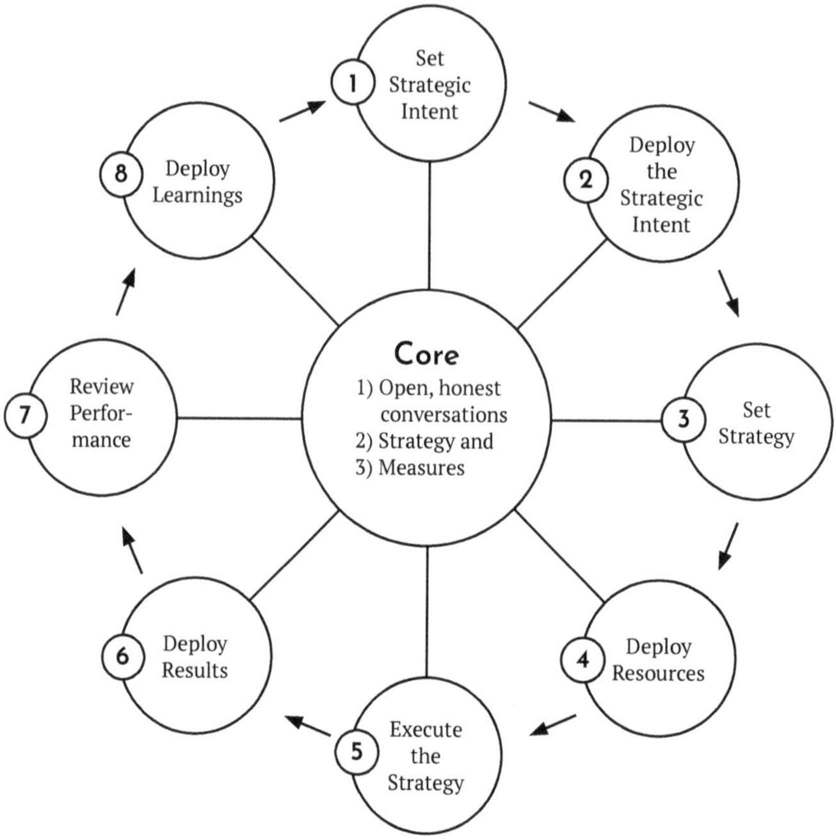

The strategic management process includes eight functions:

1. ***Set Strategic Intent***: We decide what we want to accomplish.
2. ***Deploy Strategic Intent:*** We define how we will inform everyone of what we intend to accomplish and then we inform them.
3. ***Set Strategy***: We define how we will accomplish what we want to accomplish and how we will know if it's working.
4. ***Deploy Resources***: We allocate funding for accomplishing the things we want to accomplish.
5. ***Execute the Strategy***: We do the things we decided on in #1.
6. ***Deploy Results***: We measure our performance by collecting our data and converting it to information.

7. ***Review Performance***: We evaluate what we've done, then produce lessons learned and recommendations for improving our organization and/or adjusting our strategic intent.
8. ***Deploy Learning***: We put what we learned into practice to continue the work.

These functions can take place across many levels of your organization. These eight steps provide the structured process for your management team to lead and manage your strategic transformation path (i.e., continuously set strategy and make your strategy real).

Step 1: Set Strategic Intent (Strategic Planning): Decide what you want to accomplish

Strategic planning is a group process by which your organization defines or refines its strategic intent. The process involves understanding both internal and external environments (e.g., strengths, weaknesses, opportunities, threats). Strategic planning "establishes the long-term direction of the organization in the context of the vision of the future, organizationally unique mission, and a specific set of goals, objectives, and policies developed in response to customer requirements, external mandates, and the external and internal environment" (NASA 1996, 4).

The aim of strategic planning is to develop good strategy for your organization. Good strategy

- reflects the reality of the environment;
- is agreed upon by the management team;
- is implemented;
- is based on the concepts of strategic thinking;
- achieves the desired outcomes of the organization.

When setting your strategic intent, your organization will focus on two areas:

- Answer strategic questions.
- Hold strategic conversations/off-sites.

Answer Strategic Questions: The KSC management team spent considerable time articulating KSC's strategic plan. This was difficult, because at the beginning they were told to get KSC out of operations—the very core of what they did. KSC's external environment kept changing, and uncertainty was high. KSC held a series of strategic off-site conversations (see Illustration 6.1) that helped the team answer the fundamental strategic intent questions.

- Who are we?
- What is the state of our external environment?
- How did we get to where we are today?
- Where are we today?
- Why do we need to change?
- Where do we want to be in the future?
- How do we get to our future?
- How will we lead?
- What is guiding our thinking?
- What is the essence of our strategy?

These questions and their answers are more complex than they appear. The challenge is having the senior management team (and later the entire organization) answer these questions in open, honest, and meaningful conversations. KSC produced a strategic plan that discussed its core business, future state, guiding principles, and road map.

Hold Strategic Conversations/Offsites: KSC used strategic off-sites to provide the time and focus to answer the strategic planning questions. For example, during the second strategic planning off-site, the senior management team established four senior management task teams. The first team focused on understanding the needs of KSC's customers. This team was comprised of senior managers and a select group of employees. They produced a description of the items that customers liked and disliked about doing business at KSC. The other three teams produced three statements describing the ideal future state for KSC's infrastructure/capabilities, expertise, and services.

Their integrated work led KSC to update its strategic intent. The Center's original core business focus was providing operational support to the space shuttle and associated payloads. KSC defined their new future state and core business to be a development Center that focuses on providing space systems processes, test and launch techniques, and developing associated technologies.

After the task teams shared their ideal future state, the senior management team developed an initial strategic-planning road map with goals, objectives, and strategies to help KSC reach that future state. In developing its road map, KSC chose its short-term actions with care, because they would affect choices for longer-term actions, which were defined in more general terms than the short-term actions.

And, in a move that was fundamental to what he was driving and may have become even more important than the goals, KSC Director Roy Bridges defined a set of guiding principles that transcended all decisions and actions at KSC. The guiding principles were

- safety and health first;
- satisfy customer needs anytime, anywhere;
- build reliance and teamwork everywhere;
- environmental leadership (protecting the natural environment and resources).

These strategic conversations must be converted into actions. Once a strategic conversation occurs, the organization needs to act to make the strategy a reality. Without action, the conversation doesn't mean much. I've been in strategic planning meetings where the group was looking to put action items together at the end of the meeting, and the leader said, "No need to do that now, we can do that next week." At this point you could see the participants' faces turn sour. They knew they had just wasted their time. Once an action is identified, someone must be held accountable for completing it, and that accountability must be enforced. KSC developed a set of action items or strategic initiatives from the strategic off-site.

Step 2: Deploy the Strategic Intent: Define how you will inform everyone of what you intend to accomplish and then inform them

Deploying the strategic intent is the process of sharing your strategic intent with your organization and its stakeholders to ensure they understand the strategic context and intent. This understanding creates a foundation for your organization to make plans to implement your strategic intent. Also, from this shared understanding your organization raises issues and identifies challenges to successfully implementing your strategic intent.

When deploying your strategic intent, your organization will focus on two areas:

- sharing the message throughout your organization
- understanding organizational concerns with your message to ensure that the entire organization shares and understands your strategic intent

Share the Message Throughout Your Organization. Without an understanding of your strategic intent, the rest of your organization does not have the context or rationale for the actions your team is taking. The organization needs to understand the "why" and "what" of your strategy. The challenge is ensuring that your entire organization gets the same message no matter where they are in the organization, when they hear it, or who shares it with them. To share your message, your management team needs to intentionally define a communication plan.

- Who are the intended audiences for our strategic intent message?
- What is the purpose of our message?
- What is our message?
- What are the different approaches for sharing our message?

Once they understand your strategic message, employees can give their feedback so that senior management can adjust your strategy to ensure success.

KSC deployed their strategic intent by using a set of methods, the most visible of which were "CD Rollouts" and "CD Comms." CD Rollouts were all-hands meetings, where the KSC Director shared the team's strategic intent. Most CD Rollout meetings were held annually, usually after the annual strategic planning off-site. CD Comms were direct letters to the workforce from the Center Director (CD). Illustration 8.3 shows that the Center Director used this mechanism often.

Illustration 8.3—Number of CD-comms Shared per Year

Year	1997	1998	1999	2000	2001	2002
# Of CD Comms Shared	15	13	24	19	11	15

Understand Organizational Concerns. Once your strategy is shared, your organization needs to identify the challenges and issues involved in implementing it:

- What is right with our strategy?
- What do we need to be aware of?

The management team needs to share its strategic intent and get feedback from the rest of your organization. It's usually the people on the ground every day who can give you the most and best feedback. They know the challenges and obstacles in reality, not just in theory. They have insights into these issues and challenges that only those on the front lines can see and anticipate. By understanding the implementation issues ahead of time, your organization can adjust its strategic intent before it makes a mistake.

KSC deployed this strategic intent with CD Rollouts, followed by organizational/directorate rollouts, where each directorate (business unit within the organization, each responsible for a specific task) shared the message again and gathered feedback from employees. This feedback was used to drive further senior management conversations and strategy adjustments.

Step 3: Set Strategy (Implementation Planning): Define how you will accomplish the things you want to accomplish and how you will know if it's working

The aim of implementation planning is to align your organization's activities with its strategy—to ensure that what you do will be likely to achieve what you want to accomplish. Your organization will use the implementation plan to guide day-to-day behaviors and execution of

- the normal, day-to-day processes to administer today's business;
- the improvement initiatives that cut across your organization—the big projects that you as the leader will put your energy into in order to move your organization forward;
- the specific improvement initiatives each internal organization needs to execute as part of a corporate-wide initiative;
- the specific improvement initiatives each internal organization needs to execute to improve its specific responsibilities.

Your improvement initiatives need to be evaluated, selected, and resourced. Your organization does not have enough resources to invest in all initiatives, so it must focus on aligning these efforts to its strategic plan. In executing the implementation-planning function, your organization will focus on three areas:

- Define the expectations for what the existing business needs to deliver.
- Ensure each sub-organization or business unit has clear roles and responsibilities.
- Ensure the performance objectives and measures provide clarity on what needs to be accomplished.

Convert Your Strategic Intent to Operational Terms. The challenge facing your organization is to take your high-level strategic intent to where you want your organization to be in the future. To do that, you turn your strategic intent, as defined by vision, mission, goals, and transformation path, into very specific operational terms, or performance expectations—such as objectives, measures, and strategies. Your strategic intent is where you want to be; your objectives, measures, and strategies are how you intend to get there. Once you have translated your strategic intent into performance expectations, your organization must make decisions and take actions that move it from its current state to its desired state.

The best way to define your actions is to first define your objectives and measures explicitly. A quantifiable objective can be defined as

- {increase or decrease}
- {measure}
- by {amount}
- by {date}.

Your objective defines the gap to be closed—the amount of the measure to be changed by a given date. With good objectives and measures, your organization can make your strategy more realistic.

After defining objectives and measures, your organization can then define strategies. We have all probably set objectives in our personal lives. For example, how many of us start our new year out with a resolution to "Decrease my weight by 10 pounds before summer starts"? That would look like this:

- {increase or decrease} DECREASE
- {measure} MY WEIGHT
- by {amount} 10 POUNDS
- by {date} BEFORE SUMMER STARTS.

As discussed earlier, KSC used an organizational road map that defined goals, objectives, and strategies to reach the vision of a future state, all while completing the current mission.

Align Organizational Roles. In deploying your strategic intent and implementation planning, organizational sub-units—business units, divisions, or programs—and employees will want to know how they fit within the strategy. To foster understanding and commitment to your strategic intent, your management team needs to help employees see how their contributions relate to the strategy. The challenge is helping the employee answer three basic questions for the work he or she does:

- Why do I do this work?
- What do I need to accomplish with this work?
- How do I do the work?

By working with its employees, your management team aligns employee roles to your strategic intent.

To align employee roles to its strategic intent, KSC used a set of methods:

- The first method was the overall business management system. This business management system organized and linked the documents which described KSC's strategic intent with each individual directorate's (business unit's) mission, roles, objectives, and processes.
- The second method was to use flow diagrams to document processes. The connection of the processes to the directorate's mission was made in each of the directorate's Business and Objectives Agreement Document (BOA). The BOA described the directorates in terms of their mission, function, goals, objectives, and processes. As part of the effort to become ISO 9001 certified, all processes within KSC were consistently documented.
- The third method was Center-wide initiatives to highlight the important projects to move KSC forward. The owner of these initiatives routinely shared their status with the Center Director. The owner is the person accountable for making the initiative happen.

Align Objectives and Measures. Aligning objectives and measures begins with aligning your organization's overall objectives and measures with any higher-order organization (e.g., KSC had to align its objectives and measures with those of the president, Congress, NASA, and the programs KSC supports).

Your organization must then align the internal objectives and measures of each sub-unit with your organization's overall objectives and measures. As shown in Illustration 8.4, KSC had to align objectives and measures in five key areas:

1. Align KSC's objectives and measures to NASA's
2. Align KSC's objectives and measures to each other
3. Align KSC's objectives and sub-units' objectives to each other
4. Align sub-unit measures and the measures of KSC to each other
5. Align sub-unit objectives and sub-unit measures to each other

With good alignment of the objectives and measures, your organization can then better align the processes and resources to what you need to achieve.

Illustration 8.4—Aligning the Objectives and Measures

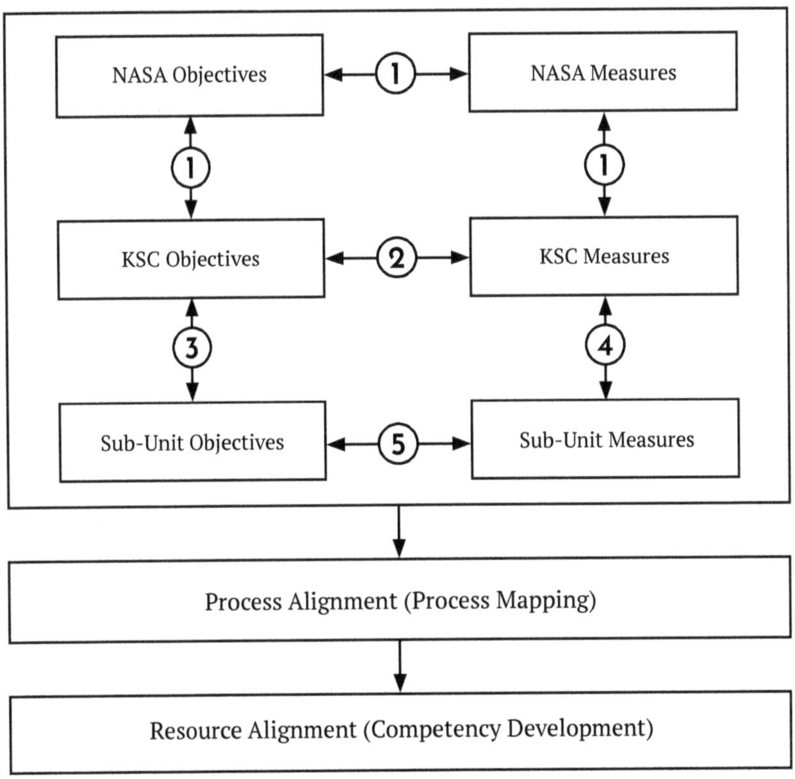

KSC used the BOA and the Goal Performance Evaluation System (GPES) to connect an individual's objectives with NASA's objectives. GPES was an automated tool to help a supervisor assign an individual's responsibilities, connect those responsibilities to higher-level objectives, and then, at the end of the year, roll up the results into an integrated scorecard of performance.

Step 4: Deploy Resources: Allocate funding for accomplishing the things you want to accomplish

Deploying resources is the process of allocating your organization's limited resources to your strategy. Deploying resources is important because

- your organization's resources are limited;
- not all activities can be funded;
- any outcome you expect to achieve must have resourced activities to deliver it. In other words, you cannot expect to achieve any outcome unless you assign or deploy resources to it.

The aim of deploying resources is to put the right resources on the right activities to move your organization forward with its strategy. Your strategy process can absolutely fail in this step. **If your organization does not explicitly devote resources and accountabilities to your strategy, the strategy will fail.** Many times, organizations hold strategic off-sites, define actions, and then fail to put the necessary resources on the strategy. Your organization must use its resources to meet today's business while investing in activities to move it to the future. Important leadership questions include

- What are our funded daily business efforts?
- What are our funded improvement ideas?
- What are the criteria for selecting and prioritizing our improvement ideas?

Deploying resources includes

- selecting efforts
- funding the investment to reach the vision.

Select Efforts. During its transformation, your organization faces the challenge of balancing multiple responsibilities with limited resources. Deploying resources is where this challenge comes to a head. Your organization will generate more ideas than you have the time and resources to execute. You will need to prioritize where you deploy your resources. We can look at deploying resources from a funnel perspective. Coming into the funnel are the potential efforts from the implementation-planning step. Coming out of the funnel are ideas to fund. Your organization needs to deploy resources across four areas:

1. administering the business—meeting the requirements of today's mission
2. building your business—investing in areas to improve and change your business
3. administering the new business while building the new business—meeting the requirements of the new products/services your organization is starting
4. catering to crisis

As part of the selection process, your organization needs to find the resources to allocate to the efforts it chooses to implement.

As discussed earlier, KSC used the BOA to document the normal, everyday work expectations. To facilitate the communication and gathering of improvement projects from across KSC, an organization within KSC developed the Kennedy Strategic Management System. Over 200 projects were submitted through this system. The implementation-planning process provided the projects for KSC to execute to move the Center forward. KSC-wide projects were managed through direct communication with the KSC Director.

KSC worked on the deploying resources function in three ways.

- The first was through its normal annual budgeting process.
- The second was through the selection of action items or major actions from each annual strategic management off-site.
- The third was through the "Top 40" technology projects.

In this process the research and development organization within KSC partnered with the operational programs (e.g., shuttle, ISS) to define the technical development areas to focus on. These potential research and development projects were defined, selected, and resourced through a formal process.

Fund the Investment to Reach the Vision. When your organization is challenged to find the resources to invest in multiple areas, it needs to find "excess" capacity to invest in emerging areas. Excess capacity can be gained from stopping current activities. Your organization needs to find the resources to fund its selected efforts. Without funding, your improvement efforts will not be implemented.

For KSC, this challenge was evident each year. As described earlier, KSC's resources were constrained. To help invest in the future, KSC was able to create a "reinvestment fund" from savings it created from its new base operations contract with the Air Force and use this reinvestment fund to move forward. They also had a KSC Center Director's discretionary fund, which was also used to make investments to move KSC forward.

Step 5: Execute the Strategy: Do the things you decided on in Step 1

Execution is carrying out the strategy and implementation plans. This process is "the means [activities and decisions] by which NASA produces outputs and outcomes for its customers" (NASA 1996, 5). Execution is where the "rubber meets the road"—delivering the products and services to the customer.

This is the point in the transformation where your organization must meet all of their requirements: the core business it has now and the strategic initiatives to move forward. It's usually easier to ensure that daily business is executed as needed, because your organization's management processes are set up to do this. But you need to ensure that the strategic initiatives are also executed.

The executing-the-strategy function includes

- aligning and executing processes,
- executing improvement projects.

Align and Deliver Processes. Processes are how the organization carries out and manages work. These processes need to be aligned to where the organization is going. The challenge is determining which processes to start, which to stop, and which to continue.

For processes that will continue, there is a second set of decisions that need to be made: whether the processes will continue as is, will be improved, or will be re-engineered. By stopping processes or improving processes, the organization can find the resources necessary to invest in future activities.

At KSC, the executing-the-strategy function was evident when KSC executed its daily, existing business and implemented improvement projects.

Execute Improvement Projects. During implementation planning and deploying resources, specific improvement projects are funded to carry out the strategy. Your organization faces the challenge of executing these projects. The day-to-day delivery of the existing mission and meeting the requirements of today's customers will often overrun the execution of the improvement projects. Your organization must maintain focus on these improvement projects and ensure that they are completed. Improvement projects are the lifeblood of the future of the organization.

At KSC, there were two types of improvement projects: cross-Center (organization-wide) and within-directorate (confined to a specific business unit). The cross-Center projects required many different people from across the Center to execute. They used cross-functional teams for these projects. For example, KSC focused an organization-wide improvement project to achieve ISO 9001 certification that documented approximately 600 processes across the Center. For the within-directorate projects, the individual unit was responsible for executing these projects as part of their assigned responsibilities or functions.

Step 6: Deploy Results: Measure your performance—collect your data and convert it to information

Deploying results is the process of gathering performance data from across your organization to determine how well your objectives are being achieved.

In deploying results, you are getting the execution results in order to understand how well you are making the strategy real.

The aim of deploying results to gain the data is to ensure you have clarity on what is working, what is not working, and what needs to be adjusted.

You are gathering the data to tell the story about your organization's performance by

- measuring performance,
- rolling up results.

Measure Performance. Measuring performance is collecting the performance data and converting it into information. The challenge is first determining what to measure and then how to get the data. **Measures are at the core of strategic management.**

In the ***Set the Strategy: Implementation Planning*** step, you translated your strategy to operational terms that defined the measurable objectives—the results you need to achieve. You are now collecting the data for the measures identified in those objectives. You are being as specific as possible to define what "good" looks like.

In deploying results, you are collecting the data to determine how well you achieved the objectives. For example, if you are focused on improving quality, then the objective could be to decrease defects. The data to collect would be the number of defects in a given time period. This data would be analyzed to see how you enhanced quality and what you need to work next.

Illustration 8.5—KSC's Measures

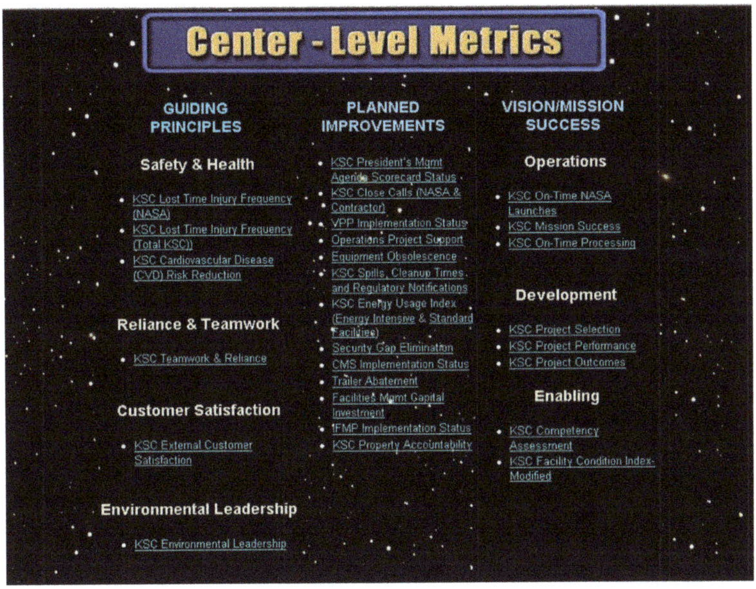

> **Figures 8.5-8.7**
>
> *Figures 8.5-8.7 were developed by teams of KSC senior managers to signify the need to change KSC.*

At KSC, the measuring of performance was evident throughout its strategic evolution. KSC developed and used an organization-wide performance measurement framework and a standard metric chart. For the performance measurement framework, it initially used a balanced scorecard (Kaplan and Norton 1996) approach and then moved to a different framework more closely aligned to the description of its business. Illustration 8.5 shows the revised framework. As shown in this framework, KSC had categories of measures (e.g., Guiding Principles, Planned Improvements, and Vision/Mission Success). Each of these categories had specific measures to describe how well KSC was performing. The bulleted items in the illustration are the measures. Each of the measures within this framework was displayed using a standard metric format. Illustration 8.6 describes the elements in this framework. These elements were the data that was used to describe and understand the measure.

Illustration 8.6—Template for Measures

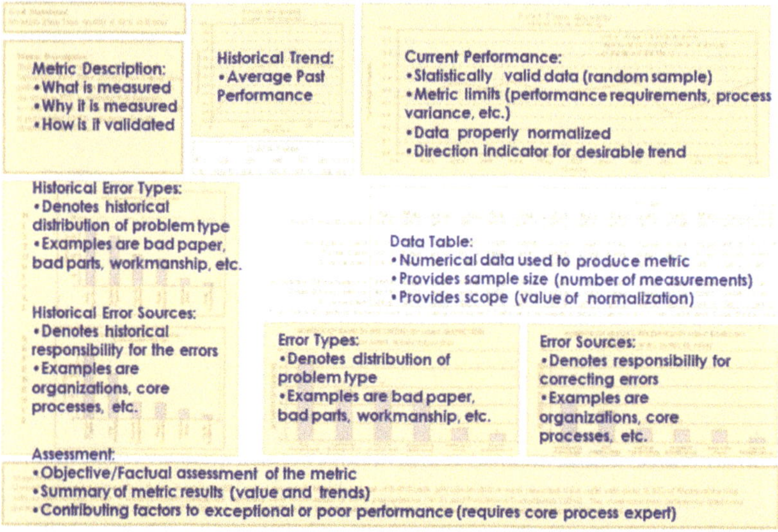

Roll Up Results. To support performance evaluation, the results from each business unit need to be rolled up—integrated into one wholistic view. The wholistic view tells the story of your organization's overall performance. This integrated view is used in performance evaluation.

The KSC Director organized important metrics and results into a three-ring binder and used it to brief his NASA boss during each performance assessment meeting. This proved to be an effective way of communicating, as it provided proof of progress and showed how any shortcomings were being addressed. These one-on-one meetings also resulted in frank and open communications about progress and problems. The increased transparency generated trust in management leadership.

KSC linked individual performance plans to KSC's overall performance and its contribution to NASA's plan. To help integrate results, KSC developed and deployed a Goal Performance Evaluation System

(GPES), which helped them develop a closed-loop system. As we discussed in more general terms earlier in this chapter, a closed-loop system connects expectations to actions to results to reflection on how the expectations were met. For example, you may set expectations to lose weight (expectations). You watch what you eat, you exercise more (actions). You take your weight at the end of three months (results). You close the loop by comparing your current weight with what you hoped to achieve when you set the objective to lose weight (reflection). This comparison tells you what you need to do next.

This closed-loop system flowed requirements from NASA's plans down to the employee's performance plans. Actions and results were rolled into an integrated reporting structure. Illustration 8.7 shows this closed-loop system.

Illustration 8.7—KSC's Closed-Loop Management System

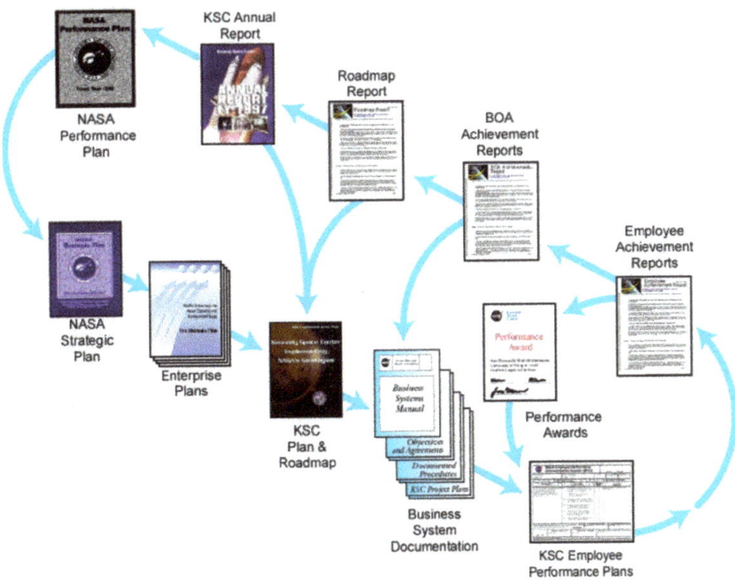

Step 7: Review Performance (Performance Evaluation): Evaluate what you've done, then use it to produce lessons learned and recommendations for improving your organization and/or adjusting your strategic intent

Performance evaluation is how the organization "measures whether the Agency achieved intended results as stated in its" plans (NASA 1996, 5). Performance measurement and evaluation produces the information that can be studied to produce lessons learned and recommendations for improving your organization and adjusting your strategic plan. The aims of performance evaluation are

1. to understand how well your strategy is being achieved;
2. to understand where the areas for improvement are;
3. to identify lessons learned;
4. most important, to drive accountability for achieving results—making someone responsible for executing the project and delivering the needed results; being clear on what is expected to be achieved by when; having clear objectives (e.g., increase/decrease measure by amount by date).

Without reviewing performance, accountability cannot be achieved.

The performance evaluation function includes

- reviewing performance,
- understanding performance gaps.

Review and Evaluate Performance. Your strategy and results need to be evaluated. Your organization must make the time, energy, and environment available to conduct the reviews. The reviews are a meeting in which basic questions are asked and answered using the measures from the deploying-results step:

- How well are we accomplishing our daily business activities?
- How well are we accomplishing our improvement initiatives?
- What are the gaps between expected and actual performance?
- What are the root causes for a performance gap?
- What are we learning from the results?

You must create the right environment for conducting your performance evaluations. To support performance evaluation, KSC used the standard metric chart discussed earlier. It also used an external auditor to provide an outside view to evaluate its management process.

Understand Performance Gaps. Given that progress has been measured, your organization needs to be able to get to the root cause of any performance gaps. However, the learning required to identify the true root cause may not happen. The challenge for your management team is to ensure that the learning loop is completed and not abandoned.

KSC worked to ensure performance gaps were understood. Some of the much-needed conversations about the organization were difficult to have in a large group setting. Many of these conversations were held with just a few individuals. The KSC standard metric chart was also used to support root-cause analysis.

Step 8: Deploy Learnings: Put what you learned into practice to continue the work

Deploying learnings is the process of sharing the results from performance evaluation to continue to share and execute the strategy throughout the organization. The aim of deploying learnings is to close the loop of the strategy process by learning from the results and making adjustments to the strategy based on what was learned. It's about continuous learning.

The deploying-learnings function includes:

- institutionalizing best practices,
- "killing" non-performing projects.

Institutionalize Best Practices. As your organization tries new approaches and implements new projects to move forward, some of these new approaches and projects will produce positive results. These internal "best practices" must be identified and the new methods institutionalized. Your organization is growing to the future; therefore, it needs to share the "seeds" that are fostering this growth.

To address this effort, KSC met routinely to review performance. When they reviewed performance, they were able to identify emerging best practices from across the Center. These best practices were shared across the directorates. KSC also used its formal rewards (e.g., Gold Dollar Awards) to highlight emerging best practices.

"Kill" Non-Performing Projects. Your organization is trying new methods, but not all efforts will meet performance requirements. Your organization needs to decide to stop these non-performing actions. As others have discussed (Royer 2003), stopping projects is not always completed. Your organization needs to stop these projects and reinvest its resources in other efforts. Strategy is a learning process, and adjusting your strategy by stopping some items is just as important as starting new ones.

Within KSC, non-performing projects tended to "die a natural death" through the lack of funding in the annual budget process. That is, non-performing projects were eliminated by slowly reducing resources over time. During the deploying-resources stage, the resources were not supplied.

Recommendations

From this chapter we offer a few recommendations and questions to engage your team with.

Your team has made the choice to think strategically. You need to convert these strategic thoughts to results by taking action. A closed-loop strategic management process (see Illustration 8.2) can help keep your team members accountable for making the changes a reality.

Next Steps

Make Targeted Moves

1. Make Use of Expertise for New Roles
2. Reduce Costs through Partnering
3. Make Investments in Capabilities
4. Reinforce Guiding Principles
5. Continuously Engage with Stakeholders

Use an Eight-step Strategic Management Process to Drive Accountability

1. Set strategic intent
2. Deploy the strategic intent
3. Set strategy
4. Deploy resources
5. Execute the strategy
6. Deploy results
7. Review performance
8. Deploy learnings

Start the Conversation

Engage your team in acting strategically by asking them to share their perspectives about:

What strategic actions or moves do we need to make?

What is our process to set and execute our strategy?

Chapter 9
Adapt the Culture

You got this

Your Situation...
Transformations Require New Behaviors

As you work the process to transform your organization, a key element you'll need to address is your organization's culture.

First, there is some part of your culture that limited your organization's ability to proactively see and respond to changes in its external environment. You need to find the gap and fix it. For example, what in your culture led to blind spots or complacency? Second, your new organization may require new beliefs, values, and behaviors. You need to lay in a new culture that is better suited to your new business model.

As you go through this process, you need to think about

> *What about our culture is hindering us from moving forward?*
>
> *How does our culture need to change to better fit our new organization?*

In this chapter, we reflect on what KSC did to understand and enhance their culture.

What's Next...
Reset Your Organization's Daily Behaviors

While the easy-to-see part of the transformation is the changes to the business model, the less visible but challenging part is the culture change. You will face the hard but crucial task of focusing on your culture. The culture provides the values, norms, and behaviors that guide how your workforce executes the processes. To truly transform, you need to change both your business model and its culture.

Next Steps

To focus on the culture you can:

- Bring Your Guiding Principles to Life
- Begin with the Positives in the Culture You Have
- Corral & Triage the Sacred Cows

Deeper Look

For a deeper look into organizational culture, see "The Culture Opportunity: NASA's NESC," in "Taking Our Learnings On the Road: how lessons learned can create a career and form a future" on page 242.

Start the Conversation

Engage your team in refining your organization's culture by asking them to share their perspectives about:

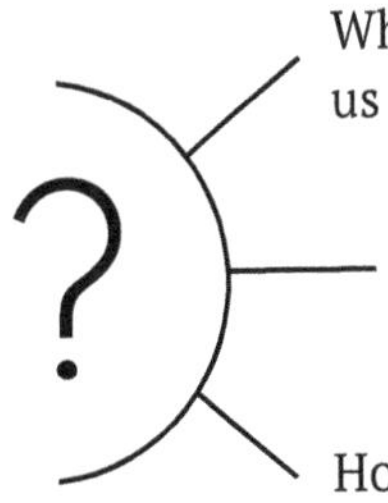

What about our culture is hindering us from moving forward?

What about our culture can help us from moving forward?

How does our culture need to change to better fit our new organization?

Dig Deeper

In this section, we provide the leader's perspective (Roy) and the consultant's perspective (Tim) on the following actions you can take:

- Bring Your Guiding Principles to Life
- Begin with the Positives in the Culture You Have
- Corral & Triage the Sacred Cows

Bring Your Guiding Principles to Life

The Leader's Experience ... Roy

When I arrived at KSC in March 1997, the Center was in an existential situation. NASA wanted to move the things that KSC did to a contractor and significantly reduce the civil service workforce. NASA did not value the expertise that KSC's civil servants were bringing to the table.

This was emotionally disheartening. As a new leader who wanted to retain the best and brightest, coming up with a plan that would attract them to stay—and doing it literally overnight—seemed hopeless. How could I design a plan they could believe in, that they would buy into with the fervor needed to make it successful? A plan that would move the organization to a place where people felt valued? How could we get them to engage and stay the task rather than see many give up and depart? Of course I was going to try to make it work, but at the beginning, it seemed an almost impossible stretch.

KSC's culture and morale were significantly improved by a wide range of initiatives, principles, and practices.

Safety & Health First: OSHA Example

We implemented best-in-class safety training for the workforce based on the DuPont safety program. We were awarded the Occupational Safety and Health Administration's (OSHA) Voluntary Protection Program Star Flag for our achievements in safety. Both NASA civil servants and the major contractors achieved this rating.

We created several projects and metrics to guide our development in this area. Each supervisor was held personally responsible for improving work conditions and eliminating safety hazards. I included myself in that quest by personally conducting safety walk-downs at different facilities each month. It wasn't an elitist culture that we were building; it was inclusive at every level, and even the guy with the most responsibility and authority wasn't sequestered away in his office. He was managing by walking around, interacting personally with every facility, every department, and people at every level. This made for a culture where people felt known, connected, and yes—valued.

Safety & Health First: Workspace Example

I decided that we could not be world class in safety and health without achieving several other major objectives. Many in our workforce were housed in offices and technical work spaces that were decades-old house trailers and railroad boxcars, including a boxcar near the launch pad, which was used by technicians. Given the hazardous weather that Florida is famous for, such as hurricanes, lightning, and tornadoes, these were unsafe. Few things dampen a workplace culture and make people feel unappreciated more than being expected to go to work in shabby, depressing, unsafe spaces, especially when there is no effort to correct the poor conditions over many, many years.

Many in the leadership at KSC were skeptical that we could talk the headquarters into new quarters but nevertheless helped me put together plans for them. When we got a close call from a major hurricane and many facilities were damaged, the projects were approved. One was a new high-rise office building to eliminate trailer parks that were well beyond their useful life. We also replaced the railroad boxcars with small facilities near worksites. People were genuinely amazed at how great the new facilities were. I toured all of them and heard that over and over again. Morale and the general atmosphere of KSC culture improved significantly.

Safety & Health First: Health and Well-being Examples

I have always been an advocate for fitness training to enhance the health and well-being of our workforce. Given how far from town we were, we remodeled and expanded our on-site fitness centers so that our people could do training without extending their workday. We also added a free rehabilitation service for those who were injured on or off duty, to save dollars and improve the fitness and long-term health of our workforce. Keeping everyone in good shape contributed to our health and safety goals.

Satisfy Customer Needs Anytime, Anywhere: Improvement Examples

I also started the Gold Dollar programs to make it easier for members of the workforce to nominate safety projects as mentioned earlier. These provided valuable insights into areas where we needed to improve. Completing the nominated projects let the workforce know how much we valued them and their ideas, which was important to this valued element of our culture.

We measured our progress in all categories, using metrics that we reviewed monthly as a leadership team and individually twice a year at performance reviews with key personnel. We rolled up metrics for individuals and lower-level organizations so that all could see how they contributed to our top-tier metrics to provide a complete picture.

We established quarterly safety and health reviews with the leadership team. We also established an annual Safety and Health Day where we stopped all work and had town meetings to review and celebrate our progress. I used the CD Comms communication tool to communicate directly with everyone in the workforce about our progress and challenges as well as to highlight contributions of individuals and organizations. Holding ourselves accountable to each other and our customers was another important value in our culture.

Satisfy Customer Needs Anytime, Anywhere: Reorganize to Update and Refresh

To improve our culture of working well together across the organization, we implemented a well-designed KSC 2000 reorganization of the Center with input from employees and leaders from across the Center. This helped us tune the organization to our goals and values as well as revitalize the leadership. It was a badly needed improvement in the organization; it had been decades since the last reorganization and much had changed in our environment as well as in our goals for the future.

Build Reliance and Teamwork Everywhere: Change Leaders

Another tool KSC deployed was the "Change Leaders Network." I started this group of managers to help drive the organization through the transformation. They were trained in *The 7 Habits of Highly Effective People*. They used this training to help be the change agents within their organization. They provided services such as change facilitation, coaching, communication, and team building. In 2001, KSC received the prestigious Franklin Covey Team Award for Synergy and Impact for the amazing progress that the team made.

The Consultant's Observations ... Tim

As Roy shared above, KSC focused a lot of energy on its culture. Illustration 9.1 summarizes how KSC enabled the transformation by establishing and reinforcing a set of core values. These values provided the foundation for how KSC government employees would work and treat each other.

A transformation takes the entire senior management team and organization working together to create the future. Shared values help the transformation to be executed more consistently. The values provide a guardrail when making decisions. These values needed to be shared within the leadership team, the entire supervisory chain across KSC, and the entire workforce. The LEAP leadership development program (shared in Chapter 12), was an approach to continue shared commitment to values and associated leadership behaviors. KSC did a great job building its leadership team and culture. NASA saw this success and started to move KSC leaders into leadership positions across NASA.

Illustration 9.1—Enabling the Transformation: Guiding Behavior

Element	1997	1998-2000	2001-2003
Guiding Behavior	• Establish process for rollouts • Establish "CD Comms" • Establish core values • Establish quarterly safety and health review • Establish new awards (e.g., Gold and Silver Dollars awards)	• Implement DuPont safety training • Establish Safety & Health Day • Pursue VPP	• Achieve VPP certification

In addition to what Roy shared, I would like to share my perspective on the culture change Roy and his team were driving towards. In thinking about culture and, more specifically, culture in the midst of a transformation, I think there are a few perspectives we can take:

- the organization's culture and the culture within the senior management team
- the positive aspects of the culture you wish to continue and the aspects of the culture that get in the way of the transformation process or the new organization you are moving toward

As leaders of the transformation, you need to focus on both.

Begin with the Positives in the Culture You Have

The Leader's Experience ... Roy

The KSC culture that we decided we wanted to preserve and enhance was incorporated into our guiding principles in our strategic approach:

- safety and health first
- satisfy customer needs anytime, anywhere
- build reliance and teamwork everywhere
- environmental leadership (protecting the natural environment and resources)

At the heart of that was achieving safety and health results that were world-class for organizations doing hazardous work every day like KSC was doing. Many initiatives as well as training for the workforce became instrumental in the road map that laid the strategic path to our goal. The major safety and health-first initiatives were discussed earlier.

KSC had always been very responsive to customers when our expertise was needed; however, we now needed to find ways to get involved in new programs when they were begun so that we could assist in the design so that, for example, it would be less expensive to be launched at KSC. Teams were organized to participate in the design of new programs such as the X-33 and to participate in the design of space shuttle upgrades. Many of these new programs were eventually cancelled primarily because of budget shortages within NASA, but we learned to meet the needs of customers at their Center and well ahead of design completion.

Building reliance and teamwork was inherent in working with customers to prepare and launch their research projects on the shuttle and ISS as well as spacecraft that we launched on expendable launch vehicles. They needed to trust us with their valuable projects and spacecraft. We also needed to build reliance with the contractor doing work on the space shuttle so that they would be very open with us on any and all issues. We needed this partnership to make a success of moving to an insight model. We did not have any major incidents caused by KSC for the life of the Space Shuttle Program; however, there were many improvements made to assure that result. For example, after an electrical short on a launch, we worked with the program and the contractor to inspect and repair wiring in the payload bay and found many incidents of damaged wiring. Also, the program allowed us to rewire some systems to provide more redundancy.

KSC existed in a wildlife refuge so it made great sense to be a full partner in protecting it. As a result of our efforts to be an environmentally responsible tenant of the refuge, they trusted us and allowed us to go forward with the industrial park initiative that we discussed earlier. As another example of our partnership, I rejected attempts by the state of Florida to run a high-speed railroad through the Center, citing the impact on the wildlife refuge. We also started an initiative to capture feral cats, which were abundant and very destructive to the birds in the refuge. We had them spayed and neutered to reduce the population as well as housing many in a facility maintained by volunteers at the Center.

The Consultant's Observations ... Tim

Roy drove the culture change. He built from what was right with the culture and tried to adjust or change parts that were not as productive. In Chapter 7 we shared the principles for thinking strategically. Roy was creating a "strategic leadership" culture within the KSC senior management team. The off-sites, working sessions, and leadership development sessions focused on developing a new leadership approach. But while strategy was an irreplaceable aspect of this transformation, an oft-repeated—and true—adage in the field of organizational consulting says, "Culture eats strategy for breakfast." In order for KSC to make the transformation succeed, it needed to change both its organizational and leadership team cultures.

KSC's senior management team shared a set of values, norms, and beliefs that drove high performance. The team shared their

1. love of the country;
2. pride in being NASA;
3. love of and devotion to the mission;
4. discipline to find solutions to technical challenges;
5. pride in sharing the NASA story with the world;
6. pride in inspiring the next generation of explorers.

These shared values supported the team well.

Corral & Triage the Sacred Cows

The Leader's Experience ... Roy

During another off-site, the group discussed the need to help influence NASA's direction to KSC. Still traditionally focused on sharing how we would meet the direction given to us, we struggled with being okay with providing future-oriented feedback to NASA. But the push to be proactive was taking place. I took the time with the team to truly own the need to change and the leadership approach that was needed to make the changes. By developing the road maps, the leadership team was being proactive in defining the future and the path to the future we wanted to take.

During a different off-site, a senior manager made a flippant comment. "We have a lot of sacred cows here," he said.

I heard this and seized the opportunity. I jumped (or launched) out of the chair and went to the flipchart to ask the team, "What are these sacred cows?" I took the marker and captured the sacred cows from the group. I saw the need to change what was getting in the way of moving to the future. The push to take ownership for the transformation was taking place.

The Consultant's Observations ... Tim

As shared earlier, KSC had good values in place. However, they had a few other values that needed to be changed to support the transformation. The items that needed to be changed within the senior management team were deeply embedded and often hard to untangle from in view of the changes the transformation was bringing:

1. The notion that they should share only good news in public. This drove KSC to have sometimes guarded conversations. Sometimes the team was not willing to challenge the status quo in larger forums. The leadership team needed to be critical and open about the issues facing KSC.
2. Self-reliance. This drove KSC to establish organizations that were not reliant on others, but this created duplication in efforts. The leadership team needed to enhance the collaboration across the Center and share resources.
3. "Follow the chain of command; do what NASA tells you to do." This drove KSC to be more responsive than proactive. The leadership team needed to continue to respect the chain of command but also be willing to influence NASA.
4. "Focus on today; focus on delivering today's mission." This drove KSC to limit its focus on the long-term future—but the leadership team needed to spend time on the future. The normal, annual budgeting process helped focus on what needed to be done for the near-term. But they needed to look further into the future, beyond the five-year budget horizon.
5. "Centers solve small problems; HQ solves big problems." This drove KSC to again be more reactive instead of proactive on solving problems directly within their control. The leadership team needed to be more intentional and explicit about how it would influence NASA as it solved the big problems. The leadership team needed to be proactive in bringing potential solutions to NASA.

These values were inherently good and served the team well up until the need for the transformation became evident. Then the team saw the need to change how they operated ... how they led KSC ... how they worked together as a team.

During one of the first off-sites, a senior manager asked for a few minutes as we began our third day. He stood up and apologized to the group, saying he was sorry for not "being strategic"—the last few days he had been thinking about the work waiting for him back in the office. This team, he said, needed to use this precious time together to "be strategic." The push to move beyond today's mission was taking place.

As you navigate your transformation you may want to ask yourself four questions about the current culture. Illustration 9.2 highlights these four questions:

1. Within the current organization, what cultural elements can we bring forward to the transformed organization?
2. Within the current organization, what cultural elements do we not bring to the transformed organization?
3. Within the senior management team, what cultural elements can we bring forward to the transformed organization?
4. Within the senior management team, what cultural elements do we not bring to the transformed organization?

These four questions help reinforce the behaviors needed for your transformation to be successful.

Illustration 9.2—Four Questions About Your Organization's Current Culture

	Organizational Culture	Senior Management Team Leadership Culture
Cultural Elements to **Bring** to the Transformed Organization	Within the current organization, what cultural elements can we bring forward to the transformed organization?	Within the senior management team, what cultural elements can we bring forward to the transformed organization?
Cultural Elements to **Not Bring** to the Transformed Organization	Within the current organization, what cultural elements do we not bring to the transformed organization?	Within the senior management team, what cultural elements do we not bring to the transformed organization?

Recommendations

From this chapter we offer a few recommendations and questions to engage your team with.

While the easy-to-see part of the transformation is the changes to the business model, the less visible but challenging part is the culture change. You will face the hard but crucial task of focusing on your culture. The culture provides the values, norms, and behaviors that guide how your workforce executes the processes. To truly transform, you need to change both your business model and its culture.

Next Steps

To focus on the culture you can:

- Bring Your Guiding Principles to Life
- Begin with the Positives in the Culture You Have
- Corral & Triage the Sacred Cows

Start the Conversation

Engage your team in refining your organization's culture by asking them to share their perspectives about:

What about our culture is hindering us from moving forward?

What about our culture can help us from moving forward?

How does our culture need to change to better fit our new organization?

PEOPLE

You got this

In this section, we explore the role of people in transformational efforts.

You know that transformations impact your team and workforce—and transformations are emotional. You will need to understand where your people are coming from. You will need to acknowledge what they are feeling. Your workforce, just like you, will have doubts, will feel unsure.

What you communicate to them is indispensable: your job as leader is to ensure they see there is a better tomorrow. You will need to find a balance between sharing a sense of urgency and at the same time giving them a sense of calmness that "we got this."

Chapter 10
Restore Pride in the Workforce

You got this

Your Situation...
Transformations Are Emotional

As you face this transformation, you already know that you will face the emotional side of change. The transformation you are embarking on will be emotional. Some folks will be excited about the change and others will resist it. As the leader, you will provide the steady calmness that understands, appreciates, and uses the emotions of the past, present, and future to energize the transformation.

As you navigate the transformation, be thinking about these things:

> "*What emotions are our employees facing regarding our past, present, and future?*
>
> *Why might the workforce and leadership team become frustrated?*
>
> *What mechanisms can we use to provide the time and space for the workforce and management team to process their emotions?*"

In this chapter we share how KSC recognized and addressed the emotional aspects of their transformation.

What's Next...
Gain Your Workforce's Commitment to the Transformation

Transformations are an emotional experience. Your team and workforce will be holding emotions such as fear, uncertainty, confusion, and sense of loss, with a sense of hope and excitement. You need to lead your organization through the emotions of the transformation.

Next Steps

To navigate and embrace the emotions you can:

- Expect Workforce Morale Hits
- Connect to the Emotions to Build Empathy
- Create Hope for the Future: Take Bold Moves and Use Strategic Initiatives to Inspire a "Run to the Future" Mindset
- Remember Your Leadership Team Will Have Frustrations as Well

Start the Conversation

Engage your team in addressing the emotions by asking the team to share their perspectives about:

What is our workforce experiencing?

What excites/worries them for today?

What are their hopes/fears for the future?

How can we keep focused on their morale?

How are we feeling as a team?

How can we support each other on this journey?

Dig Deeper

In this section, we provide the leader's perspective (Roy) and the consultant's perspective (Tim) on the following actions you can take:

- Expect Workforce Morale Hits
- Connect to the Emotions to Build Empathy
- Create Hope for the Future: Take Bold Moves and Use Strategic Initiatives to Inspire a "Run to the Future" Mindset
- Remember Your Leadership Team Will Have Frustrations as Well

Expect Workforce Morale Hits

The Leader's Experience ... Roy

One of the most emotional situations that I encountered during my 54-year career, during which I served in top-level leadership teams for 27 years, was the situation that I encountered at KSC when I arrived in March 1997. NASA had sent clear and consistent messages to the workforce at KSC that they were inconsequential. In the "Faster, Better, Cheaper" NASA, they had little to no value. Hundreds of them were asked to leave after the zero-based review.

NASA consolidated the Space Flight Operations Contracts into a single contract and gave management and control of the contract to the Johnson Space Center (JSC). KSC was ordered to evolve to a relatively small civil service workforce to provide insight over the contractor during the processing of the vehicles. They would only be in charge for the launch and landing operations. JSC controlled the budget and program for the shuttle support contractor, and the culture meant that KSC inputs were not valued highly.

So that was the vision that was being held out to them: NASA civil servants would focus on research and technology development in the future and get out of operations. KSC was not perceived to have a research role currently or in the future. As a result, KSC people were perceived by the NASA leadership as being expendable and without value for the future. Buy-outs and hiring freezes were the order of the day. The future looked bleak. Morale in the workforce was near rock bottom.

In contrast, the day-to-day job was demanding as high pressure continued to ramp up the launch rate and get ready to launch the International Space Station (ISS). The Marshall Space Flight Center had the lead on getting the ISS built and shipped to KSC. The concept for getting the ISS to orbit was initially known as "ship and shoot." KSC's role was basically to host the ISS in the new ISS Processing Facility. Testing was expected to be minimal.

The Consultant's Observations ... Tim

My first sense of the KSC emotion came while I was teaching on-site at KSC. During a project management course, a student became visibly upset. During a break in the class, I asked her what was wrong. She shared that she was disappointed and scared about the direction NASA was going.

My second sense of the KSC emotion came from focus groups we conducted with KSC employees. These focus groups provided great insights that we could use to bring to the Center Director. KSC also used these focus groups to provide the time and space for the KSC employees to process their emotions. Those emotions ranged from anger over not being viewed as adding value, to concern for their fellow workers, to excitement about creating a new, meaningful role for KSC. In addition to their emotions, the employees really wanted to know what the leadership team was doing to help create their future.

After the sessions, I walked out sharing the same emotions.

I am not a NASA employee; however, their energy and commitment were infectious. At this point, I was beginning to understand my purpose in working with KSC: to support the senior management team as they navigated a highly emotional period in its history.

My third sense of the emotions at KSC came from my interactions with the senior leaders. Depending on the subject, many emotions emerged in the team:

- pride in the KSC's accomplishments over the years
- excitement for the new path
- confusion and frustration on why KSC needed to change
- confusion and frustration on the future of KSC
- frustrations with the change taking too long

Your workforce, your team, and you yourself will experience the emotions of the transformation.

Connect to the Emotions to Build Empathy

The Leader's Experience ... Roy

The KSC transformation was emotional throughout. As we shared earlier, KSC was told to downsize because it was an operational Center and NASA didn't do operations. Some folks were excited by the possibility of evolving to a new role. Many others were confused and apprehensive about the change.

The key thing that I did was to engage the workforce and leaders in creating our strategic road map to a future that was appealing to our best and brightest. Then we gathered senior leaders often to review progress. We shared our progress regularly with the workforce to give them hope. As successes came about, we celebrated each one and used the resulting renewed hope and enthusiasm to create energy to tackle remaining strategic goals. Yes, progress generates positive emotions and willingness to push harder to achieve more.

I continuously engaged our stakeholders and the workforce to review our progress and alert them about issues where we could use their help. I gave hundreds of presentations over the six and a half years of this saga to our workforce and stakeholders.

Eventually NASA leaders appreciated our contributions to both current and future missions and stopped the downsizing well short of the original mandate. We were able to hire critical skills as well as bring on young people as interns and, after their education was completed, as new hires.

The new programs such as MEIT, JBOSC, and LSP were remarkedly successful in restoring hope for a bright future. Also, the improvements in the infrastructure, especially those housing our workforce, demonstrated that they were valued and appreciated.

At my going-away party, a person in the audience rose and addressed me after my speech. He said, "Thanks for restoring our dignity."

Looking back on KSC then and now, KSC made an amazing transformation and remained valued and vibrant throughout the period.

The Consultant's Observations ... Tim

To acknowledge, explore, and understand frustrations with the transformation, KSC used a series of tools. For example, the use of employee focus groups and interviews with leaders provided the time and space for the team to raise and process their concerns. During the senior management off-sites, the team also explored the emotional side of the change by simply asking questions that address emotions. As seen in Illustration 10.1, you can use a set of questions to explore the emotions (positive and negative) of the organization's journey.

Illustration 10.1—Six Questions to Process the Emotions of the Transformation

	Past	Present	Future
Positive	From the past, what are we most proud of? What do we need to carry forward?	In our present state, what excites us?	For the future, what are we most hopeful for?
Negative	From the past, what do we regret the most? What do we need to leave behind?	In our present state, what frustrates us?	For the future, what are we most worried for?

Asking these questions in a group setting provides time for the team to process and share their emotions. They are being heard by each other. During focus groups, training, and off-sites, the participants were asked these questions. Their responses helped us understand where the team was emotionally and what we needed to work on next. To engage the workforce, the KSC senior management team continuously involved them, using a set of approaches such as

- focus groups;
- action-learning training sessions;
- all-hands presentations;
- CD Comms.

There were certain words that we found were not good to share. They would create panic and doubt in the workforce. One sensitive phrase was "government-owned, contractor-operated." This phrase pointed to a decreased role and importance of the government employees. Another sensitive phrase was "reduction in force," or RIF. This phrase describes an involuntary layoff in the government sector. KSC needed to work both the operational and emotional fronts of the change (Beer and Nohria 2000). In addition to the changes in the processes, tools, and workforce, KSC paid attention to the overall morale of the workforce.

Create Hope for the Future: Take Bold Moves and Use Strategic Initiatives to Inspire a "Run to the Future" Mindset

The Leader's Experience ... Roy

A key aspect of finding a solution to improve NASA's opinion of KSC and shore up the Center's depleted morale was to get the total team to focus on where we could add the most value to NASA, communicate that widely within the workforce and with stakeholders, define the important things that we needed to do and then do the work, measure our progress with metrics, and celebrate progress constantly with the workforce. Surely there would be the need to make adjustments along the way and correct our approach if problems showed up in our metric reviews, but we also needed to be bold in our approach. We needed to prove our value and replenish our workforce's hope for their future at KSC.

As mentioned in earlier chapters, the key to our eventual success in giving KSC a renewed purpose was adopting a strategic approach. Over many strategic conversations, our team defined the future we wanted, the tasks that we needed to undertake, and the metrics to measure our progress. Then we communicated frequently and fully with the total workforce. We not only shared how *we* were doing, but also gathered *their* input, concerns, and ideas to bring to the ongoing conversation as well. The workforce having a say in their future and in transforming KSC was crucial to maintaining their morale and retaining their presence.

Take Bold Moves

We took a bold approach to the things that we wanted to do to assist NASA and our nation's space program. Moving the Expendable Launch Vehicle Program to KSC was probably the best example of that. Some thought that was impossible, but it was eventually sold by convincing my boss that it was the right strategic move for NASA and KSC.

KSC employees also made bold contributions to the new ISS by creating and implementing the MEIT program. The results are evident today in the ISS's third decade on orbit without major problems along the way. These results of their superb engineering expertise and careful attention to detail significantly boosted their reputation throughout NASA.

Another example of boldness was engaging the state of Florida to help us build the SERPL (Space Experiments Research and Processing Laboratory) and industrial park. This is also an example of how much the state and community valued KSC and its people. Today, there are many great jobs in manufacturing plants that have been built in the park.

As mentioned earlier, another reward for NASA and the leaders of KSC as a result of our strategic approach was that our people were sought out as leaders for other NASA organizations. Several became Center Directors or headquarters leaders, which showed everybody that our people were not only capable and skilled, but also highly valued.

Use Strategic Initiatives to Inspire a "Run to the Future" Mindset

As we detailed in other chapters, the team at KSC decided to approach this situation strategically. Initiatives were developed that successfully introduced new programs and valuable services to show NASA that the KSC team was highly critical to the success of current and future NASA programs. KSC's best and brightest were attracted to these new efforts and made them a success. The buyouts and hiring freezes were stopped.

The Consultant's Observations ... Tim

As described earlier, KSC faced a challenge with workforce morale. When they started the transformation, the workforce was told they didn't bring value any longer. The initial plan was to cut the workforce, not reshape or realign KSC. As with many change efforts, the workforce can become frustrated. They hear the words that management says about a bright future. However, they don't see actions and results that are consistent with the words.

In leading your transformation you will need to ensure the workforce sees the tangible steps you are taking to help them create their future. The bold moves and initiatives provide these very tangible examples. Yes, it is important to define these. It is also very important for the workforce to understand how these bold moves and initiatives are moving the organization forward.

Remember Your Leadership Team Will Have Frustrations as Well

The Leader's Experience ... Roy

I had several tense moments with the NASA leadership. After about a year as Center Director, I was asked to present a briefing on KSC to the NASA Administrator and his deputy. All of the other Center Directors were also in attendance. I began the briefing but almost immediately the Administrator stood up and started walking around the room and railing about something totally off the subject of KSC. After he sat down, I was told that I was out of time. I also sat down as a dejected person who felt unvalued by NASA's senior leader.

Although there were other tense moments with the NASA Administrator, such as when I found out that he was looking for someone to replace me because the JSC Center Director was irritated that I had begun a reorganization of the Center called KSC 2000, he eventually supported me and liked the progress that KSC was making. I felt relieved and appreciated.

As Center Director, I was focused on my entire team. I always invited them for personal visits whenever they had a concern. I listened and did my best to correct whatever concern that they raised. As a result, the senior leadership team at KSC remained quite stable. Few left, but those who did went to high-level positions within NASA.

The Consultant's Observations ... Tim

The emotional side of the change also impacted me. I was an external consultant with relatively limited exposure to KSC or their team. After about two years of working with them, I had a meeting with Tip, one of their senior managers. He shared some insights into the transformation: the insights pointed to problems within the team dynamics and differences of opinion on the steps to take next.

As he was sharing, I'm sure I looked like the deer in the headlights. I left his office. By the time I walked to the Deputy Director's office, Tip had called the Deputy Director to let him know that he might need to encourage me. He saw the frustration and doubt in me. In the end, it became obvious that not only was it my purpose there to support the senior management team, but also, the support and encouragement of the senior management team was crucial in order for me to stay engaged with them. I needed their support and encouragement as much as they needed mine.

Recommendations

From this chapter we offer a few recommendations and questions to engage your team with.

Transformations are an emotional experience. Your team and workforce will be holding emotions such as fear, uncertainty, confusion, and sense of loss, with a sense of hope and excitement. You need to lead your organization through the emotions of the transformation.

Next Steps

To navigate and embrace the emotions you can:

- Expect Workforce Morale Hits
- Connect to the Emotions to Build Empathy
- Create Hope for the Future: Take Bold Moves and Use Strategic Initiatives to Inspire a "Run to the Future" Mindset
- Remember Your Leadership Team Will Have Frustrations as Well

Start the Conversation

Engage your team in addressing the emotions by asking the team to share their perspectives about:

What is our workforce experiencing?

What excites/worries them for today?

What are their hopes/fears for the future?

How can we keep focused on their morale?

How are we feeling as a team?

How can we support each other on this journey?

Chapter 11
Tell the Story…Tell the Story…Tell the Story

You got this

Your Situation…
Transformations Require Continuous Communication

As the leader you will also need to play the "Chief Communications Officer." You will need to communicate with your workforce and stakeholders. They will want to be kept informed.

To plan your communication, think about

> "*Who do we need to communicate with?*
>
> *What do we want to achieve with the communication?*"

In this chapter, we explore how KSC continuously communicated with their workforce and stakeholders. We also explore how KSC continuously learned before, during, and after the transformation and documented their learnings—communication not only for the present, but also for the future.

What's Next...
Create Shared Understanding

You need to communicate continuously about the transformation. The organization needs to understand where they are in the transformation journey.

Next Steps

To create shared understanding you can:

- Communicate Up, Down, and Sideways—Continuously
- Align Your Message to the Audience
- Share Lessons Learned

Start the Conversation

Engage your team in the communication process by asking them to share their perspective about:

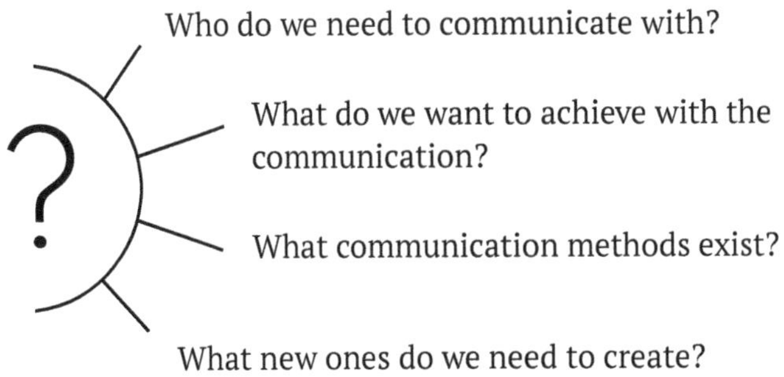

Dig Deeper

In this section, we provide the leader's perspective (Roy) and the consultant's perspective (Tim) on the following actions you can take:

- Communicate Up, Down, and Sideways—Continuously
- Align Your Message to the Audience
- Share Lessons Learned

Communicate Up, Down, and Sideways—Continuously

The Leader's Experience ... Roy

During this entire period, the drama was intense and real: how to retain our best and brightest and accomplish our mission safely while making the drastic changes required to reduce our civil servant workforce. The money to keep the workforce that we had was not in the budget, so we were forced to move forward aggressively.

To achieve these dramatic reductions, we lived with successive buyouts and hiring freezes. No one could chance a major mission failure, so we had to keep our eye on the "knitting"—the day-to-day task of assuring safe and effective processing of the space shuttle or other missions in work—at every step of the way. There were always people on the sidelines who predicted our failure and tried to halt or interrupt our strategic journey. While these people meant well, it took an amazing amount of time to keep all the stakeholders apprised and comfortable with our plans and progress. I gave well over 400 presentations to groups to keep us on track during this six-year period.

As mentioned earlier, the desired strategic outcome was to give people hope that there would be exciting work on the other side of this chasm so that our best would decide to stay with us. We needed to create some magnets for people to attract them to new work.

Earlier in the book, I detailed our major initiatives to be successful in creating these magnet programs, such as convincing NASA to consolidate the ELV programs at KSC. We as a management team worked hard at keeping us focused on bringing all our current work and new initiatives on track and producing high-quality products and services.

At KSC I made a lot of direct communications with all levels of the workforce, using a communication tool that I called CD [Center Director] Comms that went out to everyone on a frequent basis. These were in addition to hundreds of communications at meetings, all-hands, off-sites, customer visits, and stakeholder outreach. Our key themes focused on

- congratulating/thanking/acknowledging people who are displaying the behaviors that support our values;
- showing interest in the work of our people by actively visiting with them and encouraging them;
- having difficult conversations to draw out key issues/concerns and taking action to address them
- actively pursuing alternative views;
- admitting mistakes openly and in a way that shows interest in doing better;
- sharing the difficult choices we made that are consistent with our values.

The Consultant's Observations ... Tim

KSC proactively engaged both its workforce and its stakeholders in the transformation process. They learned from them and kept them informed. Communication throughout the transformation is crucial. As we shared earlier, transformations are emotional. KSC's transformation was emotional. In fact, KSC faced a morale challenge. Communication was critical to bringing the workforce along on the transformational journey.

As well as you think you are communicating, you may not be doing enough. The value of communication can't be oversold. For example, as part of a LEAP training program (discussed in Chapter 12), KSC offered a class reflecting on the KSC transformation. In this class, we had the participants see how the events in the country led to drivers on NASA and then KSC's responses. The participants were able to track the major events across the years of the transformation. As much as KSC communicated, there probably could have been even more—or different—communication. Sometimes it was just hard for the employees to connect the dots. Your communication needs to help them see the bigger picture.

Align Your Message to the Audience

The Leader's Experience ... Roy

During my tenure at KSC, I communicated up, down, and sideways (to stakeholders outside of NASA). I wanted everyone to understand what we were trying to accomplish, progress toward our strategic goals, and issues that we were working to solve.

For the workforce we used strategic off-sites for senior leaders as well as weekly strategic reviews to review progress and issues. We had periodic all-hands sessions with the broader workforce. We had a special annual stand-down day for an in-depth focus on safety. I used CD comms to communicate via email to all employees with an account on immediate concerns and significant events. I met with program managers for our major programs, Space Shuttle and ISS, one-on-one, often.

I met with my boss at NASA HQ to brief him on issues and progress often as well, either in his office in DC or when he visited KSC. Each year I presented a detailed review of our performance to my boss, using a three-ring binder full of metrics. I traveled to brief the JSC Center Director one-on-one on any critical issues or initiatives. The NASA Administrator had meetings with all Center Directors several times a year. I would be asked to brief about once per year to the group. There was an annual Space Day in the Florida capital, and I briefed them on our progress toward our strategic initiatives and presented ideas where they could help, such as progress in establishing the industrial park. I met with our elected officials in the Congress periodically, and usually one-on-one.

All of these communications were critical to assure support for our strategic goals. There were also plenty of informal communications, such as when senior leaders attended space shuttle launches or flight readiness reviews. I put a high priority on all of these events and tailored my message for each different type. I made it clear that my door was open to anyone who wanted to discuss something with me. I also did as much managing by walking around as time permitted, including dropping by to visit leaders in their offices. Finally, I often went for a late-in-the-day jog around the Center. If I saw anything out of the ordinary, I would email the leader as soon as I returned to my office.

The Consultant's Observations ... Tim

A simple communication equation defined by Louis I. Middleman helps us think about how to communicate: Audience + Purpose = Design (Middleman 1981). For KSC, the audience was primarily the KSC workforce. Some were demoralized by the need to transform. For example, the first employee focus groups wanted to see that the KSC leadership team was working the problem. They wanted to believe that someone was looking out for them.

Additional audiences included stakeholders such as other Centers, NASA headquarters, and local partners. In reflecting on their transformation communication, we can see the purpose of the communications included

- reducing uncertainty about the transformation;
- "connecting the dots" of the drives, actions, and emerging results of the transformation;
- celebrating the "victories" along the journey ... showing how recent accomplishments are part of the overall transformation;
- gathering feedback from the workforce on the state of the transformation;
- reinforcing the journey that the organization is on.

All these communications help demonstrate to the workforce that the leadership have the transformation under control and are focused on supporting the workforce. For example, KSC communicated the strategic direction and core values in all-hands meetings. These all-hands provided an opportunity for the KSC director and other managers to share the reason for change, what the strategic direction was, and the progress made. KSC communicated strategic issues via CD comms. CD comms were one- to two-page letters from the KSC Director to the KSC community.

Share Lessons Learned

The Leader's Experience ... Roy

As previously mentioned, our communications expanded beyond KSC and NASA. I hosted other leaders both within and outside of NASA or visited them on a regular basis and discussed progress and issues. We also shared our story with the external community. As part of our work with Stephen Covey, we shared our story with their community. The Covey folks formally recognized KSC for their transformational efforts. We had periodic lunch and dinner events with the National Space Club of Florida. The group consisted of members of the community and elected officials as well as members of contractor organizations, educational organizations, and KSC. I gave updates on our progress as well as information on upcoming events. One evening event was a festive occasion with an annual award presented to someone who had distinguished themselves in a significant aerospace achievement in Florida during the year. It was named after the first KSC Center Director, Kurt Debus.

Across this broad community, with people in a wide range of positions, the goal of all our communications was to be as transparent as possible about our achievements as well as any issues, with an emphasis on any lessons learned that would be critical for the future.

One serious lesson learned about an issue which was presented in Chapter 9 was about the electrical short on a space shuttle launch.

We had to do a lot of corrective actions to repair damage to wires in the payload bay. The lesson learned was to put protective covers over any areas when workers would need to be in the payload bay and to inspect the area after the work to assure no damage.

As you could imagine, given how complicated the shuttle was, there were many lessons learned over the years—some of them only after shortages of funding and time led to catastrophes. Unfortunately, following the Columbia accident, the accident board determined that both Challenger and Columbia accidents had a similar contributing cause, which was termed normalization of deviation. This term meant that the O-ring problem in the solid rocket boosters and the foam strikes on the heat shields were thought to be just maintenance issues since neither had resulted in significantly critical damage. Concerned engineers and safety experts had to prove that these incidents were unsafe but they couldn't without detailed programs to address the root causes and potential damage to critical systems. Given the severe budget and time constraints on the program, there was never enough money to address these issues in depth—until after the fatal accidents.

Clearly space is hard, and lessons learned were critical to prevent accidents. I was assigned to transfer to the Langley Research Center as Center Director to set up a new agency to solve this problem. The new agency was named the NASA Engineering and Safety Center. They had enough budget to do detailed studies of potential problems and recommend solutions that were mandated on programs. I attended their tenth reunion and heard that they had done 500 in-depth studies on a variety of NASA programs to look into issues nominated by chief engineers at NASA Centers. Since the inauguration of the NESC, NASA's safety record has been excellent.

The Consultant's Observations ... Tim

Throughout the transformation you will continue to learn from your efforts. Some things will work well and others will not. You can capture the lessons learned along the way. To think about your learning approach, you may want to think about

- How well am I learning from my experience now?
  How well is our team learning from our collective experience?
- How can we improve our reflecting, capturing, and sharing of our lessons learned?

As we shared earlier, transformations are hard. As you go through the transformation, you will need to reflect and learn about how well the transformation is going. You need to learn about what is and is not working so well for changing your organization and for leading its transformation. KSC reflected on both during the transformation and after the transformation. During the off-sites, the senior leadership team would reflect on the progress and challenges since the last off-site. They used this time to adjust their approaches for the next move.

As Roy was getting ready to go to his next assignment, KSC engaged with the workforce to help them process, reflect, and learn from the transformation. As part of their supervisory leadership training program, we put together an action-learning workshop to reflect on the transformation. We shared a ten-year history map of the world, NASA, and KSC. We shared what was going in the world that drove KSC to change. This reflection helped folks see the events, connect the dots, and reflect on the learnings.

Through these sessions, the KSC supervisors developed their set of transformational lessons learned to carry forward to their next experience. These lessons learned were also shared with the KSC senior management team for them to use in the future. These lessons learned are provided in Illustration 11.1.

Illustration 11.1 –Supervisor's Transformational Lessons Learned

1. Strategy Takes Time

- Long-term gains from small steps over time

2. Keep the Strategy Flexible

- Learn-as-you-go spiral development approach to strategy
- Evaluate and adjust the strategy

3. Develop a Strategy

- Positions and aligns KSC's contibutions to the external environment and initiatives
- Focuses on KSC's mission, strengths
- Diversifies work
- Builds on core competencies
- Invests in new roles
- Focuses on employees
- Provides a long-term vision

4. Implement the Strategy

- Tell the story
- Communicate the strategy
- Align actions
- Partner

5. Focus on Results

- Focus on measurable performance gains
- Gain credibility
- Improve KSC
- Develop leadership succession
- Get KSC involved early in new programs

6. Build and Implement a Strategy Process

- Drives KSC to be proactive & influence external strategy
- Involves, listens to, and communicates with employees
- Lead by an engaged and unified senior management team
- Frames the big picture and strategic issues

They also reflected on the transformation and developed a set of lessons learned for leading change and transformations. At the end of one of the sessions, an individual came up to me and said, "It is a damn shame I have to be in this class ... to understand what we did, why we did it, and the results." He was lamenting that, before this class, he couldn't connect the dots of the drivers-actions-results from events across the country, to NASA, to KSC, to the transformation. Until the class, he was unable to see the connections.

This is why communication needs to be continuous, clear, relevant, and intentional—and why keeping learning at the core of your transformation and documenting those learnings are so important. On their own, your workforce will not be able to understand how the pieces fit together. Communication is key. You need to ensure that the workforce and stakeholders understand the why, what, how, performance, and lessons learned about the transformation.

Citations

Citations for this list are in "Reference List for papers published during the KSC transformation," which can be found in the "For Inquiring Minds... The Details" section on page 293.

During the transformation we also published a series of papers about what we were learning. Documenting your transformation is an essential form of both learning and communication—not only in the present but also for the future.

Recommendations

From this chapter we offer a few recommendations and questions to engage your team with.

You need to communicate continuously about the transformation. The organization needs to understand where they are in the transformation journey.

Next Steps

To create shared understanding you can:

- Communicate Up, Down, and Sideways—Continuously
- Align Your Message to the Audience
- Share Lessons Learned

Start the Conversation

Engage your team in the communication process by asking them to share their perspective about:

Who do we need to communicate with?

What do we want to achieve with the communication?

What communication methods exist?

What new ones do we need to create?

Chapter 12
Lead as a Team

You got this

Your Situation...
Transformations Require Leadership

Transformations are not easy. Your transformation will require a strong set of leaders acting as a unified team. The senior management team also needs to be supported. They will need to feel confident that they can lead this transformation. You will balance both challenging and encouraging your leadership team. Think about your mentors, coaches, or teachers who were able to do this for you. You are now playing the challenger-encourager role.

As you think about your team, here are some questions to answer:

> *How well do we work together?*
>
> *Who can support the senior management team with this transformation?*

In this chapter we explore how KSC engaged and supported their senior management team.

What's Next...
Provide Strong Leadership Presence

Transformations are hard and taxing on your leadership team. Your leadership team will need new skills to navigate the journey. You need to invest in building your leadership team.

Next Steps

To build your leadership team you can:

- Build the Leadership Skills Throughout the Organization...Including Your Leadership Team
- Provide a Pit Crew

Start the Conversation

You can engage your team in enhancing their capability to lead by asking them to share their perspectives about:

> **Deeper dive**
>
> *For a deeper dive into this concept, read Case Study #2, "Build the Leadership Team: NASA's LaRC Transformation," in the section "Taking Our Learnings On the Road: how lessons learned can create a career and form a future" on page 249.*

Who is on our team?

What experience do we have with change and transformations?

How well do we work together?

Who can support the Senior Management Team with this transformation?

Dig Deeper

In this section, we provide the leader's perspective (Roy) and the consultant's perspective (Tim) on the following actions you can take:

- Build the Leadership Skills Throughout the Organization... Including Your Leadership Team
- Provide a Pit Crew

Build the Leadership Skills Throughout Your Organization...Including Your Leadership Team

The Leader's Experience ... Roy

At KSC, we explored several leadership training opportunities, and all of them helped us to be better leaders. For example, we deployed seminar training based on *The 7 Habits of Highly Effective People* by Stephen Covey. As a NASA-wide initiative, we deployed safety training developed by the DuPont company. We also deployed LEAP training, which is described below.

A crucial part of the transformation was to (1) have a set of leaders drive the change throughout the organization and (2) ensure the leadership bench was strong throughout all levels of KSC. To accomplish these outcomes, we established the Leadership Excellence Achievement Program (LEAP). The program was developed by an internal team who conducted internal analysis, external benchmarking, and a review of best practices. The program included classroom sessions, outdoor activities, "outward bound" activities, books, various trainers, and a multi-rater feedback tool, and *7 Habits* was included in the training. The LEAP program focused on the following elements:

- Behavior Characteristics of a Leader
- Forging the Vision
- Strategic Management
- Empowerment
- The Leader's Toolbox

All supervisors within KSC participated in the program. The sessions also provided the opportunity for the supervisors to reflect on the current transformation and provide feedback to the senior management team.

The leadership team responded well to our training, and they led and managed well.

I had been trained previously in the Deming Management Method, which was a well-constructed set of techniques for continuous process improvement. At KSC we decided to become ISO 9001–certified as a major initiative to document all our processes and engage in continuous process improvement. We were successful in our certification effort, and the process of getting certified improved our own processes significantly.

Most important, we created a management team that learned together how to manage strategically. Many of the young people on this team at the beginning now occupy high-level leadership positions across NASA. Those who are still at KSC are doing a great job of tackling the new challenges of the day.

One thing that is certain, beyond death and taxes, is change. I was pleased to have an opportunity to lead this great team during a very difficult time. Truly the position of being the KSC Center Director was the best in my career. As I was fond of saying, living on the beach and launching rockets for a living is a great way to live.

What I learned at KSC helped me to be a better leader and successfully lead transformations at two other large technical organizations later in my career.

Deeper dive

For a deeper dive into this concept, read Case Study #2, "Build the Leadership Team: NASA's LaRC Transformation," in the section "Taking Our Learnings On the Road: how lessons learned can create a career and form a future" on page 249.

The Consultant's Observations ... Tim

As the person accountable for making your transformation a success, you need to rely on your senior management team and a set of folks supporting them. You need to build your senior management team and provide a "pit crew" to support your transformation process. Yes, KSC focused a lot on the overall KSC culture. They drove this change with the specific actions Roy outlined above. In addition to this, I think the biggest culture change was within the KSC senior management team. An organization has only one overall culture, but it is strongly influenced by the microcultures that comprise it, and vice versa. And to accomplish this transformation, some of the values, norms, and beliefs held by the senior management team regarding how they wanted to lead had to change.

Your senior management team is crucial to managing and leading your entire organization. They will drive the changes throughout their domain of responsibility. The senior management team, in addition to their daily management and leadership skills, need transformational skills and will also need to work well as a team; transformations require cross-functional coordination and changes.

As discussed earlier, KSC proactively engaged the senior management team in the strategic conversations. The Executive Team—Roy Bridges and Jim Jennings—also provided individual leadership and team-collaboration training. During every off-site there was some sort of development experience, and these experiences also occurred in between the off-sites. The Executive Team brought in a series of executives who led transformations to share their lessons learned. They provided formal training programs as well. To help build the team camaraderie, they engaged in social activities. Some of the skills focused on strategy, change/change management, transformations, leadership, and communication. Roy and Jim also brought in speakers to share their perspectives on the state of NASA and the space industry. All these development experiences provided the senior management team with a set of new perspectives, skills, and tools. Illustration 12.1 summarizes these learning opportunities.

Illustration 12.1—Enabling the Transformation by Learning

Element	1997	1998-2000	2001-2003
Learning: Self-assessment	• Initial focus groups and interviews • Loyalty Study by Right Management Associates identified key concerns over KSC's strategic uncertainty, ongoing career confidence, communication issues, workplace stress, KSC's future mission, involvement and teamwork, organization change • President's Quality Award application and feedback process provided insight into management system practices • Best Manufacturing Practices Oct. 1996 assessment of KSC's best practices • Senior managers talking with customers • Senior managers developing views of expertise • Right Management Consulting study to baseline organization before rollout of strategic implementation plan • CD directs KSC to review supervisory training practices, leads to the development of Leadership Excellence Achievement Program	• Action research in support of off-site • Data collection as part of the LEAP training sessions • KSC civil service employee survey	• Economic Impact of NASA on Central Florida
Learning: External Views	• Various leaders from external organization shared insights as part of the annual strategic retreats	• Various leaders from external organization shared insights as part of the annual strategic retreats	• Various leaders from external organization shared insights as part of the annual strategic retreats
Learning: Building Leadership and Change Management Skills	• Various leaders from external organization shared insights as part of the annual strategic retreats	• Leadership Excellence Achievement Program (LEAP) developed • Covey-based training on change management	• Continue to support implementation and use of LEAP and Covey training

Provide a Pit Crew

The Leader's Experience ... Roy

I experienced many difficult situations in my Air Force career, but the existential situation at KSC was the worst. NASA was under so much pressure to build the ISS within existing budget resources, which were scarce and getting worse with every review. That meant that we needed to fly the space shuttle as often as possible and with no additional mishaps. Clearly that day job was first in the minds of every senior leader involved with these efforts. But on top of that we were in a downsizing crisis and needed to define and achieve a future that would be attractive to our best and brightest so that they would stay and contribute to NASA's future programs.

Fortunately, my deputy Jim Jennings brought to my attention a consultant, Tim Kotnour. Tim was an expert in how to manage strategically. I agreed with that approach, and he became the chief of our pit crew. He helped us lead our first strategic off-site where we all agreed on the basic approach of how to define a future that would be attractive and come up with the vision and strategic goals that we have shared in this book. We selected Jenny Lyons to be our Strategic Planning Manager. She had an office near mine. She structured and set up the details of our many weekly meetings to review progress and take necessary corrective action as well as help me to generate communications both inside and outside the Center. I also decided to add an intern to my staff who would keep me informed about how our actions were being received by the workforce and assist with preparing communications. This was the basic pit crew for Jim and me. We were fortunate that they were so very talented.

As we progressed, there were others added to the pit crew to assist in accomplishing major initiatives. For example, when we decided to reorganize the Center, we set up a KSC 2000 team to work the details. Tim mentions these and several others in the next section.

I had never been in an Air Force position long enough to experience a complete strategic transformation, but I had six and a half years at

KSC. It was amazing what the pit crew helped us to accomplish. KSC survived and flourished. I look back with great fondness on what the team achieved.

The Consultant's Observations ... Tim

KSC enabled the transformation by establishing and providing a change infrastructure—the set of people focused on helping the senior management team make the transformation happen. One issue facing the organization was how to provide the resources to take the actions needed for transforming. Sink and Morris (1995) highlighted the need for establishing a change infrastructure. KSC implemented four types of infrastructures—people with the skills to provide internal change resources. KSC used different teams to provide a pit crew to help the organization drive the changes:

- ***Business Innovation Group.*** This group was responsible for developing the overall business management system and helping lead the effort to become ISO 9001–certified.
- ***Change Leader's Network.*** This group was trained in the Covey approach to provide help to managers in leading change efforts in organizations.
- ***Informal Focus Groups.*** These groups were tasked to address specific challenges facing KSC.
- ***Strategic planning manager.*** This position was responsible for supporting the leadership team in running the strategic management process.

KSC used formal and ad hoc teams systematically to achieve improvement results. The executive team's desire to institute real change led to establishing the Business Innovation Group (BIG). Their primary focus was to gain ISO 9001 certification.

To encompass all Center activities, BIG worked with the senior management team and formed an informal employee task team called the ISO 9001 Implementation Team. Strategic off-sites were held with the senior management team to instruct them about ISO 9001 benefits and how obtaining certification supported KSC's goals.

BIG also visited directorate and organizational all-hands meetings to hold question-and-answer sessions with employees. BIG led monthly management reviews with the senior management team to report the status of the ISO 9001 implementation effort and to bring problems and issues before the senior management team for resolution.

Senior management team involvement demonstrated to employees KSC's commitment to ISO certification. BIG assembled the ISO 9001 Implementation Team to have one member from each of KSC's 19 directorates and organizations. The ISO 9001 Implementation Team was chartered to build an ISO-compliant management system. Each team member took lessons learned and program decisions back to their own directorate or organization. This informal task team also proved invaluable in disseminating information in real time to each directorate and organization.

The informal task team existed for twelve months, initially meeting every two weeks, but meeting every week for six months prior to certification. Integrating informal and formal task teams allowed KSC to apply the needed resources at the right time to lead, manage, learn about, and systematically implement ISO 9001 certification.

KSC used many other formal and ad hoc teams throughout its transformation. KSC also established the Manager of Strategic Planning position. This position provided a continuous focus on the strategic management process. Illustration 12.2 summarizes how KSC provided a change infrastructure.

Illustration 12.2—Enabling the Transformation: Providing a Change Infrastructure

Element	1997	1998-2000	2001-2003
Providing a Change Infrastructure	Informal employee focus groups Business Innovation Group Strategic Planning Manager	Change Leader's Network	Covey Award for Change Leader's Network

Recommendations

From this chapter we offer a few recommendations and questions to engage your team with.

Transformations are hard and taxing on your leadership team. Your leadership team will need new skills to navigate the journey. You need to invest in building your leadership team.

Next Steps

To build your leadership team you can:

- Build the Leadership Skills Throughout the Organization...Including Your Leadership Team
- Provide a Pit Crew

Start the Conversation

You can engage your team in enhancing their capability to lead by asking them to share their perspectives about:

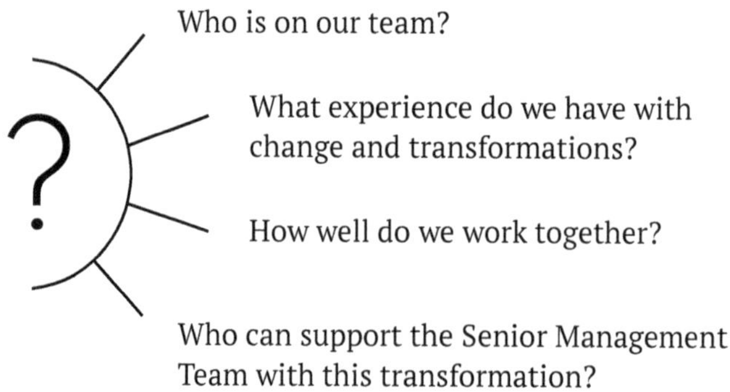

DIGNITY

You got this

In this section, we explore the significance of dignity as the heart and soul of your transformation efforts. We are transforming for our customers, stakeholders, and, most importantly, our workforce and ourself.

Chapter 13
Double Down on Dignity

You got this

Your Situation...
Transformation Leadership... It's All About Dignity

Transformations are hard.

You will become tired and perhaps frustrated at times. Know that this is an important journey you are on. Your workforce and stakeholders are counting on you to lead the organization through this. As you navigate your transformation, be clear with yourself about why you are doing this:

> "*What do I hope to achieve for the organization?*
>
> *What do I hope to achieve for the workforce?*
>
> *What do I hope to achieve for the leadership team?*
>
> *What do I hope to achieve for myself as a leader?*"

In this chapter, we end our journey in this book with a perspective on the core reason to follow a systematic approach to your transformation.

What's Next...

Ensure Your Organization Knows and Believes Their Actions Are Making a Difference

You must keep dignity (in addition to the performance gaps) as a primary driver for the transformation.

Next Steps

To keep dignity as a focus you can:

- Make It Personal to You
- Accept Your Leadership Calling ... Double down on Dignity
    - Create a Sense of Dignity in the Workforce
    - Create a Sense of Dignity in the Leadership Teams
    - Create a Sense of Dignity in the "Pit Crew"

Start the Conversation

What do I hope to achieve for the organization?

What do I hope to achieve for the workforce?

What do I hope to achieve for the leadership team?

What do I hope to achieve for myself as a leader?

Dig Deeper

In this section, we provide the leader's perspective (Roy) and the consultant's perspective (Tim) on the following actions you can take:

- Make It Personal to You
- Accept Your Leadership Calling ... Double Down on Dignity
  - Create a Sense of Dignity in the Workforce
  - Create a Sense of Dignity in the Leadership Teams
  - Create a Sense of Dignity in the "Pit Crew"

The Leader's Final Experience... Make It Personal to You ... Roy

In this book we explored the adoption of a strategic management approach. I must admit that it was a new approach for me. I had used some elements of it during my Air Force positions, but many of those were comparatively short, with little time to complete an organizational transformation. I had six and a half years at KSC. We had the time and the best of reasons to attempt and be successful with a major transformation.

The journey was a tough one, going from the existential crisis that greeted me when I arrived to a successful conclusion. As we presented in Chapter 1, the list of successes was lengthy and crucial to NASA's overall success.

All these results are important and long-standing.

From my high school days, my dream was to be part of opening the space frontier. The focus of that, given my love of aviation and testing new aircraft, was to become an astronaut. I was successful in flying the eight-day Spacelab 2 mission as the pilot of Challenger. Following the subsequent Challenger crash, I was recalled to the Air Force and had to reinvent myself as a leader, first in several Air Force command positions, then, after I retired from the Air Force, at NASA and Northrop Grumman.

I was thrilled to be offered the opportunity to lead KSC for NASA. The people were incredibly good at what they did, and the mission was critically important to the future of space exploration. Helping them be successful drove me to be the best leader that I could be.

I thought that NASA was wrong about getting rid of our talented civil servants and moving to a contractor-operated Center. The whole logic of "Faster, Better, Cheaper" was illogical for a workforce that needed to get today's job done *and* prepare for the next generation of space vehicles. I wanted to save as many of the best of KSC's people as possible to have the best opportunity for success with the space shuttle, the ISS, ELV, and new vehicles after the shuttle retired, to mention just a few of their important efforts.

During the seven years of KSC's transformation, many leaders learned how to lead strategically, and that paid huge dividends to KSC and NASA. Those people were not only successful at KSC; many of them moved to important positions and top-level leadership jobs in other Centers and NASA headquarters, where they have contributed to NASA's many successes over the years. For me personally, leading the KSC team and then going to LaRC to set up the NESC were highlights of my leadership career.

There were going-away parties for Benita and me to thank us for our contributions at KSC. One gift that started out as a joke by Jim Kennedy still exists. Jim declared that the Banana River Bridge would be named the Roy D. Bridges Bridge, and a sign was erected. This was to signify that the JBOSC contract had "bridged" the waters separating KSC and Cape Canaveral Air Force Station. Many people have since commented that they had traveled over "my bridge."

Now, with the first launch of the Artemis program behind us, NASA is leading the way back to the moon, and eventually headed to Mars, with humans. KSC people continue to add their unique expertise to each of NASA's programs to assure continued success.

The Consultant's Final Observations... Accept Your Calling ... Double Down on Dignity ... Tim

While supporting the transformation, I saw the frustration, confusion, anger along with the joy and sense of purpose. Within NASA, the mission is key ... the love of the mission is core to the NASA workforce. When KSC was told to downsize and their role devalued, I could feel the emotional hit in the workforce. But Roy and his leadership team turned the emotions to the positive.

Create a Sense of Dignity in the Workforce

In the moment, I didn't fully realize what the transformation meant to the leadership team and the workforce. It was some years after Roy left that I was working with a consultant to help me figure out my next professional move. In my discussions with the consultant, I reflected on the KSC transformation project. She asked a simple question: What did this mean to you? I shared the following story with her:

KSC and the KSC community had a series of celebration/goodbye celebrations for Roy. They appreciated his leadership and desired to say thank you. During the last celebration, we collectively shared a very cool and unique moment. The event was held in the Saturn V facility, which houses a Saturn V rocket laid down on its side. You can walk under it. The experience is amazing. It was fitting for the celebration to be held there. The facility was filled with the KSC workforce and partners. Once this event was done, Roy and his wife would be hopping on a plane to Langley (his next NASA assignment).

After probably an hour or so, the event ended. We all just sat there in our seats in silence. We didn't know what to do. Should we go? Should we stay? What do we say?

The silence was broken by a single individual, Richard Stevens. He shouted to Roy:

"Roy, thank you ... you gave us dignity."

After he said this we still just sat there. We had to let his message sink in. Roy and his team brought KSC dignity.

Richard provided the perfect ending to Roy's tenure at KSC. He succinctly put into words whatever everyone was feeling but didn't know how to express: Roy and his team provided dignity to the KSC workforce. The organization and workforce wanted to know that their work was valued and meaningful, and that it was contributing to the future of NASA. **We transform to bring dignity to our organization, our workforce, our senior management team, and ourselves.**

Create a Sense of Dignity in the Leadership Teams

The senior management team needed to know that they were leading together as a team to transform the organization. They needed to feel like they had some power to create their workforce's future.

As for Roy and the individual leaders, they needed a sense of purpose and effectiveness in leading the transformation. Before Roy came to the Center, the management team understood the challenge but weren't sure what to do. The level of complexity was significant, given the level of changes KSC was being asked to make while also flying the shuttle safely: transform while also ensuring the risks don't increase.

There was this one senior manager who had rubbed/scratched a patch on the side of his head until it was bald. As he sat listening, the scratching seemed to help him process the conversation. Maybe it was the stress; perhaps he just didn't know how to manage or lead through this large-scale transformation. But he was searching for how to bring value to KSC and the KSC workforce. And through Roy, he was able to help the senior management team develop a structure for leading the transformation.

The workforce saw that the role they were playing today—and would be playing in the future—was important. They knew their purpose was to deliver the mission today. Successful mission delivery and changes would create their future. They knew the senior management team was looking out for them. They saw hope for their future.

The senior management team was able to proactively engage in leading their workforce. The workforce had confidence in them—they knew this team would work together and take the right steps to navigate KSC through the transformation. The leadership team accepted their purpose to lead the transformation. They felt a sense of control over the Center's destiny. KSC's leadership no longer felt helpless.

Everyone got a sense of dignity ... a sense of purpose.

Create a Sense of Dignity in the "Pit Crew"

As for me, I did (and still do) get a sense of dignity and purpose by supporting NASA. I've shared many times that the NASA work gives my work meaning ... it gives me purpose. In fact, NASA just gave me an Outstanding Public Leadership Medal—all because Roy trusted me and mentored me. (Thanks, Roy.) I continue to learn. I continue to share these learnings with my students at the university and with other leaders. Roy "launched" my career.

I can't speak for Roy. But my sense was that he had a strong sense of dignity and confidence coming into this situation. This sense of dignity and confidence became the walking role model for others in KSC to see and perhaps emulate. In his own words, "A signal that we had been successful in our cultural change came at my going-away party when a member of the workforce stood up and said, 'You restored our dignity.'" Roy knew his purpose was to lead KSC through this transformation and to also build the team. His legacy goes far beyond the changes made at KSC.

Roy Bridges's legacy is the set of leaders he mentored.

Recommendations

From this chapter we offer a few recommendations and questions to engage your team with.

You must keep dignity (in addition to the performance gaps) as a primary driver for the transformation.

Next Steps

To keep dignity as a focus you can:

- Make It Personal to You
- Accept Your Leadership Calling ... Double down on Dignity
    - Create a Sense of Dignity in the Workforce
    - Create a Sense of Dignity in the Leadership Teams
    - Create a Sense of Dignity in the "Pit Crew"

Start the Conversation

What do I hope to achieve for the organization?

What do I hope to achieve for the workforce?

What do I hope to achieve for the leadership team?

What do I hope to achieve for myself as a leader?

Final Reminder

We started Chapter 1 with some advice. We are going to end this book with a final reminder:

We believe you are here at this time and place for a reason. Be confident and draw on your previous experiences. Everything you have done up to this point has prepared you for this moment. You got this.

You can and will bring dignity to your organization, workforce, leadership team, and yourself.

Godspeed, transformational leader.

You got this

Tim

Roy D. Bridges, Jr.

Epilogue
Taking Our Learnings On the Road

You got this

How lessons learned can create a career and form a future

We can't overestimate the impact that lessons learned can have on your life—and especially on your future. These case studies tell the stories of transformations Roy led after leaving KSC. Each study is followed by Tim's commentary on how the learnings carried forward from the KSC transformation informed those future transformations and Roy's career. We hope that you will see that you bring value to your work in the form of lessons learned from your past experience, and that everything you experience now you carry with you into your own future.

Epilogue

Case study #1

The Culture Opportunity: NASA's NESC

Roy's View ... Focus on the Root Cause

I took my learnings from the KSC transformation and continued to apply and update the learnings to other organizations. The following case study tells another story and shines a light on the transformations of another organization. This case study focuses on the establishment of the NASA Engineering and Safety Center (NESC) at the Langley Research Center.

After the Columbia Accident Report was published, I got a call from the NASA Administrator. He said, "I am going to reassign your Deputy Director, Jim Kennedy, as the Center Director at the Langley Research Center to set up a NASA Engineering and Safety Center as a key action to prevent future accidents."

I protested. I said, "My background is aeronautical research as an engineering test pilot and former space shuttle astronaut. Jim does not have that type of experience. Also," I added, "he would be great as the future Center Director of KSC." The Administrator agreed and ordered me to get ready to report to Langley.

I could have kept quiet and ended my NASA career at KSC, which was my true personal desire. But I felt that would not be best for all concerned. So off to Langley and another adventure.

Understand the Culture

Had I not been selected as an astronaut, I could have been a test pilot for the rest of my career and been happy. I was that enamored with the test pilot profession and aeronautical research, which was the focus at Langley. I thought that I would like the work at Langley but honestly, I was parachuting into another unknown. I had never been there. I didn't know the people. I didn't know the stakeholders. Maybe I had a clue about one of the challenges, setting up the NESC, but there were more challenges that came as a surprise.

I was given only a few months to get up to Langley Research Center and set up the NESC. In addition, I was directed to show up at Langley without letting anyone know that I was coming. This restriction prevented me from checking with the current leadership at Langley on what other challenges they were facing. On my first day, I showed up onstage at the auditorium and was introduced to the workforce by the NASA Administrator.

Build a Team that Believes in the New Culture

One of the smartest early decisions that I made in planning for Langley was to invite Ralph and Lesa Roe to join me as key members of my staff. Ralph was previously the head engineer for the Space Shuttle Program at KSC and was currently working in the Space Shuttle Program Office at JSC. I wanted him to be the Director of the new NASA Engineering and Safety Center. Lesa would initially oversee our business operations as a direct report to me. After I completed a reorganization of the Center, she became my Deputy Center Director. Both proved to be excellent choices. Ralph did a great job in setting up the NESC and making it effective. Lesa was an excellent deputy in all ways.

Work The Cultural Root Causes

Before getting into broader issues facing LaRC, let me describe the transformation that the NESC would bring to NASA.

Ralph and I worked to make sure that the NESC addressed the root causes of the issues that led to not only the Columbia tragedy, but also played a role in the Challenger tragedy. Both had so changed the course of my career and killed 14 of my colleagues. The Columbia Accident Investigation Board Report (Columbia Accident Investigation Board 2003) detailed the role that NASA culture played in both mishaps. I have often summarized the basic issue as the one on the sign over the Johnson Space Center Mission Evaluation Room, which is where experts convened to work issues during space missions. It read, "In God we trust. All others bring data." Alas, given the pressures of time and strained budgets, there was no capability to give time and money to resolve potential problems that arose during the Space Shuttle Program, where the shuttle was declared an operational vehicle after only four missions, rather than the experimental vehicle that it was.

The accident report noted that the culture also made managers more dominant in the decision-making process than engineers and safety experts. Managers placed problems that had not led to a serious mission issue to the sidelines. This technique was labeled "normalization of deviation" by the accident report. Both the solid rocket booster O-ring issue and the damage caused by foam strikes on the heat shield of the orbiter had been observed many times, but nothing was done to fix the underlying causes until after the tragedies. Management perceived the numerous foam losses as a maintenance issue. The O-rings that were damaged on earlier missions were dismissed as something that would not lead to major damage.

One could say that the entire human space program was always about schedule and budget. "Go to the moon before the end of this decade" was just the beginning. Three astronauts of Apollo 1 were killed in a ground test. Imagine putting people in a capsule with an inward opening hatch that could not be opened easily in an emergency. Then fill it with 100% oxygen, flammable materials, and numerous ignition sources. It sounds like an accident waiting to happen, and it was.

The shuttle was given the go-ahead only if NASA agreed to do everything for everybody. Expendable launch vehicles were abandoned since the shuttle would haul everything to orbit. A steady and increasing launch schedule was required. Additionally, NASA began to rely more and more on contractors rather than a robust in-house engineering corps. NASA managers argued with Morton Thiokol engineers and managers that it would be okay to launch Challenger on an abnormally cold day. The Morton Thiokol folks relented, since they couldn't prove that it was unsafe. Later we saw a member of the Challenger Accident Board dip an O-ring into a cold solution. He showed how it lost all its flexibility, rendering it less capable of performing its function, and that previous damage to O-rings on launches already showed the design to be ineffective. Clearly, it didn't take much of a test to show that this was an accident waiting for a really cold day to happen.

Then, even after Challenger, when NASA was relieved of doing everything for everybody and expendable launch vehicles were again used, the International Space Station (ISS) was over budget and behind schedule. A vigorous launch schedule was required to finish the ISS sooner.

On the day after the Columbia accident, I asked my KSC expert on foam damage to meet me at the Vehicle Assembly Building and bring any photos that he had of previous foam damage to the vehicle. Standing next to a Solid Rocket Booster (SRB), he showed me a photo of a significant dent into the solid cork ramp at the bottom of the SRB that had occurred on a recent mission. I knew then that a piece of foam could result in significant damage to critical pieces of the heat shield. Tests run during the accident investigation showed that a piece of foam could easily penetrate the heat shield on the leading edge of the wing. Why wasn't that test run before the accident? No time or money for things like that. The dent into the cork was dismissed as just another minor maintenance issue and set aside. It was not even mentioned at a subsequent Flight Readiness Review (FRR).

Raising concerns at an FRR was discouraged. I brought up an issue at an FRR for discussion and was severely criticized afterwards by a NASA leader for disrupting the proceedings. The culture was to work issues outside of final reviews. Shuttle managers often dismissed opinions outside of program boundaries as not worthy of consideration.

Align Resources with the New Culture

Ralph and I argued for a robust budget for the NESC so that when managers, engineers, or safety experts raised concerns about potential issues, there would be resources to bring in the best minds in industry, academia, and government to study the issue and do any necessary tests. Despite early pushback, we were eventually successful. Also, the chief engineer at each Center reported to the NESC and was encouraged to bring any issue to the NESC for review. I saw the NESC as the Supreme Court of Engineering and Safety. They prioritized their abundant resources to address the most critical problems in NASA.

I was invited to speak at the tenth anniversary of the founding of the NASA Engineering and Safety Center (NESC) at Langley. I learned that in the ten years since its creation, they had completed over 500 in-depth technical studies of potential safety issues that had been nominated by the chief engineers at NASA's Centers.

If only we'd had the vision to set up the NESC after Challenger, we might have prevented the Columbia tragedy.

The lesson learned is that successful transformations must get to the root causes of issues and assure that the corrective actions are sufficient to correct them. Also, it is critical to address the cultural issues as well as any hardware or engineering issues.

The NASA Administrator required all NASA Center Directors to have every civil servant in the workforce read the accident report and develop a report of any cultural problems at each Center that needed correction. At Langley, we organized focus groups to meet and develop a report that was delivered by each team to the entire organization at a town hall meeting. One issue that the teams identified was the prevalent use of "fear of retaliation" as the predominant management technique to keep the workforce in line. I will address the resolution to this issue as part of a discussion of the broader Langley transformation.

Another lesson learned is that even a wonderful organization such as NASA that did so much to inspire me to join in exploring our universe can become blind to cultural issues. These can be extremely destructive when dealing with space vehicles. Space is hard, and to do it successfully requires an organization like the NESC, which can force managers to pay attention to seemingly minor anomalies before they become tragedies.

Tim's View … It Is About the Hard Choices to Change the Culture

(Note: I was not directly supporting Roy in this case and I am reflecting on the journey he led the organization through.)

This case is a great reminder that you must address the organization's culture as you transform. Culture may be one of the hardest things to change but also one of the most important. Culture is deeply ingrained in an organization and probably in some way is an underlying driver for its transformation. Your organization's culture provides the values, norms, and beliefs that inform how you and your team answer fundamental transformational questions:

- Do we take the transformation on or not?
- Who is on our leadership team to take the transformation on?
- What is the core problem we need to solve?
- How will the core problem be addressed (e.g., the way it always has been or in a new way)?

Roy and his team realized that solving the issues associated with the Columbia accident required a culture problem to be addressed. They saw they needed a new way to deliver the technical excellence and authority that NASA needed. They also saw that the NASA culture would require them to deploy a new way to implement the new model. Roy and his team worked to ensure the current culture would not stop the needed transformation. You may need to see what in your culture is limiting your organization and its ability to change.

Making these culture changes will require you to have both the right leadership team and the resources to invest in the changes. Roy spent considerable time building his team and their skills. Building this team turned out to be critical to the NESC moving forward. Roy also needed to get dedicated resources to support NESC. This change could not be a fad of the year. It had to be sustaining. And so will yours. You will need to build your team and provide the resources it needs.

Case study #2

Build the Leadership Team: NASA's LaRC Transformation

Roy's View ... Leaders Can Transform, Too

When I parachuted into Langley to set up the NESC, I had been told it was the best-run Center in NASA.

Well, there were a few problems.

The first hint of trouble brewing was President Bush's announcement in January 2004 of the new Vision for Space Exploration. It was a response to the Columbia accident to regain public enthusiasm for space exploration. The plan was to send humans back to the moon by 2020 in preparation for the human exploration of Mars. I was excited about it.

The NASA Administrator told me to talk to our congresswoman to get her support and to begin a campaign of public engagement. He assured me that the project would be funded with more top-line budget—budget increases that NASA would request from Congress rather than funding it by cutting existing programs. Our aeronautical research budget would not be cut because of it.

The plan called for the International Space Station to be completed by 2010 and the space shuttle retired in the same year. A new capsule, Orion, would be built along with investments in a lot of new technology.

A month later, when the president's budget was announced, Langley's budget was cut by $100 million from the previous year's $800 million. Several major projects were canceled. My congresswoman was angry with NASA and me because I had unknowingly communicated a lie to her about Langley's budget not being a target to fund the president's new program. She had already promoted it to her constituents. But, to her constituents, budget cuts in their district because of the program felt like she was not supporting and advocating for them.

My workforce was extremely upset. I learned that they felt entitled to their top-line budget and projects. They had been protected through the years. They could not see a way forward. I needed to help them adjust to this new reality and get them engaged in the new work. After all, Langley managed the Viking spacecraft, which was the first to touch down on Mars. The human space program with the Mercury astronauts resided at Langley until JSC was established in 1961 as the Manned Spacecraft Center. We needed to reconnect to our legacy.

One of our first efforts to engage was to deploy a senior manager to JSC, where he embedded himself in the Shuttle Program Office. He helped them to understand how we could help with the Return to Flight projects. Langley picked up a lot of work as a result. We also worked hard to bring new technology projects to the Center which were focused on the return to the moon and on to Mars programs. These were great additions. We soon found enough work to survive the first budget cut. I knew that we weren't out of the woods yet. I needed to do a lot more to make us nimble enough to not just survive, but thrive.

Improve Your Self

I have had a lot of leadership training, given my time at the United States Air Force Academy, professional-development training during my 31-year Air Force career, and several specialty training courses that I attended, such as the Deming Management Method. I didn't think that I needed any other leadership training until I attended the Learning As Leadership seminars while at NASA's Langley Research Center (LaRC).

That was an eye-opening experience. It not only helped me adopt a more effective leadership style for working with scientists and researchers in my workforce at LaRC, but it even helped me be a better husband, father, and grandfather. It also played a critically important role in jelling the entire leadership team that excelled under the most severe circumstances.

Basically, it gave me insight into how my very direct management style was often not effective and could shut down communications with my leadership team and inhibit many from expressing their issues with me. This direct style was okay in a military culture but was problematic when dealing with scientists, who tended to be more introverted. By recognizing it as a problem, coming to grips with why I acted that way, and recognizing triggers that tended to make me react in this way, I was able to change my management style. It helped me hear and understand issues and problems that were troubling my people so that I could undertake corrective actions across the organization. It also gave me techniques to change and avoid sliding back into bad habits.

Build the Senior Leadership Team

I had been successful at KSC by approaching challenges strategically. At our first leadership retreat at Langley, we all got on the same page about our strengths and areas where we needed to improve. We began to build a road map to achieve future successes. We had many other off-site leadership retreats to keep everyone engaged as well as to adjust to the changing external environment.

After I had heard all of the inputs from the participants, we took a break and I summarized the main points on large flip charts. I presented this to the team, and they agreed with my summary and that was the beginning of our road map.

As I was preparing to depart the retreat, I ran into Langley's chief scientist. I asked him what he thought of the summary that I had presented. "It was the best example of leadership excellence that I have ever witnessed," he said. I was humbled by his remark. Now all we had to do was implement it and as quickly as possible. That would be the true test of my leadership and the team.

The leadership team decided that we needed to reorganize the Center to focus on our strengths and the new direction for NASA. I realized that our most senior leaders needed a dose of new blood. Those at the highest rank, Senior Executive Service (SES), acted like they had jobs for life. I needed them to feel some of the pain that people working for them were feeling. Also, we didn't need as many SESs, which would save us some budget dollars in the long run.

I convened a meeting with them in September 2004 and told them they would have to compete for an SES position in the new organization, and there would be fewer slots than we currently had. Each of them would be allowed to compete for three of the new positions.

I invited the Office of Personnel Management to approve our selection process. I also asked them to set up a leadership assessment exercise to score each applicant on their leadership capabilities.

In addition to the selection board, I interviewed each of them for a different reason. I asked them to tell me which positions at the next level under SES they would like if they weren't successful in winning one of the SES positions. No one would lose pay, just prestige.

We stood up the new organization and announced the winners of the SES competition in October 2004 at a senior leadership retreat.

Quite a few people were upset with me. That was understandable, as we had several disappointed leaders. The amazing thing was that, before I retired from the Center, several of them told me that the change was the best thing that had ever happened to them because they felt reinvigorated by their new duties.

We hit bottom in February 2005 when the president's new budget was announced. We suffered another budget cut of $300 million. Such a drastic cut would most likely require a reduction in force.

Now people were really scared.

Build the Leaders' Skills

We held another senior leadership retreat to create the Center Transformation Project to address the budget cuts. When I briefed him, the NASA Administrator gave it his gold star award.

We also started a major leadership development project that was instrumental in the eventual success of our transformation.

I stumbled into this leadership development training, Learning as Leadership, when the head of our research organization, who reported to me directly, asked permission to take his seven direct reports to a leadership training program in California for ten days in November 2003. He said that they weren't working well as a team, and he had talked to someone who had attended Learning as Leadership with great results. Despite the time and expense, I gave my approval. When they returned, I interviewed the participants. All but one described the training as life-changing. The other one refused to go to the remaining three seminars because he described it as a cult religion.

I decided to attend the next offering in March 2004 to see for myself. It fell into the category of life-changing. Despite my years of leadership training and experiences during my Air Force and NASA careers, I discovered that my leadership style, which had been effective in those operational organizations, was not as effective in a research organization like Langley. In an operational organization, people expected the leader to be direct. At Langley, I joked that you could tell the extroverted scientists because they looked at my feet when they were talking to me instead of their own feet. To say that they were inhibited by my direct style was a gross understatement. The training helped me to recognize my behaviors that were not effective and to reinvent my leadership style to be effective in a research organization. I also had the advantage of frequent coaching calls that kept me informed of what others were seeing in my behaviors so that I could correct any issues immediately.

We expanded the group of attendees to include all of those who reported directly to me. Over the course of the four seminars during the year, we jelled as a team and were able to select and fully engage with effective long-term strategies that proved to be highly successful.

Later, we brought the same leadership training to the Center and offered it to the next several levels of management. It made a huge difference in the overall performance of the Center.

Turn the Leadership Team Loose

Our leadership team became a team of entrepreneurs. The Kick-Start Teams that we had created developed into effective marketing organizations and began to bring new work to the Center. The new NASA Administrator, who arrived in 2005, made a wise decision to have healthy NASA Centers as opposed to paying for the new Constellation Program, an early part of the Vision for Space Exploration (which was eventually canceled) out of the Aeronautical Research Centers' budgets. He basically reversed the cutting of our budget to the degree that it had been done under previous leadership and restored a lot of that money by more equitably engaging the Center in new work. So, we did not have to have those draconian workforce reduction programs that it looked like we were going to have to pursue. We picked up a lot of new work for the exploration program, just as we had done to help the Space Shuttle Program Return to Flight. Things began to improve rapidly. The future looked bright.

Engage the Workforce

As I mentioned earlier, we discovered that another serious culture problem at Langley was widespread use of fear of retaliation as a management technique. To help cure this problem, in addition to the leadership training and selection of new leaders, I tried an unusual experiment.

I created a position called the Center Ombuds, which people could access if they wanted an issue worked anonymously. I also set up a special small seminar that I called "Can We Speak." These were held in small, remote conference rooms to provide some extra privacy. People could access a website to reserve a space. I would meet with the group as the only manager in attendance. The ground rule was that I would listen. I promised not to expose anyone publicly or any issue that was raised unless the person wanted me to work it with them. If they wanted to have it worked anonymously, I referred them to the Center Ombuds.

What I heard at these sessions was amazing. It gave me an excellent grounding on what was going on in the workforce. While I didn't identify anyone who brought up an issue, it made me much more aware of budding problems so that I could discuss them in general with our leadership team and develop broad solutions.

Tim's View ... You Are Never Done

(Note: I was not directly supporting Roy in this case and I am reflecting on the journey he led the organization through.)

This case is a reminder that all transformations at a macro level carry some common elements:

- Leadership presence
- Systematic change
- Change management.

This case brings out an important lesson learned about leadership. I believe that leadership is the hardest, least thanked, and loneliest position in an organization. It is also the most important role. Your transformational leadership role will be pushing the organization and its leaders to do things it may not know how to or want to do. You will be challenging your leadership team. You will need to manage stakeholders that may be pushing their own agenda. You will need to make the hard decisions: remember, the easy decisions don't come to the boss ... only the hard ones. As I said, leadership is the most important role. You are here at this time and place for a reason. Roy was here at that time and place for a reason. He was able to bring his past experiences to guide another organization through a transformational journey. As the leader, you will also need to adjust your leadership style as Roy did. He took the time to learn about himself, his leadership style, and his team. This investment enabled him to work with his team to drive fundamental changes in the organization. You may need to adjust your style to fit the transformational situation and team.

This case also reminds us that we need both a systematic change approach and a change management approach for the transformation. In this case, Roy worked both of these approaches. For the systematic change approach, Roy had to

- recognize the need to change;
- set a compelling vision to inspire the workforce, and see the need to change from a positive perspective;
- find the unique ways the organization can be relevant going forward;
- engage stakeholders continuously, and deal with stakeholders that were not always as supportive as he wished they would be.

The systematic change in this case was driven by a compelling reason to change that was both negative (i.e., the need to downsize) and positive (i.e., the opportunity to be part of the Vision for Space Exploration). You will need to help your team and workforce see both sides of the need to change. The negative points to what needs to be improved. The positive points to the hope for the future. You will need to provide both perspectives.

For the change management approach, Roy focused on building a mentality of continuous working of the transformation. He knew better than to assume he and his team were done when they solved one or two problems. The problems would continue to emerge. You will need to know this and instill in your team that they will be in a continuous cycle of seeing the symptom, finding the root cause, taking action, reflecting on the results, making adjustments, and working the next problem. The leadership team is in a never-ending problem-solving cycle.

Remember, this case brings out an important lesson learned about leadership: Leadership is the hardest, least thanked, and loneliest position in an organization. It is also the most important role. You got this.

Case study #3

Leadership Presence Makes the Difference: NSTec Transformation

Roy's View ... Digging for Root Causes After a Really Bad Day

See the Need for Change

After retiring from NASA at the end of 2005, I accepted a job offer to be a director at Northrop Grumman in their government services sector. After a short time with them, I became a director of one of their business units. One of the contracts that we won was as the managing partner in a limited liability company named National Security Technologies (NSTec) that operated the Nevada Test Site (NTS), now called the Nevada National Security Site (NNSS), for the Department of Energy's National Nuclear Security Administration (NNSA) in Nevada.

NNSS is run as a government-owned, company-operated entity. NSTec had approximately 2500 employees to run a very large site 65 miles northwest of Las Vegas in a remote area. NNSS was the site of our nuclear weapons tests aboveground from 1951 until 1963, when a test ban treaty was signed with the Soviet Union. Testing continued underground until all full-scale testing was stopped by treaty with Russia and France in 1992. From the beginning of testing until the treaty in 1992, NNSS completed a total of 828 underground tests and 100 above-ground tests.

It continues to do a lot of scientific testing of materials and components of nuclear weapons as well as other hazardous tests of things such as chemicals used by terrorists around the world. It also operates the Remote Sensing Laboratory, which has capabilities to respond to emergencies in support of counterterrorism and radiological incidents. There are many interesting facilities supporting the mission, such as a test facility 963 feet below ground.

My role at the NNSS initially was as the chair of the Parent Organization Oversight Committee , which performed approximately six in-depth technical and safety reviews each year and reported the results to the company, Board of Managers, and the federal field office overseeing the contract.

Be Present and Listen

In the spring and summer of 2014, NSTec experienced several minor safety incidents and one major incident with injuries to a worker. This was a really bad day for the company, and the federal oversight team threatened to terminate the contract. My boss asked me to lead a team to do a deep dive and develop a plan to eliminate the root causes.

I formed an eight-person team, and we traveled to North Las Vegas, set up shop in a spacious conference room, and began work. Over the next two months, we dug up the underlying root causes and created a long-term get-well plan to achieve and sustain a culture of operational excellence. We called the plan the Five Pillars of Operational Excellence. It included detailed strategies to make large improvements in the five areas. After out-briefing the company leadership and our board of managers, I returned to my home and office in Colorado and resumed my day job.

Unfortunately, during subsequent trips by a smaller team and me to observe progress, we concluded that the company was moving far too slowly in implementing the changes that we had recommended. My boss was extremely concerned, as we were on the verge of re-competing the ten-year contract and a good reputation was crucial to winning it again. He decided to create a new position, Vice President for Strategic Management, and asked me to commute to Nevada to fill the position and get the company moving in the right direction faster.

Sustain the Changes

Initially, the NSTec leadership was a little wary of my role in the company and of me. But they soon warmed up to me, and we began to make real progress. The company appointed top-level managers for each of the five pillars, and I met with them weekly to review the implementation of the plans. We also had frequent communications to all levels of the company on what we were doing, why we were doing it, and progress.

I thought that I would be able to return to my day job after a few months, but, alas, that wasn't to be. Near the end of 2015, the president of NSTec retired, and we began a leadership shuffle. I was asked to become the Vice President for Operations, which would also include my duties from my previous position as Vice President for Strategic Management.

Build the Leadership Team

Over the next two years, the company made rapid improvements and achieved the highest award fee score in the complex during our last performance period. I convinced all the company's top leaders to attend the leadership training at the same company, Learning As Leadership (LaL), that I had used at NASA Langley. I was even able to convince the federal customer leaders to attend. After training the senior leaders, we had the company bring training on-site for the next level of company and federal management. The improvement in leadership resulted in an impressive increase in employee engagement, measured by annual surveys.

LaL Training

The effects LaL training had on this transformation and its participants are further detailed in Case Study #4: Changes in Behaviors of Key Persons in Case Study 3 Following LaL Training on page 264.

LaL developed a case study of the improvement in leadership in the company as well as between the company and the federal customer team. They changed the names of all the players in the study so that it could be used to illustrate the dramatic good changes in behaviors that are possible with other clients. The study was created using inputs from the trainers based on interactions at the seminars as well as the extensive follow-up coaching calls with all of the participants.

Engage the Workforce

Measuring employee engagement was a best practice that I imported from Northrop Grumman. Basically, we used the Gallup Survey to measure the percentage of employees who were engaged. We taught managers and supervisors how to make changes to improve engagement, as companies with more engaged employees demonstrated better results in all categories such as safety and quality.

When the contract was competed after 10 years, which was normal, we fielded a strong team for the competition of the contract and wrote a good proposal. We didn't win. Perhaps we asked for too much fee, since our proposal was graded well in all other areas. Our contract ended on November 30, 2017. The good news was that I could stop commuting to Las Vegas every other week and spend more time at home.

Clearly the new contractor inherited a strong leadership team at all levels because of our leadership training and our focus on operational excellence and employee engagement. The NNSA Administrator awarded me his highest award, the Distinguished Service Gold Medal. I had to lead the transition to the new contract and team, and our people did a great job. We finished strong.

Tim's View...Leadership Presence is Key

(Note: I was not directly supporting Roy in this case and I am reflecting on the journey he led the organization through.)

This case is a reminder that all successful transformations at a macro level carry some common elements:

- Leadership presence and listening
- Sustaining changes
- Building the leadership team.

Be Present & Listen

One of the common elements is leadership presence to (1) see the need to change, (2) drive to find the core issues/root causes, (3) drive action, and (4) hold people accountable for making changes. Your role in leading the team is to bring your presence to your team and to build a relationship with them. Roy again drew on his experiences to lead an organization through a transformation. He provided the presence and perspective to guide the organization in seeing a new way to operate. He laid the foundation for fundamental culture change.

Sustain the Changes

The intent of transformations is to not just "Band-Aid" the symptoms. You need to lead the organization through solving the deep root causes. You will need to provide the leadership presence to enable or invite the team to do deep-dive analysis. Your organization may not know how to or want to do this analysis. Your presence will be needed to drive them to do this. Roy's presence enabled the team to take the time and space to make systematic change. He led the team in gathering the right performance data and used that data to understand the root causes. Once the root causes are identified, you will need to lead the team in making the necessary changes to find and then eliminate the problems impacting your organization's performance.

Roy had the team develop an individual action plan for each of the Five Pillars of Operational Excellence:

1. Management Engagement and Communications Process Improvement
2. Safety/Quality Prioritization and Hazard Identification
3. Management Focus and Integration of Programs and Operations Process Improvement
4. Enterprise Work Management, Planning, and Control Process Improvement
5. Issues Management & Continuous Improvement.

Each of these pillar action plans provided solutions to the systemic root causes. Furthermore, the leaders/participants of these five teams had to personally sign their action plans. Roy was driving personal accountability for the change. You will need to drive and hold your team accountable for making the needed changes.

Build the Leadership Team

Remember, Roy again "parachuted" into the organization. He needed to be trusted by this new team to enable the above transformation activities. Roy had to connect with the leadership team. As you come into the organization or leadership role for the transformation, you will need to build relationship with your leadership team. They will need to trust you. You will need to trust them. This takes time and will be tested as your team works through tough challenges. The investment in team building will pay off.

Case Study #4

Changes in Behaviors of Key Persons in Case Study 3 Following LaL Training

Originally "Cultural Transformation and Performance Improvement at a High Hazard, Contractor-run DOE site"

—Courtesy of Learning as Leadership

All names have been changed. Intended as a supplement Case Study to *Ego Free Leadership: Ending the Unconscious Habits that Hijack your Business.*

The Problem: Daunting Challenges and Poor Performance

In 2012, a managing and operating contractor running a major national security site for the Department of Energy faced daunting challenges. The complex—larger than the state of Rhode Island—was one of the biggest weapons testing facilities in the country, with over 2,000 employees and a government contract worth $500 million per year.

Like most government contractors, the company was facing pressure to reduce costs and remedy a litany of safety concerns, all while operating within a tight time frame and conforming to stringent government regulations.

Operational improvements, however, were stymied by conflicts between key programs and divisions that were supposed to collaborate on highly complex and hazardous projects. According to John Hall*, Vice President of Operations, the atmosphere had become toxic to the point of dysfunction. "Directors just did not like each other," says John. "They were only interested in taking care of their own departments. And honestly, I was among them."

Although each leader wanted the organizational culture to improve, it had been this way for as long as they could remember. "Historically, the organization was very stove piped, with little cooperation taking place beyond the boundaries of each silo," explains Rob Miller*, a senior VP who had joined the client from its parent company, Northrop Grumman, after careers with the US Air Force and NASA. "The operating site was created forty years ago by rolling three different contractors into one company, and it never really integrated them."

Tasked with carrying out highly critical government programs, including testing new technologies to detect weapons of mass destruction and safely maintaining national stockpiles of nuclear weapons, each program director ran his or her department with little cooperation between divisions: all while struggling to meet cost controls, deadlines, and profit margins.

This lack of collaboration made the organization more expensive to run: unshared resources caused redundancies in personnel, and fighting over budgets made it difficult to invest strategically for the larger enterprise. When issues arose, finger pointing slowed down process improvements and productivity— sometimes to a complete halt.

John recalls a particularly dysfunctional relationship between the director of Operations and Infrastructure and the director of Global Security, one of the site's two major programs. "They weren't speaking to each other," says John, "and their lack of coordination affected everything. Projects weren't getting done on time, or within budget. Sometimes they failed to cooperate entirely, which meant experiments didn't get completed and data went uncollected. We were failing the mission."

At one point, a key facility had to halt productions entirely because they were unable to maintain minimum quality standards.

In addition to issues *within* the company, the organization was also entangled in a long-standing conflict with its government oversight organization. The company operated under strict surveillance by the Department of Energy, where the manager of their field office, Pete Patterson*, had become aggravated by the poor performance.

"The two organizations were at total odds with each other," says John. "We believed Pete and the government were creating unnecessary work for us, while they were convinced that we were doing the bare minimum to make a buck.

"Nobody was focused on the mission."

The Intervention: Working on "Ego"-Driven Behaviors

Vice President Rob Miller was a senior executive on loan from the contractor's parent company, Northrup Grumman. A veteran experienced in running large government contracts, Rob was no stranger to infighting and tense relationships with headquarter organizations. Fortunately, he also knew these dynamics could change.

In his previous role leading a NASA Aeronautics Center, Rob had faced similar personnel challenges, and recalled going through a program that had helped his executive team to work more cohesively. When industry veteran David Jenkins* was brought in as a new CEO, and communication continued to deteriorate, Rob suggested that the team reach out to this company, Learning as Leadership (LaL).

John Hall thought it would be a waste of time. As a veteran executive of the national security industry, punitive micro-management from a government counterpart was an expected part of the job. There was no changing that. In particular, John held a negative view of NFO manager, Pete Patterson.

"I thought Pete was incredibly close-minded," recalls John. "He always needed to be in charge, didn't want to listen, and dictated exactly how he thought things should be done. Whenever a mistake occurred, he became angry and vindictive."

The relationship was so distant that Pete recalls John later telling him, "I thought you were the devil."

John, Rob and Pete, along with CEO, David Jenkins, were part of a five-person executive team that attended LaL's one-year program as a pilot.

The 360° feedback process and rigorous seminar methodology provided a crucial window for the team to examine their own leadership tendencies. Rather than focusing on what the other leaders were doing wrong, they were encouraged to identify how their own fears and unchecked assumptions were causing them to lash out or shut down, thus blocking productive communication.

They learned to speak in a frank, non-confrontational way, about the beliefs and judgments they held about each other, as well as the mission critical operational issues they had struggled to resolve. They mapped out how their behaviors were negatively affecting performance and the broader organization.

"All of us, but Pete and I in particular, dove into delicate topics, that in my 30 years working in the national lab complex, I had never seen discussed," recalls John. "Until going through LaL, I would have never thought it was possible."

As often is the case in conflict situations, each executive saw the other in simplistic and one-dimensional terms. "I'm a very technical person," explains John. "I'm deeply involved in the intricacies of the programs we run here at the site. I saw Pete as a compliance person who only cared about checking boxes." Pete, meanwhile, viewed John as overly-focused on driving revenue, and not caring about quality.

A major issue they surfaced was how the contractor leadership team operated in fear of retribution from Pete. "We didn't want to surface issues because we didn't trust him to respond reasonably," recalls the CEO David Jenkins. "Meanwhile, he operated in a 'gotcha' mode, because he didn't trust us to surface issues."

The team put their charged perspectives on the table, sometimes realizing they were false, at others honing them into important feedback that had never really been delivered. The leaders were able to see that while each of them had a different style of interacting, they all cared deeply about the overall mission. This sense of alignment opened up a new set of possibilities.

"That engagement," Pete says, "set John and I on a new path toward understanding each other. We finally saw that we were both trying to achieve the same goal, but using a different focus. Moreover, LaL challenged each of us to acknowledge how we were contributing to the problem, and that no progress could be made until we started changing ourselves."

Today, their relationship has shifted dramatically. "Much to my surprise, Pete actually changed his management style," admits John. "Now, he and I can talk about anything regardless of the issue, which has been a tremendous advantage for the organization."

For Pete, the difference has also been transformational. "Today, when we have a conversation on a sensitive topic," says Pete, "I no longer have negative reactions. John and I have positive dialogues where we're both focused on trying to work things out. Before, I was just focused on pushing my own agenda."

The Outcome: Improved Safety, Productivity, and Profit

Although rigorous oversight by DOE was non-negotiable, the strained interpersonal dynamics made everything slow-moving and costly. When Pete and John began having healthier interactions, it quickly impacted outcomes in multiple areas of the company.

Nuclear Safety was one such program. "Nuclear safety is a complex function on which we spend millions of dollars every year," explains John. Responsible for providing safety analysis for nuclear operations, the area is so complex that the contractor produces a 1,200-page report each year detailing and assessing levels of hazardous risk.

Typically the company would devote extensive resources to developing this report, only to have the DOE oversight team tell them that "everything was wrong." The contractor would then re-do the report three, four, sometimes more, times. The whole process was expensive, time-consuming, and a source of bitter animosity for both organizations.

"The federal side was not specific with us about their expectations for the nuclear safety documents," explains John. "We would do the work, hand it to them for approval, and they would throw it back in our faces, telling us that we were incompetent."

Pete and his colleagues, on the other hand, saw the situation differently. "We would give them feedback, they would go back and work for a while, and then give us something that didn't take into account anything we had said," Pete recounts. "It was aggravating." When he and John met to discuss nuclear safety, Pete experienced John's questions and issues as complaining: "Finally, I'd just tell him, 'I'm the Federal Senior Manager. I don't care what you think. Here's what you need to do.' It was a very unproductive relationship."

While this level of interpersonal dysfunction may seem extreme to an outsider, it is quite pervasive in public and private sector leadership. Both John and Pete saw the other person as incompetent and/or ill-intended, and solely responsible for the gridlock. Neither could recognize that their negative beliefs about the other were causing them to behave in ways that provoked the very actions they most criticized. This is a central characteristic of "self-fulfilling prophecies," in which leaders, teams, and even entire departments blame the "other side" for problems they have both created. When a leader has partners, customers, or peers who "just don't get it," chances are, he or she is unconsciously perpetuating one of the many disruptive cultural dysfunctions that can undermine performance.

As John and Pete acknowledged and worked through their beliefs about each other, they began to communicate more effectively. Issues that used to take them months to resolve, and thousands of dollars to "do over," began to be handled in a matter of days.

Today, before the client even runs its report, the two men sit down to discuss expectations and potential areas of discrepancy. As a result, the nuclear safety function operates on a more timely and productive schedule, thus requiring less costly oversight. "Now that we understand what their perspective is ahead of time," explains John. "The whole process is much more efficient. And, the end product is better."

The Shift: From "I want to Win!" to "How Can I Help?"

Equally critical to a government contractor's performance are its internal relationships between program directors and the employees they manage. At this M&O contractor, no one had a reputation for being more impossible to work for than deputy director Rick Moranis*.

Among his colleagues, the impressions of Rick were almost universally negative. "Rick was a leader who ran you over," recalls Mary Black*, a deputy who oversaw the nuclear stock pile, and was a peer of Rick. "He always had to be right, and wanted to prove that he was in charge. I don't think he ever partnered with anybody. He told us what he needed, when he needed it, and expected you to get it done exactly how he wanted it done."

Before coming to LaL, Rick was oblivious to how his style was impacting others. "If there was trouble, I was the guy who would fix it," Rick recalls. "I always got the job done, and I didn't much care about the effect I had on anyone around me."

Fallout from Rick's authoritative management style included a revolving door of employees who worked for him. "I gave people very little flexibility about how to get things done," admits Rick. "If you didn't do something exactly how I wanted it, or if you didn't work the hours that I worked, I simply turned you out of my projects." When people operate in this manner, they may produce an impressive amount of work themselves as individual contributors, but as leaders they also generate a lot of unengaged and unhappy associates, as well as high rates of employee turnover.

> According to The Gallup Organization, employee engagement has a direct correlation to a business' bottom line. In one study, Gallup examined 49 publicly traded companies from 2008-2012, finding that businesses with a critical mass of engaged employees significantly out- performed their competition, in terms of earnings per share.
>
> The research studied the differences in performance between engaged and actively disengaged work units and found that those scoring in the top half of employee engagement nearly *doubled* their odds of success, compared with those in the bottom half. Those in the 99th percentile had *four times* the success rate of those in the first percentile.

The Takeaway: The Importance of Engaging Employees

"I knew intellectually that not allowing others to have a say creates an unsustainable environment where people don't feel engaged in their work," explains Rick. "But I hadn't ever really examined *how* I was shutting others down."

Rick had always justified his abrasive behavior as an unavoidable cost of being results-oriented. At LaL, Rick learned to question this assumption, and found that his leadership style actually derived from a long pattern of learned behaviors, driven in large part by his own need to appear strong, competent, and in control. He so dreaded feeling or appearing weak or incompetent that, whenever his self-image was threatened by circumstances or colleagues who disagreed with him, he overpowered them using force and control tactics. While he had long believed that his "hard edge" was a key part of his success as a leader, he began to realize that exactly the opposite of this was true: his fear of appearing incompetent was holding him back.

The first major impact LaL had on Rick came from his 360° feedback. The feedback—which included comprehensive input from numerous colleagues, as well as from his wife—was a major revelation. It opened his eyes to hear how his ego-driven behaviors were also impacting his personal life. Because of his intense desire to get his vacation "right," his kids had begun referring to him as the "Vacation Nazi." As he began to connect the dots between his personal and professional life, Rick could suddenly see the damaging effects of his behavior.

At work, his reports were disengaged and afraid of him while his peers avoided him and assumed he had ill intent. His behavior, intended to achieve success, was undermining his organization's performance.

"It was deeply impactful to hear from a third-party person," says Rick, "the specific, personal costs of how I behaved. It was a turning point for me."

Rick emerged from his LaL seminar with a new awareness. He began treating people who worked alongside him and underneath him differently. He listened more carefully to his coworkers, especially when they disagreed with him. He admitted when he felt vulnerable about his competence or position, thus revealing a humanity his colleagues didn't think he had. He took in their opinions, and allowed them to come up with their own solutions.

VP John Hall supervised Rick and witnessed this transformation up close. "I saw Rick change his entire style," shares John. "He completely altered the way he interacted with others."

Upon noticing the changes, one employee admitted to Rick, "When I heard I had to work for you, I cringed and started looking for a new job. All I knew about you was the Rick of yesterday. Today, you are nothing like that. You don't carry a hammer with you anymore, and you've given me the opportunity to run my organization."

Rick always had a reputation as a powerhouse, but with the perspective gained at LaL, he learned to use his strong will and determination to empower and enable his team. No longer exclusively concerned with looking out for himself, Rick worked to ensure that *everyone* came out on top. Rather than just driving results for just his organization, he now operates with the entire enterprise in mind.

The changes in Rick's management style were so apparent, he was later promoted to Director of Operations and Infrastructure, a position in which he manages close to half the workforce.

"Rick is in a role that fits him to a T," says Mary. "He's a functional manager who provides operations and infrastructure support that enables all of us to pursue our missions. He often comes into my office, asking, 'What can I do to help you?' He knows what his role is, and he executes it well."

The Goal: One Mission—One Organization

At the site, each deputy works beneath a director, who heads up a division. Because directors usually interact with clients in the capitol, it is often the deputies who manage operations and interact with people across the company.

In her role as a deputy, Mary Black had the challenging task of ensuring that the nation's nuclear weapons stockpile remained safe and secure. With a large organization of technical experts spread over remote locations, her work required close collaboration with other departments to facilitate the movement and hiring of staff resources.

To her dismay, Mary frequently experienced other deputies as being "oppositional," when it came to responding to her department's needs. Rather than receiving help, she perceived her colleagues as pushing back against her: citing rules, regulations, and their department's own priorities as reasons to avoid cooperation. Widespread distrust between the deputies and their respective organizations existed for years, even decades, making progress on improving operations nearly impossible.

Having witnessed significant breakthroughs in different pockets of the organization, CEO David Jenkins decided to bring all the company's deputies to the same LaL team-building seminar that he, John, Pete, and Rob had completed several years earlier. He felt that incremental improvement was not sufficient to achieve his vision of operational excellence at the site. He wanted to create a step function change in the cultural dynamics across their organization.

Rick vividly recalls the five deputies, before the seminar, as a pretty dysfunctional group. "We had very distinct opinions of one another," says Rick, "and we each felt that the others were self-motivated, self-interested, and working only for their own gains, rather than the gains of the organization."

With some reluctance, the deputies examined their ego triggers, raised issues honestly with each other, analyzed their strengths and weaknesses, and gave each other feedback.

Mary clearly recalls an exercise in which they openly told one another where they needed to improve. "I typically take on a lot of responsibility," she recalls, "and sometimes I fall short in following through on commitments." She had always thought it was no big deal, just a necessary byproduct of being results-driven and over-committed. But when she heard her teammates share how her behavior was directly affecting them and the company's goals, it stopped her short.

With the help of her colleagues, Mary was able to see how her desire to feel "needed" and successful was causing her to be unrealistic, and then let other people down. In turn, she was able to offer feedback to her colleagues about their own flaws. For the first time, she felt the input was received in an unguarded and self-reflective way.

The team saw that they each feared being judged, and their defensive tendencies in turn contributed to the lack of openness. Though uncomfortable at times, they surfaced the specific reasons they distrusted each other, and examined how it was hurting the broader organization.

Clearing up the sources of their tension and misalignment was inspiring, and the team rallied around why they had come to work for the client organization in the first place. *One of the unfortunate consequences of ego-driven workplace dysfunction is that jockeying for power, control or acknowledgment causes an organization's mission and purpose take a back seat.*

The team of deputies committed to reversing this trend, re-prioritizing the organization and its mission over their own personal gains. They also agreed to address issues directly with each other, rather than letting problems fester by assuming the other had ill intent, or lapsing into conflict avoidance.

"We made commitments to each other that we wouldn't do it alone," recalls Mary. "We pledged to have weekly conversations to support one another." That made all the difference.

A New Cohesive Culture

"When our deputies returned from LaL," recalls John Hall, "it was clear they were committed to interacting differently. They began to work out problems that the directors above them couldn't resolve."

As the deputies became more cohesive, they built a new wall of accountability and teamwork that had ripple effects on the core cultural dynamics and performance of the company at large.

Their success at solving problems went quicker and deeper than that of senior management. "They would make things happen without any friction or delay," recalls John. "After decades of silos and gridlock at this site, they began breaking down barriers, and performance took off."

Within one year of completing the course, each of the five deputies was promoted to director level. "It was pretty extraordinary," says John. "I've never seen five deputies get promoted to senior management all at once. I'm convinced that LaL gave them the insight, ability, and opportunity to come together and form a team that supported each other in leading change, even when their bosses weren't interacting. In the end, they were promoted because they were the ones demonstrating the leadership the organization needed."

"When we had a reorganization and were promoted to directors," says Mary, "All of the work we had done making commitments to each other set the foundation for how we interacted as a senior management team."

Executives recall how different the company felt almost overnight when the leadership team changed. "Many of us commented on it," says Rob. "You went into a meeting with senior management, and all the tension and stress were gone from the room. It really felt like 'gosh, people are enjoying coming to work again'."

At the same time the deputies were promoted, John Hall became the new CEO of the company. He also noticed the change. "In my 30 years of work in the nuclear industry, this is the highest-performing team I've ever been a part of," he shares. "Not because I'm president—but because of all the work we've done on our beliefs, behaviors, and relationships."

The new positive management culture rippled throughout the organization, continuing to improve the company's performance ratings by DOE. "Experiments were being completed on-budget and on-schedule," recalls John. "We had better performance and we better understood our cost factors. We could identify stumbling blocks in a project's execution, as well as who (or what) was really making things happen. Our alignment as a team allowed us to make adjustments and move people around to the greatest benefit for our customers. Everything has improved, from performance to safety to security to how we comply with all requirements."

Turning Around a Company in More Ways Than One

Between 2012-2015, close to one hundred executives and middle managers from the contractor and oversight organizations participated in LaL leadership and culture change programs. The majority received a 360° feedback, as well as attending multiple leadership seminars. Many attended reluctantly, convinced it would be a waste of their time. "How could a workshop possibly improve communication between people who disliked each other so intensely?" they wondered.

The improvements the contractor made affected both its people and its bottom line. Here's how:

- Improved Gallup Employee Engagement – the percentage of engaged employees *increased by 70%*, while the number of not engaged and actively disengaged employees fell by 18% and 43%, respectively.
- Increased Profit – By communicating more effectively with its Federal Oversight organization, the client completed projects more quickly— without having to redo reports numerous times to satisfy the field office.
- Higher Quality Work —"Our Planning is better, Quality is better, packages work better. It's made it easier for the program directors to actually get the work done." John Hall, CEO
- Reduction in Safety Incidents — The client has improved its ability to meet federal safety standards while reducing the rate of safety violations. Timeouts increased by 76% from 2012 to 2016.
- Improved Productivity – When a company is dysfunctional, cross-organizational issues often get stalled, shutting down operations. When organizations begin to collaborate across silos, problems are ironed out more quickly, and productivity increases. "We've never been so busy, and are getting more work done with the same number of employees. More time is spent devoted to the mission." John Hall
- Pooling Resources—In the "old" organization, people rarely moved between divisions. "Now we move people around regardless of who they work for. We'll move them to a different organization to support the other organization, when they need to even though it may have some impacts to the original organization." John Hall
- DOE Performance Rating—In fiscal year 2016, the organization was rated the top performing, high hazard site in the complex. In FY 2017, the client was rated "Excellent" in all 6 areas of performance evaluation and were scored 100% in two areas: Science, Technology and Engineering; and Leadership. "I have never heard of any organization receiving a 100% PEMP rating, much less two." John Hall

Learning to Strengthen a New Muscle

As the organization continues to make unprecedented improvements in performance and employee satisfaction, they are also quick to admit that it's an ongoing process. When executives temporarily forget their common goals, as they inevitably do, shares Mary, they have built-in mechanisms to remind them that their primary goal is to support one another.

On the federal government's side, Pete Patterson believes the time spent improving communications has been well worth the effort. "There's a more stable mission now at the site, and it's growing by leaps and bounds, which is good for the entire workforce," says Pete.

The organization has since achieved one of their biggest goals coming into LaL, which was to create a new, and more functional, governance model in its relationship with the Federal Government. "The relationship with our contract partners has improved significantly," says Pete. "The work we did with LaL helped each of our organizations to stop using how we fought with the other to not do the work we each needed to accomplish. They began addressing their internal problems, and I began addressing those in the oversight organization."

LaL's leadership training, coaching and consulting allowed the contractor and the DOE oversight organization to come together and embrace a shared mission, for the first time in in its 40-year history. "Working together as a united site leadership team," says Pete, "is the way we *should* do business."

Acknowledgments

From Roy

Achieving successes in transforming organizations as presented in the case studies in this book all depended on the amazing employees and consultants who participated in making necessary changes while getting the day job done, day after day. I salute and thank all who served with me during those difficult times. Because of your contributions we made the progress needed to make each of them successful in the short and long term.

I want to thank Tim Kotnour for his expert help in transforming KSC during my tenure and documenting the success in his book, *Transforming Organizations: Strategies and Methods*, and now in this book. I think his expertise will be of great assistance to other leaders who face situations demanding a transformation, and I am happy to be of support in that quest. Tim remained closely connected with KSC after my tenure and has played a key role in KSC's continued success over the years to today.

What I learned from Tim at KSC helped me be successful with transformations presented in the case studies for NESC, LaRC, and NSTec. I also want to single out others who were key to the success of these other transformations that I led. Ralph Roe was key to the creation and success of the NESC over the years as its first Director. Lesa Roe as my Deputy Center Director at LaRC was a major factor in the success of the transformation during my tenure and beyond as she succeeded me as Center Director. I also want to thank the members of the Learning as Leadership team for playing a major role in helping me with the LaRC and NSTec transformations.

I want to also pay tribute to my late wife, Benita, for her role in raising our kids and supporting me in my rather hazardous career as a fighter pilot, test pilot, and astronaut. She was a wonderful first lady at two USAF commands that I held plus KSC and LaRC. My career was not always as kind to her and my children as I would have liked as we moved many times and often at inconvenient times for them.

From Tim

This book grew out of an ongoing, multi-year partnership between National Aeronautics and Space Administration's (NASA) Kennedy Space Center (KSC). Many KSC individuals have given their time, efforts, energy, and honest opinions throughout the partnership. Without their openness and willingness to learn with each other and the author, the strides in strategic management and this book would not have been possible.

KSC Center Director Roy Bridges provided the freedom and never-ending support for us to truly engage in implementing the strategic management process. His leadership provided us with an on-going challenge—trying to keep the process at the same pace he was setting and following the vision he was building within KSC.

James Jennings provided the reality to our process and efforts, and continued to be the glue that held the organization and strategic management process together. Jim understands the political actions necessary to successfully implement the strategic management process.

Two other people deserve special mention—the KSC Strategic Planning Managers I worked with on a daily basis: Saul Barton and Jenny Lyons. Saul provided the mentorship on how to get things done in the KSC environment. He knows how to "plant the seeds" and nurture them for others to see the results as their own. Jenny Lyons understands the process work to ensure alignment of goals and people. I thank all of them for providing the environment to learn, grow, and achieve.

Finally, I thank my family (Mary Lynn, Jessica, and Andrew). I thank them for their unending support and encouragement. My family reminded me of the significance of our journey. They gave up numerous evenings and weekends as we supported KSC's transformations. I thank them for going on the journey with me.

From both of us:

Many senior managers throughout KSC have provided their thoughts and knowledge about strategic management and NASA/KSC. Without their openness, the strategic management process would not have been successful. A few people deserve special recognition:

KSC Center Director Jay Honeycutt provided the initial support to begin the effort. James Jennings, KSC Deputy Director, provided the initial and continuing support for the strategic management efforts. Several other leaders were instrumental in the success of the KSC transformation.

Dan Goldin, NASA Administrator, allowed KSC to keep the savings from JBOSC in our budget as an incentive to pursue the initiative. That was key to providing the resources to pursue other strategic projects.

Joe Rothenberg, Associate Administrator for Space Flight and Roy's boss, made the decision to transfer the LSP program to KSC, which finally gave KSC a major program.

Governor Jeb Bush and the government of FL were key to the success of the initiative to establish an industrial park and build the Space Experiment Research and Processing Facility as the first building in the park.

We thank all of them for significant contributions to the success of the transformation

We thank the folks who helped prepare this document through their feedback on the content and formatting. Lori Brown and Lisa Norman expertly pushed us to produce a useful document. Artūrs Bremanis expertly made the book more accessible with the formatting and illustration work. If you want a team to encourage you, gently nudge you, push you when you need it, get you to think, and care about your project as much as you do—if you want a team to make you better then this is the team for you. We cannot overstate the difference they made for us. They brought this work to life. Thank you.

For Inquiring Minds... The Details

In this section, we include details that take you deeper into the history of the story and its authors.

Illustration 1.5—Summary of Key KSC Mission Accomplishments

Element	1997	1998-2000	2001-2003
Shuttle Launches per Year	• 1997: 8 • Transition to SFOC	• 1998: 5 (John Glenn Flight) • 1999: 3 • 2000: 5	• 2001: 6 • 2002: 5 • 2003: 1
ISS Elements Integrated and Tested	• 1st of incremental design reviews • Shuttle-Mir phase I • Shuttle docked with Mir • Fabrication of Node 1 and 2 and U.S. lab module • Shuttle-Mir phase • Shuttle-Mir phase I • Node items to KSC Elements delivered to KSC • Z1 Truss • Pressurized Mating Adaptor 3 • Control Moment Gyros • Node 1 (Unity)	• Shuttle-Mir phase I completed • Node I checkout Major assembly • Unity • Z1 Truss • P6 Truss • Logistics support • Elements delivered to KSC • Leonardo Multi-Purpose Logistics Module • Raffaello Multi-Purpose Logistic Module • Quest Joint Airlock • US Laboratory Destiny • Space Station Remote Manipulator System • Truss/Photovoltaic Module Solar Arrays Integrated testing • Multi-Element Integrated Test (MEIT) I completed • Began MEIT-2	Major assembly • Destiny Lab • Robotic Arm • Joint Air Lock • S0 Truss • Mobile Transporter • Mobile Base System • P1 Truss • P6 Solar Arrays • Logistics support Integrated testing • Multi-Element Integrated Test (MEIT) 2 completed
Launch Services Program Launches per Year	• 1997: 5	• 1998: 7 • 1999: 6 • 2000: 6	• 2001: 6 • 2002: 6 • 2003: 6

Element	1997	1998-2000	2001-2003
Technology Devel-opment Efforts	• Focused on enhancements to existing processing equipment	• Cryogenic testbed estab-lished • Latest new addition, the Vapor Containment Facility which is located next to the Space Station Processing Facility. • The Checkout and Launch Control System at the Hypergolic Maintenance Facility was declared operational in a ribbon cutting ceremony. • Construction of Life Sci-ences Research Facility. • The Florida legislature passed a budget that included $30 million for a space research laboratory at KSC and the roads thru the new industrial park. • Advanced Spaceport Technologies Working Group (ASTWG) estab-lished • Advanced Range Tech-nologies Working Group (ARTWG) established	• Presidential Directed Com-mission of the "Future of the US Aerospace Industry "calls for the federal gov't to assume the responsibility for sustaining, modernizing, and providing critical technolo-gies--space launch infrastructure

Illustrations 4.1–4.4: deeper details about KSC's business model changes

Illustration 4.1—Summary of KSC's Operational Business Model Changes

		SFOC Transition	ISS MEIT	LSP Transition
Required Business Model Changes	Situation	Perform more integrated and comprehensive testing of ISS module	Move civil service from the day-to-day hands-on work and move contract management to JSC	Consolidate NASA's Expendable Launch Vehicles (ELV) efforts to KSC
	Business Model Concept Changes	Create new products, services, and methods	Create new methods	Create new products, services, and methods
Business Model Concept Alignment	External Need	Partial	Yes	Yes
	Internal Desire	Yes	Partial	Yes
	Internal Capability	Partial	Partial	Partial
Enablers for Successful Implementation	External Advocacy	Partial	Yes	Yes
	Resources: Dollars	Yes	Yes	Yes
	Resources: Human Capital	Yes	Yes	Yes
	Resources: Time	Yes	Yes	Yes
	Control: Changing Environment	Yes	Yes	Yes
	Control: Ability to Influence the Environment	Partial	Partial	Partial

		SFOC Transition	ISS MEIT	LSP Transition
Summary of Critical Success Factors	Alignment	Partial	Partial	Partial
	Advocacy	Partial	Yes	Yes
	Resources	Yes	Yes	Yes
	Control	Partial	Partial	Partial
Outcome	Short-Term (early 2000s)	SFOC transition successfully made	MEIT successfully completed	LSP transition successfully made
	Long-Term (a 2020 perspective)	ISS remains in orbit KSC continues to support the ISS utilization by processing cargo	The lessons learned on novel approaches for the government to be involved in mission assurance continue to be applied to LSP and the Commercial Crew program	LSP continues to be a vital organization to acquire launch services for NASA LSP lessons learned and people have been transferred to other commercial programs in NASA (e.g., Commercial Crew Program)

Illustration 4.2—Summary of KSC's Operations Business Model Changes

		Office Space for KSC Employees	Industrial Park Outside of KSC Gates
Required Business Model Changes	Situation	Part of the KSC workforce was working in trailers	KSC was looking to invite more partners to the space coast. They needed the ability to be close to KSC without having the security requirements
	Business Model Concept Changes	Create new methods	Create new products, services, and methods
Business Model Concept Alignment	External Need	Partial	Yes
	Internal Desire	Yes	Yes
	Internal Capability	Yes	Yes
Enablers for Successful Implementation	External Advocacy	Yes	Yes
	Resources: Dollars	Partial	Partial
	Resources: Human Capital	N/A	N/A
	Resources: Time	Yes	Yes
	Control: Changing Environment	Partial	Partial
	Control: Ability to Influence the Environment	Partial	Partial
Summary of Critical Success Factors	Alignment	Partial	Partial
	Advocacy	Yes	Yes
	Resources	Partial	Partial
	Control	Partial	Partial
Outcome	Near-Term (early 2000s)	• Built a new building...Operations Support Building 2 that enhanced the working conditions	• Established the Exploration Park
	Long-Term (a 2020 perspective)	• Actively being used for current operations support	• Enables expanded presence for commercial space companies

CCS Master Plan	JBOSC
Develop a long-term master plan for the integrated Cape Canaveral Spaceport (KSC and Cape Canaveral Air Force Station) with industry and government involvement	Establish a joint contract with the Air Force for the institutional or base operation services of KSC and the Cape Canaveral Air Force Station
Create new products, services, and methods	Create new methods
Yes	Yes
Partial	Partial
Partial	Partial
Yes	Yes
Yes	Yes
Yes	Yes
Yes	Yes
Yes	Yes
Partial	Partial
Partial	Partial
Yes	Yes
Yes	Yes
Partial	Partial
• Master plan established	• JBOSC was implemented • JBOSC received recognition from external entities
• KSC continues to take a long-term perspective to the spaceport • After the shuttle, KSC focused on making the spaceport a multi-user spaceport	• KSC continued to adjust the base support contract approaches to reduce cost • Using the lessons learned and outcomes, KSC has transformed itself to be more than government launches; there are significant commercial operations now occurring at KSC

Illustration 4.3—Summary of KSC's Development Business Model Changes

		Spaceport & Range Technologies	Shuttle Upgrades
Required Business Model Changes	Situation	Support design and development of technology to enhance the spaceport's capabilities	Support design and development of technology to enhance the shuttle's capabilities
	Business Model Concept Changes	Create new products, services, and methods	Create new products, services, and methods
Business Model Concept Alignment	External Need	Partial	Partial
	Internal Desire	Partial	Partial
	Internal Capability	Partial	Partial
Enablers for Successful Implementation	External Advocacy	Partial	Partial
	Resources: Dollars	Partial	Partial
	Resources: Human Capital	Partial	Partial
	Resources: Time	No	No
	Control: Changing Environment	Partial	Partial
	Control: Ability to Influence the Environment	Partial	Partial
Summary of Critical Success Factors	Alignment	Partial	Partial
	Advocacy	Partial	Partial
	Resources	Partial	Partial
	Control	Partial	Partial
Outcome	Short-Term (early 2000s)	KSC provided real-time enhancements to the processing… funding was limited	The project was assigned to KSC The project was later cancelled
	Long-Term (a 2020 perspective)	This expertise is recognized as important to the SLS launch. KSC is assigned the Exploration Ground Systems programs to build the infrastructure for processing and launching the SLS	KSC continues to use its launch vehicle expertise to support the development of the SLS and enhancements to the commercial launch services

CLCS	Life-Sciences	ASTWG & ARTWG
Develop new technologies and systems associated with the checkout and launch control system used during testing, countdown, and launch	Conduct life sciences research aligned to NASA and ISS needs	Create a national partnership focused on defining advanced technologies for spaceports and ranges
Create new products, services, and methods	Create new products, services, and methods	Create new products, services, and methods
Partial	Yes	No
Partial	Partial	Partial
Partial	Yes	Partial
Partial	Yes	No
Partial	¥es	Partial
Partial	Yes	Partial
No	Yes	No
Partial	Yes	No
Partial	Partial	No
Partial	Yes	No
Partial	Yes	No
Partial	Yes	Partial
Partial	Yes	No
The project was assigned to KSC The project was later cancelled	Successful in the short term in that KSC received funding and made contributions	The importance of ground operations infrastructure being recognized in VSE
As part of the Exploration Ground Systems program (led by KSC), KSC is developing a new launch control and checkout system for SLS	KSC continues to conduct research and technology development on plant systems. These systems are crucial to a sustainable human presence on the Moon and Mars	This expertise is recognized as important to the SLS launch. KSC is assigned the Exploration Ground Systems programs to build the infrastructure for processing and launching the SLS

Illustration 4.4—Summary of KSC's Enabling Business Model Changes

		Safety Focus	ISO/Business System	Strategic Management Process
Required Business Model Changes	Situation	Safety is a continuous focus area for NASA and KSC	Enhance the KSC strategic and business management systems aligned to ISO 9001 and Baldrige criteria	KSC senior leaders saw the need to lead in a different way
	Business Model Concept Changes	Create new methods	Create new methods	Create new methods
Business Model Concept Alignment	External Need	Yes	Yes	Yes
	Internal Desire	Yes	Partial	Yes
	Internal Capability	Yes	Partial	Yes
Enablers for Successful Implementation	External Advocacy	Yes	Yes	Yes
	Resources: Dollars	Yes	Yes	Yes
	Resources: Human Capital	Yes	Yes	Yes
	Resources: Time	Yes	Yes	Yes
	Control: Changing Environment	Yes	Yes	Yes
	Control: Ability to Influence the Environment	Yes	Partial	Yes
Summary of Critical Success Factors	Alignment	Yes	Yes	Yes
	Advocacy	Yes	Yes	Yes
	Resources	Yes	Yes	Yes
	Control	Yes	Yes	Yes
Outcome	Near-Term (early 2000s)	KSC achieved VPP certification	KSC received ISO 9001 certification	KSC deployed the strategic management process to guide their transformation
	Long-Term (a 2020 perspective)	KSC continues to focus on safety Safety is a core part of the KSC culture	KSC continues to use the business and remains ISO certified	The KSC strategic management process continues today and was transferred to other NASA programs and organizations

Reference List for our original book and other previously published articles about the KSC transformation

- Hacker, Marla E., Tim Kotnour, and Larry A. Mallak. 2001. "Formalizing deployment processes in the US Government." *International Journal of Public Sector Management* 14 (3): 221-240.
- Kotnour, Tim. 2001. "Building knowledge for and about large-scale organizational transformations." *International Journal of Operations & Production Management* 21(8): 1053-1075.
- Kotnour, Timothy George. 2009. *Transforming organizations: Strategies and methods.* CRC Press.
- Kotnour, Tim. 2011. "An emerging theory of enterprise transformations." *Journal of Enterprise Transformation* 1(1): 48-70.
- Kotnour, Tim, Saul Barton, Jim Jennings, and Roy D. Bridges. 1998. "Understanding and leading large-scale change at the Kennedy Space Center." *Engineering Management Journal* 10 (2) : 17-21.
- Kotnour, Tim, and Tim Bollo. 2007. "Strategic management in a multi-program technology program involving convergence and divergence of programs: Observations from NASA." In *PICMET'07-2007 Portland International Conference on Management of Engineering & Technology*, pp. 105-112. IEEE, 2007.
- Kotnour, Tim, Jean Matkovich, and Rob Ellison. 1999. "Establishing a change infrastructure through teams." *Engineering Management Journal* 11 (3): 25-30.

Reference List for papers published during the KSC transformation:

- Hacker, M., Kotnour, T. G. and Mallak, L. 2001. "Turning Strategic Plans into Reality through Formalizing Deployment Processes: Three U.S. Federal Government Case Studies." *International Journal of Public Sector Management* 14 (3): 221-242.
- Kotnour, T. G. "A Project Management Approach to Organizational Transitions." Industrial Engineering Research Conference, Miami, FL, May 1997.
- Kotnour, T. G. "Measuring Organizational Alignment in a Project Environment." Industrial Engineering Research Conference, Phoenix, Arizona, May 1999.

- Kotnour, T. G. 2001. "Building Knowledge for and about Large-Scale Organizational Transformations." *International Journal of Operations and Production Management* 21 (8): 1053-1076.
- Kotnour, T. G., Saul Barton, Jim Jennings, and Roy D. Bridges. 1998. "Understanding and Leading Large-Scale Change at the Kennedy Space Center." *Engineering Management Journal* 10 (2): 17-21.
- Kotnour, T.G. and M. Hjelm. "Understanding Leadership Support for Learning Within Project Teams." The International Conference on Computers and Industrial Engineering and The International Conference on Industry, Engineering, and Management Systems, Cocoa Beach, Florida, March 2001.
- Kotnour, T.G. and J. Lenzini. "Understanding Supply Chain Management of a Spaceport." The International Conference on Computers and Industrial Engineering and The International Conference on Industry, Engineering, and Management Systems, Cocoa Beach, Florida, March 2001.
- Kotnour, T. G. and J. Lyons. "Strategic Management Thinking For Driving Large-Scale Transformation: Processes and Lessons Learned From The Kennedy Space Center." Industrial Engineering Research Conference, Phoenix, Arizona, May 1999.
- Kotnour, T.G. and J. L. Lyons. "Strategic Management Challenges and Lessons Learned from KSC's Transformation." Institute of Industrial Engineers, Orlando, Florida, 2002.
- Kotnour, T.G. and B. McIlrath. "Process Alignment to Meet Strategic Goals." The International Conference on Computers and Industrial Engineering and The International Conference on Industry, Engineering, and Management Systems, Cocoa Beach, Florida, March 2001.
- Kotnour, T. G., J. Matkovich, S. Barton, S, and J. Jennings. "The Engineering of Strategic Management Systems." Industrial Engineering Research Conference, Canada, May 1998.
- Kotnour, T. G., Jean Matkovich, and Rob Ellison. 1999. "Establishing a Change Infrastructure through Teams." *Engineering Management Journal* 11 (3): 25-30.
- Nunez, J. and T. G. Kotnour. "Knowledge Management in the Internal Space Station." Space Congress, April 2002.

Biography: Roy Bridges

Major General (Ret.)
Roy D. Bridges, Jr.

Roy retired from Northrop Grumman on January 31, 2019. Prior to his retirement he was Northrop Grumman Technology Services' Director responsible for DOE business. Previously Roy was the Vice President for Operations for National Security Technologies, LLC (NSTec), which was the company managing and operating the Nevada National Security Site (NNSS) for the Department of Energy's National Nuclear Security Administration. NSTec was a Northrop Grumman Technology Services (NGTS) managed Joint Venture. Roy was seconded to the company and remained a NGTS employee. NSTec had annual sales of over $450 million annually and a workforce of over 2000. Prior to that assignment Roy led the Mission Solutions Business Unit. He provided management direction and oversight of contracts for customers in the DOD, DOE, DHS, and NASA. Project locations included Huntsville AL; San Bernardino and Seaside CA; Aurora, Colorado Springs, and Lakeside CO; Panama City FL; Baltimore, Lanham and Princess Anne MD; Las Vegas NV; Layton UT; NASA Langley Research Center; and many others. Roy led a workforce of over 1000 people and was responsible for profit and loss of this $300 million business unit. He also had a role on the Board of Managers for NSTec. Roy's board responsibilities included being the chair of the Parent Organization Oversight Committee, which was the expert technical staff for the board.

Prior to joining Northrop Grumman in February 2006, Roy served as the Center Director of NASA's Langley Research Center in Hampton, VA, where he directed aeronautical and space research programs. Prior to that position, he was the Center Director of NASA's Kennedy Space Center in Florida, where he was responsible for NASA's space shuttle and International Space Station launch processing and operations as well as the acquisition and launch of NASA's expendable launch vehicle missions.

Bridges is a retired U.S. Air Force Major General. Prior to his last USAF assignment at Wright-Patterson AFB, OH, as the Air Force Materiel Command Director of Requirements, he was the Commander, Air Force Flight Test Center, Edwards Air Force Base, CA. In prior assignments, he also served as the Commander, Eastern Space and Missile Center, Patrick AFB, FL, and Commander, 412th Test Wing, Edwards AFB, CA.

As a NASA Astronaut, he piloted the space shuttle Challenger on the eight-day Spacelab 2 mission in July 1985.

As a pilot, test pilot and astronaut, he flew 4460 hours in a variety of aircraft including the following: F-100, F-104, YA/A-10, A-37, OV-99 (space shuttle Challenger), C-11, F-15, T-37, T-33, and T-38.

Bridges is a distinguished graduate of the U.S. Air Force Academy, Colorado Springs CO, where he earned a Bachelor's Degree in Engineering Science. He received a Master of Science Degree in Astronautics from Purdue University IN, in 1966 and, in May 2001, he received an honorary Doctorate of Engineering Degree from Purdue. He was a distinguished Graduate of USAF Pilot Training and top graduate of the USAF Aerospace Research Pilot School. He was inducted to the Georgia Aviation Hall of Fame. He was honored by the Florida Institute of Technology with an honorary Doctorate of Science Degree.

He has received numerous awards and honors. Most recently, he was inducted into the Astronaut Hall of Fame. Previously, he was awarded the National Nuclear Security Administration's top honor, the Administrator's Distinguished Service Gold Award. He was awarded NASA's Outstanding Leadership Medal, the Presidential Meritorious Executive Award, the Northrop Grumman Award for Excellence and many military honors including the following: Distinguished Service Medal, Defense Superior Service Medal with oak leaf cluster, Legion of Merit with oak leaf cluster, Distinguished Flying Cross with two oak leaf clusters, Meritorious Service Medal, Air Medal with 14 oak leaf clusters, Air Force Commendation Medal, and the NASA Space Flight Medal.

Born in Atlanta, Georgia, he now lives in Colorado Springs, Colorado.

He authored a book about his life, titled *An Improbable Astronaut: How a Georgia farm boy wound up flying the space shuttle.*

Biography: Tim Kotnour

Tim Kotnour, PhD

Tim Kotnour's CV includes the Lockheed Martin St. Laurent Professor in the Department of Industrial Engineering and Management Systems at the University of Central Florida and Director of the UCF Engineering Leadership and Innovation Institute (eli2) and the Professional Engineering Management Program. He completed his doctorate in Industrial & Systems Engineering from Virginia Tech. His core work focuses on "making strategy real." He integrates both corporate and academic settings by partnering with senior management teams to develop solutions through technical assistance, education, training, and research.

Corporate Setting. Tim focuses on strategic management, organizational transformations, and solution delivery. He provides professional presentations and strategic conversation facilitation to leadership teams as large as 200+ people. He has been actively engaged with multiple executive teams in leading significant transformations including:

- A 25+ year relationship with NASA's Kennedy Space Center (KSC) to lead and execute multiple transformations including commercializing shuttle operations, responding to the Columbia accident, enabling the Vision for Space Exploration, transitioning out of the Space Shuttle Program, moving to a multi-user spaceport, and using commercial launch services.
- A 25+ year relationship with NASA's Launch Services Program to enable the continuous evolution to a customer-focused, learning-based organization.
- The development and execution of a project-based organization to deliver large-scale systems development for NASA's Exploration Ground Systems.
- The transformation of the packaged-goods model to a mobile, social, and direct-to-consumer business model within the video-game industry.

In 2023, Tim was awarded a NASA Outstanding Public Service Medal in addition to the NASA Public Service Medals he was awarded in 2016, 2005, and 2001 for the partnership work with KSC. He is author of the book *Transforming Organizations: Strategies and Methods* and co-author of the book *Inspiring the Leader Engineer: Instilling the Burning Desire & Confidence to Change the World.*

Academic Setting. As described in the co-authored book *Inspiring the Leader Engineer—Instilling the Burning Desire and Confidence to Change the World*, Tim has led significant transformations:

- Securing over $2.7 million for practice-oriented research and training.
- Creating a balanced portfolio of undergraduate programs with significant annual touch points and impacts (e.g., increases in students' practice of creativity (80%), innovation (78%), collaboration (79%), accountability (72%), and solution delivery (84%)).
- Creating the graduate, executive-style Engineering Management Cohort Program with 197 alumni, $5.8 million in revenue, 75% of the alumni having significant job responsibility increases, and significant return on investment for the partnering organizations (e.g., L3Harris, Kennedy Space Center, Lockheed Martin, Raytheon, Siemens, and Walt Disney World).
- Creating executive programs such as the Chief Information Officer learning community with industry partners for 10 years that generated over $1.3 million.
- Building philanthropic relationships in partnership with the Dean/Development Office to raise over $1.17 million.
- Building sustainable capability to enable consistent, repeatable delivery of the programs.

Tim teaches Technology Strategy, Project Engineering, and Engineering Management. He has taught strategy for the European School of Management and Technology. He served as the Editor of the *Engineering Management Journal* and is a Fellow of the American Society for Engineering Management.

Abbreviations

ARTWG: Advanced Range Technology Working Group
ASTWG: Advanced Spaceport Technology Working Group
BIG: Business Innovation Group
BOA: Business and Objectives Agreement Document
CCAFS: Cape Canaveral Air Force Station
CD: Center Director
CD Comms: direct letters to the workforce from the Center Director
CD Rollouts: all-hands meetings, where the KSC Director shared the team's strategic intent
CLCS: Checkout and Launch Control System
ELV: Expendable Launch Vehicle
FY: Fiscal Year
GPES: Goal Performance Evaluation System
HQ: Headquarters
ISO: International Standards Organization
ISS: International Space Station
JBOSC: Joint Base Operations and Support Contract
JSC: Johnson Space Center
KSC: Kennedy Space Center
LaRC: Langley Research Center
LEAP: Leadership Excellence Achievement Program
LSP: Launch Service Program
MEIT: Multi-Element Integrated Test
NASA: National Aeronautics and Space Administration
OSHA: Occupational Safety and Health Administration
OSP: Orbital Space Plane
PGOC: Payload Ground Operations Contract
RFP: Request for Proposal
SERPL: Space Experiment Research and Processing Laboratory
SFOC: Space Flight Operations Contract
STS: Space Transportation System
UCF: University of Central Florida
VPP: Voluntary Protective Program
ZBR: Zero-based Review

Glossary

action learning: *small groups working to together to develop shared understanding and learning to solve problems*

all-term: *the relationship of the current, short-term, and long-term states of an organization*

bad day: *something is seriously disrupting or threatening your business. Examples: a mission failure, a space shuttle crashing, a rocket failing to reach orbit, a satellite failing to operate, a significant loss in revenue market share, a failure of a new product, a failure of a core technology, etc.*

change infrastructure: *a team that provides internal consulting to support the senior management in making the transformation happen*

change management: *the set of activities to ensure your workforce goes on the transformation journey and your organization's limited resources are used on the efforts most likely to lead to the successful transformation*

core business: *the primary customers, products, and services that define how the organization brings value to the industry*

culture: *shared attitudes, values, goals, morale, and practices—mutual respect for fellow workers, kindness, compassion, treating everyone equally and with dignity—that characterize an institution or organization*

desired outcomes: *the results your organization needs to achieve from the perspective of its customers, key stakeholders, and employees*

Directorates: *the individual, internal organizations that comprise the Center, each responsible for a specific task*

Directors: *heads of major organizations (i.e., directorates) reporting to the Center Director*

drive accountability: *making someone responsible for executing the project and delivering the needed results; being clear on what is expected to be achieved by when*

employees: *civil servants working in the organizations at KSC*

escalate/escalation philosophy: *a plan describing why, when, and how to bring awareness of a disruptor to the attention of the leader and team*

external environment: *the set of factors (e.g., political, legal, economic, competition, demographics, etc.) outside of an organization that can impact its performance*

focus area: *issues that are important for the organization to address*

focus group: *a small group of employees that provide their perspective to the issues facing the Center*

future state: *what the organization will be in the future*

goals: *long-standing outcomes the Center delivers to its primary stakeholders; enduring statements of how the organization impacts the industry*

honest broker: *a consultant or internal trusted rep who brings data with very little bias for a specific course of action*

improvement initiatives: *a set of initiatives/program to help solve the transformation problem*

leadership team: *the team of people assigned to manage a transformation (a.k.a. senior management team, management team, transformation team)*

management team: *see leadership team*

MEIT: *Multi-Element Integrated Test--a protocol for connecting the modules destined for ISS on the ground to make sure that all the interfaces and systems were tested to assure that they would work well when attached in space*

metric: *a unit by which something is measured. What exactly a metric is, is determined by whatever you are trying to measure, whether that thing is tangible or intangible.*

objectives: *describe what needs to be accomplished; the ideal structure for an objective is (increase/decrease) (measure) by (amount) by (date)*

off-sites: *meetings or retreats away from the usual work environment to provide the time and space for the leadership team to hold strategic conversations*

oversight/insight: *In the oversight mode, the government is in charge of all activities and is supported by the contractor. In the insight mode, the contractor is in charge of all day-to-day processing activities, and the government is only fully in charge of the launch countdown and landing*

payload: *something that is taken into space via a rocket...payloads could include cargo, scientific instruments, or a human crew*

range: *the "cone" of airspace that defines the path through which a launch vehicle traverses...the FAA and Space Force ensure this space is safe for the launch vehicle to fly through. Also includes the infrastructure to support launches such as radars, weather stations, telemetry systems, photographic systems, flight termination systems. All together, it becomes the Eastern Space and Missile Range that supported both NASA and Air Force launches.*

relevancy: *how well the market values your organization's products and services*

responsiveness: *how well the products and services are delivered within the customer's expectations regarding cost, quality, and timeliness*

road map: *a description of how the organization changes over time*

rolling up [results]: *taking the data from each sub-unit and combining the data to provide a wholistic look that tells the story of the organization's overall performance*

scenario: *a combination of both projections of what is known and extrapolations beyond what is known in order to imagine potential future environments your organization may face. Scenarios are a "story" of what the world and/or your organization could be like in the future, so you can plan for it in the present.*

senior management team: *see leadership team*

shuttle processing: *all things that must be accomplished between landing from one mission and launch on the next mission. It includes extensive inspections, investigation and fix of any anomalies on previous mission, periodic maintenance required for each system, stacking the vehicles in the VAB, transporting to pad, installing payload into payload bay (some of which is done on launch pad), fueling, launch countdown and launch. When vehicle clears the tower, mission control at JSC assumes command until landing.*

spaceport: *the infrastructure used to process, launch, and land the launch vehicle and spacecraft...a spaceport can be thought of as an "airport" for space travel*

stakeholder: *anyone who can impact or be impacted by the organization, both internal and external—some are more important than others.*

strategic conversations: *conversations that the senior management team engages in to understand the internal and external environment and define the overall strategy of your organization, in order to adjust your strategy to your external business environment.*

strategic initiatives: *the efforts to enhance existing or develop new products, services, or capabilities*

strategic plan: *the description of your organization's strategic intent (mission, vision, goals, values), objectives, and strategies to accomplish its mission*

strategic response: *A strategic response involves implementing a strategic transformation path containing four focus areas/swim lanes: execute today's mission, continuously set strategy, make the strategy real, and enable the transformation.*

strategies: *the set of efforts or tasks to accomplish an objective*

strategic: *very important to the success of the organization*

strategic transformation: *a complex process that will fundamentally and intentionally change your business model, involving understanding its current state and defining its ideal future and transition states.*

sub-units: *business units, divisions, or programs within your organization*

transformation team: *see leadership team*

transition state: *the time when your organization is balancing its current- and future-state missions and core businesses*

zero-based review (ZBR): *a budgeting method in which all expenses, projects, etc. must be evaluated and justified for a new period, starting from zero instead of beginning with the previous budget and making adjustments to it*

Works Cited

- Ackoff, Russell Lincoln, Jason Magidson, and Herbert J. Addison. 2006. *Idealized Design: How to Dissolve Tomorrow's Crisis... Today*. Wharton School Publishing.
- Anthony, Scott D., Matt Eyring, and Lib Gibson. 2006. "Mapping Your Innovation Strategy." *Harvard Business Review* 84 (5): 104-13. https://hbr.org/2006/05/mapping-your-innovation-strategy?autocomplete=true.
- Appelbaum, Steven H., Roger Simpson, and Barbara T. Shapiro. 1987. "The Tough Test of Downsizing." *Organizational Dynamics* 16 (1): 68–79. https://doi.org/10.1016/0090-2616(87)90033-7.
- Argyris, Chris, and Donald A Schön. 1978. *Organizational Learning : A Theory of Action Perspective*. Reading, Massachusetts: Addison-Wesley.
- Barthélemy, Jérôme. 2006. "The Experimental Roots of Revolutionary Vision." *MIT Sloan Management Review* 48 (1): 81.
- Becker, Karen. 2008. "Unlearning as a Driver of Sustainable Change and Innovation: Three Australian Case Studies." *International Journal of Technology Management* 42 (1-2): 89-106. https://doi.org/10.1504/IJTM.2008.018062.
- Beer, Michael, and Nitin Nohria, eds. 2000. *Breaking the Code of Change*. Vol. 78 (3). Harvard Business School Press.
- Bowonder, B., Anirndha Dambal, Shambhu Kumar, and Abhay Shirodkar. 2010. "Innovation Strategies for Creating Competitive Advantage." *Research-technology Management* 53 (3): 19-32. https://doi.org/10.1080/08956308.2010.11657628.
- Brinberg, David, and Joseph E. McGrath. 1985. *Validity and the Research Process*. Sage Publications.
- Brynjolfsson, Erik, Amy Austin Renshaw, and Marshall Van Alstyne. 1997. "The Matrix of Change." *MIT Sloan Management Review* 38 (2). https://sloanreview.mit.edu/article/the-matrix-of-change/.
- Cameron, Kim S., Sarah J. Freeman, and Aneil K. Mishra. 1993. "Downsizing and Redesigning Organizations." In *Organizational Change and Redesign*, edited by George P. Huber and William H. Glick. Oxford University Press.
- Champy, James. 1995. *Reengineering Management: The Mandate for New Leadership*. HarperBusiness (a division of HarperCollins Publishers).

- Chan, Jeffrey K., Sara L. Beckman, and Peter G. Lawrence. 2007. "Workplace Design: A New Managerial Imperative." *California Management Review* 49 (2): 6-22.
- Christensen, Clayton M., and Michael Overdorf. 2000. "Meeting the Challenge of Disruptive Change." *Harvard Business Review* 78, no. 2: 66-77. https://hbr.org/2000/03/meeting-the-challenge-of-disruptive-change.
- Christensen, Clayton M., Matt Marx, and Howard H. Stevenson. 2006. "The Tools of Cooperation and Change." *Harvard Business Review* 84, no. 10: 72-80. https://hbr.org/2006/10/the-tools-of-cooperation-and-change.
- Crol, Johannes B. 2000. "Creating Support for a Change in Strategy." *International Journal of Technology Management* 19 (6): 586-596. https://doi.org/10.1504/IJTM.2000.002833.
- Cunningham, John B. 1993. *Action Research and Organizational Development.* Praeger.
- D'Aveni, Richard A. 2007. "Mapping Your Competitive Position." *Harvard Business Review* 85 (11): 110-20. https://hbr.org/2007/11/mapping-your-competitive-position.
- Davidson, W. H. 1993. "Beyond Re-engineering: The Three Phases of Business Transformation." *IBM Systems Journal*, 32(1). https://doi.org/10.1147/sj.321.0065
- Day, George S. 2006. "Aligning the Organization with the Market." *MIT Sloan Management Review* 48 (1). https://sloanreview.mit.edu/article/aligning-the-organization-with-the-market/.
- Deming, W. Edwards. 1986. *Out of the Crisis*. Massachusetts Institute of Technology Center for Advanced Engineering Study.
- Dotlich, David L. and James L. Noel. 1998. *Action Learning.* Jossey-Bass, Inc.
- Drucker, Peter F. 1993. *Post-Capitalist Society*. HarperBusiness, a division of HarperCollins Publishers, Inc.
- Eisenhardt, Kathleen M. 1989. "Building Theories from Case Study Research." *Academy of Management Review* 14 (4): 532-550. https://cin.ufpe.br/~in1037/leitura/eisenhardt-1989-BuildingTheoryFromCaseStudies.pdf.
- Eskew, Mike. 2007. "Stick with Your Vision." *Harvard Business Review* 85 (7/8), : 56-57.

- Filippini, Roberto. 1997. "Operations Management Research: Some Reflections on Evolution, Models and Empirical Studies in OM." *International Journal of Operations & Production Management* 17 (7): 655-670. https://www.emerald.com/insight/content/doi/10.1108/01443579710175583/full/html.
- French, Wendell L. and Cecil Bell. 1999. *Organization Development: Behavioral Science Interventions for Organization Improvement (Sixth Edition)*. Prentice-Hall.
- Gadd, Ken W., and John S. Oakland. 1996. "Chimera or Culture? Business Process Reengineering for Total Quality Management." *Quality Management Journal* 3 (3): 20-28. https://www.tandfonline.com/doi/abs/10.1080/10686967.1996.11918740.
- Gehman, Harold W. 2003. *Columbia Accident Investigation Board Report*. Vol. 1. Columbia Accident Investigation Board. https://sma.nasa.gov/SignificantIncidents/assets/columbia-accident-investigation-board-report-volume-1.pdf.
- George W. Bush. "A Renewed Spirit of Discovery: The President's Vision for U.S. Space Exploration," January 14, 2004, NASA Headquarters, Washington, DC, https://georgewbush-whitehouse.archives.gov/news/releases/2004/01/20040114-3.html
- Grover, Varun. 1999. "From Business Reengineering to Business Process Change Management: a Longitudinal Study of Trends and Practices." *IEEE Transactions on Engineering Management* 46 (1): 36-46. https://doi.org/10.1109/17.740036.
- Hahn, Dietger. 1991. "Strategic Management—Tasks and Challenges in the 1990s." *Long Range Planning* 24 (1): 26-39. https://doi.org/10.1016/0024-6301(91)90021-F.
- Hamel, Gary. 2002. *Leading the Revolution*. Harvard Business School Press.
- Hammer, Michael. 2004. "Deep Change: How Operational Innovation Can Transform Your Company." *Harvard Business Review*, 82 (4), pp. 84-93. https://hbr.org/2004/04/deep-change-how-operational-innovation-can-transform-your-company.
- Hammer, Michael. 2007. "The Process Audit." *Harvard Business Review* 85 (4): 111. https://hbr.org/2007/04/the-process-audit.
- Hatch, Nile W., and David C. Mowery. 1998. "Process Innovation and Learning by Doing in Semiconductor Manufacturing." *Manage-*

ment Science 44 (11-part-1): 1461-1477. https://doi.org/10.1287/mnsc.44.11.1461

- Hedrick, Terry E., Leonard Bickman, and Debra J. Rog 1993. *Applied Research Design: A Practical Guide*. Sage Publications, Inc.
- Henderson, Joan, Rodney McAdam, and Steven Parkinson. 2005. "An Innovative Approach to Evaluating Organisational Change." *International Journal of Technology Management* 30(1-2): 11-31. https://doi.org/10.1504/IJTM.2005.006343.
- Hill, Terry, Alastair Nicholson, and Roy Westbrook. 1999. "Closing the Gap: A Polemic on Plant-based Research in Operations Management." *International Journal of Operations & Production Management* 19 (2): 139-156. https://doi.org/10.1108/01443579910247400.
- "History of NASA's Spaceport." Kennedy Space Center, n.d., accessed April 12, 2024, https://www.nasa.gov/kennedy/kennedy-space-center-history/. Accessed previously on November 16, 2008, as *Kennedy Space Center Story*, http://www.nasa.gov/centers/kennedy/about/history/story/kscstory.html (now inactive).
- Huber, George P. 1991. "Organizational Learning: The Contributing Processes and the Literatures." *Organization Science* 2 (1): 88-115. https://pubsonline.informs.org/doi/10.1287/orsc.2.1.88.
- Huber, George P., and William H. Glick. 1993. "What Was Learned About Organization Change and Redesign." In *Organizational Change and Redesign: Ideas and Insights for Improving Performance*, edited by George P. Huber and William H. Glick. Oxford University Press. 383-391.
- Huy, Quy Nguyen, and Henry Mintzberg. 2003. "The Rhythm of Change." *MIT Sloan Management Review* 44 (4). https://sloanreview.mit.edu/article/the-rhythm-of-change/
- Jackson, Cody, and Mike Schneider. 2022. "Once in the Doldrums, Florida Coast Hums With Space Launches. APNews September 1, 2022. https://apnews.com/article/space-launches-technology-science-unemployment-cfc56cf6d94b33b4340214cad8f3cfa2. (Accessed September 2, 2022, reprinted in part as shown in text, as "Florida's Space Coast Returns to Life with Increase in Kennedy Space Center Launches," 9/2/2022, Associated Press.)
- Johnson, Mark W., Clayton M. Christensen, and Henning Kagermann. 2008. "Reinventing Your Business Model." *Harvard*

Business Review 86 (12): 50-59. https://hbr.org/2008/12/reinventing-your-business-model.

- Johnstone, Paul M., Richard D. Blomberg, George J. Gleghorn, Norris J. Krone, Richard A. Voltz, Robert F. Dunn, Charles J. Donlan et al. 1996. *Review of Issues Associated with Safe Operation and Management of the Space Shuttle Program.* No. NASA-TM-111835.
- Kanter, Rosabeth Moss, B. A. Stein, and T. D. Jick. 1992. The Challenge of *Organizational Change: How Companies Experience It and Leaders Guide It.* The Free Press.
- Kanter, Rosabeth Moss. 1983. *The Change Masters: Innovation for Productivity in the American Corporation.* Simon & Schuster.
- Kanter, Rosabeth Moss. 2008. "Transforming Giants." *Harvard Business Review*, Vol. 86 (1), pp. 43-52. https://hbr.org/2008/01/transforming-giants.
- Kaplan, Robert S., and David P. Norton. 1996. *Balanced Scorecard: Translating Strategy Into Action.* Harvard Business School Press.
- Kaplan, Robert S., and David P. Norton. 2007. "Using the Balanced Scorecard as a Strategic Management System." *Harvard Business Review*, Vol. 85 (7/8), pp. 150-161. https://hbr.org/2007/07/using-the-balanced-scorecard-as-a-strategic-management-system.
- Kaufman, Robert S. 1992. "Why Operations Improvement Programs Fail: Four Managerial Contradictions." *MIT Sloan Management Review* 34 (1): 83. https://www.proquest.com/openview/e3c74b36b3eae04a5fd8f0daf7ad41d4/1?pq-origsite=gscholar&cbl=26142 .
- Kennedy Space Center. 1997. *Kennedy Space Center Implementation Plan*, 1997. In *Kennedy Space Center Annual Report FY* 1997, p3. https://ntrs.nasa.gov/api/citations/20060016437/downloads/20060016437.pdf
- Kianto, Aino. 2008. "Development and Validation of a Survey Instrument for Measuring Organisational Renewal Capability." *International Journal of Technology Management* 42 (1-2): 69-88. http://dx.doi.org/10.1504/IJTM.2008.018061.
- Kim, W. Chan, and Mauborgne, Renée. 2004. "Blue Ocean Strategy." *Harvard Business Review*, Vol. 82(10): 76-84. https://hbr.org/2004/10/blue-ocean-strategy .
- Kleiner, Art, and George Roth. 1997. "How to Make Experience Your Company's Best Teacher." *Harvard Business Review* 75 (5): 172-178. https://hbr.org/1997/09/how-to-make-experience-your-companys-best-teacher.

- Kotnour, Timothy George. 2009. *Transforming Organizations: Strategies and Methods*. CRC Press.
- Kotter, John. 1996. *Leading Change*. Harvard Business School Press, Canada.
- Kurstedt, Harold. A. 1993. *Management Systems Theory, Application, and Design*. Management Systems Laboratories.
- Lawler, Edward E., Allan M. Mohrman Jr., Susan A. Mohrman, Gerald E. Ledford Jr., Thomas G. Cummings et al. 1999. *Doing Research That Is Useful for Theory and Practice*. Lexington Books.
- Lawler, Edward E., and Worley, Christopher G. 2006. "Designing Organizations That Are Built to Change." *Sloan Management Review*, 48 (1): 19-23. https://sloanreview.mit.edu/article/designing-organizations-that-are-built-to-change/.
- Lawler, Edward E., Mohrman, Susan A., and Ledford, Gerald E. 1998. *Strategies for High Performing Organization*. Jossey-Bass Publishers.
- Lawrence, Thomas B., Bruno Dyck, Sally Maitlis, and Michael K. Mauws. 2006. "The Underlying Structure of Continuous Change." *MIT Sloan Management Review* 47 (4). https://sloanreview.mit.edu/article/the-underlying-structure-of-continuous-change/
- Lincoln, Yvonna S., and Egon G. Guba 1985. *Naturalistic Inquiry*. Sage Publications, Inc.
- Marshall, Robert, and Lyle Yorks. 1994. "Planning for a Restructured, Revitalized Organization." *MIT Sloan Management Review* 35 (4): 81. https://sloanreview.mit.edu/article/planning-for-a-restructured-revitalized-organization/.
- McCurdy, Howard E. 2003. *Faster, Better, Cheaper: Low-Cost Innovation in the U.S. Space Program*, The Johns Hopkins University Press.
- Middleman, Louis I. 1981. *In Short: A Concise Guide to Good Writing*. St. Martin's Press.
- Mintzberg, Henry. 1994. *The Rise and Fall of Strategic Planning*. The Free Press.
- Montgomery, Cynthia A. 2008. "Putting Leadership Back into Strategy." *Harvard Business Review* 86 (1): 54. https://hbr.org/2008/01/putting-leadership-back-into-strategy
- Mukherjee, Amit Shankar, Michael A. Lapré, and Luk N. Van Wassenhove. 1998. "Knowledge Driven Quality Improvement." *Management Science* 44 (11-part-2): S35-S49. https://doi.org/10.1287/mnsc.44.11.S35

- NASA and US Air Force. 2003. *Advanced Spaceport Technology Working Group: Baseline Report, November 2003.*
- NASA and US Air Force. 2004. *Advanced Range Technology Working Group: Baseline Report, March 2004.*
- NASA. 1995. NASA HQ RELEASE: 95-73, Headquarters, Washington, DC, 1995b.
- NASA. 1995. *The Report of Space Shuttle Management Independent Review Team, 1995a.* https://ntrs.nasa.gov/api/citations/19950018046/downloads/19950018046.pdf
- NASA. 1996. *Review of Issues Associated with Safe Operation and Management of the Space Shuttle Program, Nov. 1996.* https://ntrs.nasa.gov/api/citations/19970010486/downloads/19970010486.pdf
- NASA. 1999. *Space Launch Vehicles Broad Area Review Report Nov 1999.* http://klabs.org/richcontent/Reports/Failure_Reports/Space_Launch_Vehicles_Broad_Area_Review.pdf (accessed November 16, 2008; site no longer active). Cited in "Air Force Completes Launch Review," Tech. Sgt. R. R. Getsy, *Space Daily*, December 1, 1999, https://www.spacedaily.com/news/launchers-99u.html
- NASA. 2001. *Concept Of Privatization Of The Space Shuttle Program, September 2001.*
- National Academy of Public Administration. 1996. "Effective Downsizing: A Compendium of Lessons Learned for Government Organizations." National Academy of Public Administration. https://dopdfdownload.com/effective-downsizing-a-compendium-of-lessons-learned-for-government-organizations.pdf
- National Academy Of Public Administration. 2002. *A Review of the Joint Base Operations and Support Contract: Kennedy Space Center/45th Space Wing.* National Academy Of Public Administration. https://napawash.org/academy-studies/a-review-of-the-joint-base-operations-and-support-contract-kennedy-space-ce.
- National Aeronautics and Space Administration. 1996. *NASA Strategic Management Handbook.* Washington, D.C: National Aeronautics and Space Administration
- National Aeronautics and Space Administration. 2006. *NASA Strategic Management & Governance Handbook (NPD 1000.0)*, Washington, D.C: National Aeronautics and Space Administration.
- Office of Science and Technology Policy and National Security Council. 2000. *The Future Management and Use of the U.S. Space Launch*

Bases and Ranges, Report of the Interagency Working Group, February 8, 2000.

- Osterwalder, Alexander, and Yves Pigneur. 2010. *Business Model Generation: A Handbook for Visionaries, Game Changers, and Challengers.* John Wiley & Sons.
- Pascale, Richard Tanner, and Jerry Sternin. 2005. "Your Company's Secret Change Agents." *Harvard Business Review* 83 (5): 72-81. https://hbr.org/2005/05/your-companys-secret-change-agents
- Pekar Jr, Peter, and Stan Abraham. 1995. "Is Strategic Management Living Up to Its Promise?." *Long Range Planning* 28 (5): 32-44. https://hbr.org/2005/10/the-hard-side-of-change-management
- Right Management Associates. 1996. "Organization Measurement Consulting Services offered to NASA Kennedy Space Center." Prepared by Right Associates, February 1996.
- Roberto, Michael A., and Lynne C. Levesque. 2005. "The Art of Making Change Initiatives Stick." *MIT Sloan Management Review* 46 (4). https://sloanreview.mit.edu/article/the-art-of-making-change-initiatives-stick/
- Rouse, William B. 2011. "Necessary Competencies for Transforming an Enterprise." *Journal of Enterprise Transformation* 1 (1): 71–92. doi:10.1080/19488289.2010.548905.
- Royer, Isabelle. 2003. "Why Bad Projects Are So Hard to Kill." *Harvard Business Review* 81, (2): 48-57. https://hbr.org/2003/02/why-bad-projects-are-so-hard-to-kill
- Ruff, Frank. 2006. "Corporate Foresight: Integrating the Future Business Environment into Innovation and Strategy." *International Journal of Technology Management* 34, (3-4): 278-295. https://www.inderscienceonline.com/doi/abs/10.1504/IJTM.2006.009460
- Sandy, William. 1991. "Avoid the Breakdowns Between Planning and Implementation." *The Journal of Business Strategy* 12 (5): 30–33. https://doi.org/10.1108/eb039440
- Schwartz, Peter. (1991) 1996. *The Art of the Long View.* Crown Currency. [reprint edition]
- Schwartz, Peter. 1991. *The Art of the Long View.* Doubleday Business. [first edition]
- Senge, Peter M. 1990. *The Fifth Discipline: The Art and Practice of the Learning Organization.* Doubleday/Currency.

- Sidky, Ahmed. 2007. "A Structured Approach to Adopting Agile Practices: The Agile Adoption Framework." PhD diss., Virginia Polytechnic Institute and State University. https://vtechworks.lib.vt.edu/server/api/core/bitstreams/4ff25112-51c4-4ce7-86f3-ee3e0c84100a/content
- Simon, Herbert A. 1960. *The New Science of Management Decision.* Harper and Brothers. https://doi.org/10.1037/13978-000
- Simons, Robert. 1994. "How New Top Managers Use Control Systems as Levers of Strategic Renewal." *Strategic Management Journal* 15 (3): 169-189. http://www.jstor.org/stable/2486965.
- Sink, D. Scott and William T. Morris. 1995. *By What Method?* Industrial Engineering and Management Press.
- Sirkin, Harold L., Perry Keenan, and Alan Jackson. 2005. "The Hard Side of Change Management." *Harvard Business Review* 83 (10): 108. https://hbr.org/2005/10/the-hard-side-of-change-management.
- Space News. 2003. "Boeing Updates Assessment of Launch and Satellite Businesses in Weak Commercial Space Markets." http://www.boeing.com/news/releases/2003/q3/nr_030715a.html (accessed November 16, 2008).
- Stanke, Alexis K. 2006. "Creating High Performance Enterprises." PhD diss., MIT, USA. https://dspace.mit.edu/bitstream/handle/1721.1/83207/PLN_06_BO03_Stanke_CreatingHighPerformanceExtendedEnterprises.pdf?sequence=1&isAllowed=y
- Stewart, T. (2006), "Architects of Change." *Harvard Business Review,* 84 (4): 10.
- Strebel, Paul, and Anne-Valerie OHLSSON-CORBOZ. 2006. "The Art of Making Smart Big Moves." *MIT Sloan Management Review* 47 (2): 79–83. https://shop.sloanreview.mit.edu/store/the-art-of-making-smart-big-moves
- Sull, Donald N. 2005. "Strategy as Active Waiting." *Harvard Business Review* 83 (9): 120. https://hbr.org/2005/09/strategy-as-active-waiting
- Taylor, Bernard. 1984. "Strategic Planning—Which Style Do You Need?." *Long Range Planning* 17 (3): 51-62. https://doi.org/10.1016/0024-6301(84)90008-6.
- United States Congress. 1998. "Commercial Space Act of 1998." PUBLIC LAW 105–303—OCT. 28, 1998. https://www.congress.gov/105/plaws/publ303/PLAW-105publ303.pdf.
- United States General Accounting Office. 1995. "Workforce Reductions: Downsizing Strategies Used in Selected Organizations." United

States General Accounting Office, March. https://www.gao.gov/assets/ggd-95-54.pdf.

- Van Wingerden, Robert G. 2001. "Managing Change." *International Journal of Technology Management* 21 (5-6): 487-495. https://dx.doi.org/10.1504/IJTM.2001.002928
- Waalewijn, Philip, and Peter Segaar. 1993. "Strategic Management: the Key to Profitability in Small Companies." *Long Range Planning* 26 (2): 24-30. https://doi.org/10.1016/0024-6301(93)90132-Y
- Wilson, Ian. 1994. "Strategic Planning Isn't Dead—It Changed." *Long Range Planning* 27 (4): 12-24 https://doi.org/10.1016/0024-6301(94)90052-3
- Wyatt Company, The 1993. "Best Practices in Corporate Restructuring." The Wyatt Company.
- Yin, Robert K. 1989. *Case Study Research: Design and Methods (Revised Edition)*, Sage Publications.
- Zook, Chris. 2007. "Finding Your Next Core Business." *Harvard Business Review* 85 (4): 66-75. https://hbr.org/2007/04/finding-your-next-core-business

Index

(Page numbers in ***bold italic*** refer to illustrations.)

D

E

H

I

J

K

L

M

N

O

P

R

S

Design and the Reader

We always knew that the design of this book would be crucial in connecting with our readers. We wanted you to be able to easily digest this important information. We were looking for the "sweet spot" of making the book accessible while also providing the details. We found it in the hard, creative work of our designer, Artūrs Bremanis. The resulting design enables the book to be welcoming and comprehensible—not overwhelming. We thank Artūrs for truly caring about our project.

About the Authors

Roy

Roy D. Bridges Jr.'s life reads like a mythical story of a boy with an infallible work ethic and unstoppable determination who set his sights on space, earned the rank of Major General, and achieved his dream of reaching the stars. Then he helped many others reach the stars as Center Director of NASA's Kennedy Space Center.

Born in Atlanta, Georgia, Roy now lives in Colorado Springs, Colorado. His home has a view from his deck of the US Air Force Academy, which was a major factor in enabling his successful career. He is also close to his immediate family, which he enjoys. He authored a book about his life, titled *An Improbable Astronaut: How a Georgia farm boy wound up flying the space shuttle*. And after a long and literally stellar career, in May of 2023, Roy was inducted into the US Astronaut Hall of Fame.

Tim

Tim Kotnour, PhD continues to focus on his calling to help his students and customers "make their strategy real." As of this writing, he has served his students, NASA, and other customers for 30 years.

Born in Chicago, Illinois, Tim settled in Orlando, Florida, early in his career. He believes he has the "best gig" in the world translating the learnings and models across both the university and industry. His robust academic history includes being appointed the Director of the Engineering Leadership & Innovation Institute at the University of Central Florida. His experience with NASA launched his career and now enables him to share those learnings with the next generation of technical leaders. In 2023, he was awarded the NASA Outstanding Public Service Medal.

www.ingramcontent.com/pod-product-compliance
Lightning Source LLC
LaVergne TN
LVHW072350240926
848802LV00018B/12/J
9781631070778